THE POLITICS

Additional Volumes in Prometheus's

Great Books in Philosophy Series

THE POLITICS

ARISTOTLE

Translated by
William Ellis

PROMETHEUS BOOKS
700 East Amherst St., Buffalo, New York 14215

Published 1986 by Prometheus Books
700 East Amherst Street, Buffalo, New York 14215

Library of Congress Catalog Number: 86-70378
ISBN 0-87975-346-3

Printed in the United States of America

ARISTOTLE was born in the northern Greek town of Stagira in 384 B.C., where his father was the personal physician to the great-grandfather of Alexander the Great. At the age of eighteen Aristotle entered Plato's Academy and soon became recognized as its most important student. He remained under Plato's tutelage for nearly twenty years.

After his teacher's death in 347 B.C., Aristotle cultivated associations with other Academy students throughout Greece and Asia Minor. Then in 342 B.C., Aristotle was asked by King Philip II of Macedonia to become the tutor for his young son Alexander, who was later to become the conqueror of much of the known world at that time. The young prince remained under Aristotle's supervision until 336 B.C., when he acceded to the throne after his father's death. Two years later Aristotle returned to Athens and founded his own school, which he called the Lyceum. This intellectual center flourished during the years when Alexander the Great ruled Greece as part of his large empire. But upon Alexander's death in 323 B.C., Aristotle was charged with impiety by Athenians who resented his associations with the Macedonian conqueror. Rather than risk the same fate as Plato's mentor Socrates, Aristotle fled to the city of Chalcis, where he died in 322 B.C.

Aristotle's interests, like those of Plato, were diverse and his writing cast its shadow on many fields, including logic, metaphysics, epistemology, ethics, politics, and the sciences. Among his most well-known works are: *The Categories, The Prior and Posterior Analytics, The Physics, The Metaphysics, De Anima, The Nicomachean Ethics,* and *The Politics.*

A TREATISE ON GOVERNMENT

BOOK I

CHAPTER I

As we see that every city is a society, and every society is established for some good purpose; for an apparent good is the spring of all human actions; it is evident 1252*a* that this is the principle upon which they are every one founded, and this is more especially true of that which has for its object the best possible, and is itself the most excellent, and comprehends all the rest. Now this is called a city, and the society thereof a political society; for those who think that the principles of a political, a regal, a family, and a herile government are the same are mistaken, while they suppose that each of these differ in the numbers to whom their power extends, but not in their constitution: so that with them a herile government is one composed of a very few, a domestic of more, a civil and a regal of still more, as if there was no difference between a large family and a small city, or that a regal government and a political one are the same, only that in the one a single person is continually at the head of public affairs; in the other, that each member of the state has in his turn a share in the government, and is at one time a magistrate, at another a private person, according to the rules of political science. But now this is not true, as will be evident to any one who will consider this question in the most approved method. As, in an inquiry into every other subject, it is necessary to separate the different parts of which it is compounded, till we arrive at their first elements, which are the most minute parts thereof; so by the same proceeding we shall acquire a knowledge of the primary parts of a city and see wherein they differ from each other, and whether the rules of art will give us any assistance in examining into each of these things which are mentioned.

CHAPTER II

Now if in this particular science any one would attend to its original seeds, and their first shoot, he would then as in others have the subject perfectly before him; and perceive, in the first place, that it is requisite that those should be joined together whose species cannot exist without each other, as the male and the female, for the business of propagation; and this not through choice, but by that natural impulse which acts both upon plants and animals also, for the purpose of their leaving behind them others like themselves. It is also from natural causes that some beings command and others obey, that each may obtain their mutual safety; for a being who is endowed with a mind capable of reflection and forethought is by nature the superior and governor, whereas he whose excellence is merely corporeal is formed to be a slave; whence it follows that the different state of master 1252b and slave is equally advantageous to both. But there is a natural difference between a female and a slave: for nature is not like the artists who make the Delphic swords for the use of the poor, but for every particular purpose she has her separate instruments, and thus her ends are most complete, for whatsoever is employed on one subject only, brings that one to much greater perfection than when employed on many; and yet among the barbarians, a female and a slave are upon a level in the community, the reason for which is, that amongst them there are none qualified by nature to govern, therefore their society can be nothing but between slaves of different sexes. For which reason the poets say, it is proper for the Greeks to govern the barbarians, as if a barbarian and a slave were by nature one. Now of these two societies the domestic is the first, and Hesiod is right when he says, " First a house, then a wife, then an ox for the plough," for the poor man has always an ox before a household slave. That society then which nature has established for daily support is the domestic, and those who compose it are called by Charondas 'ομοσιπνοι, and by Epimenides the Cretan 'ομοκαπνοι; but the society of many families, which was first instituted for their lasting, mutual advantage, is called a village, and a village is most naturally composed of the descendants of one family, whom some persons call 'ομογαλακτες, the children and the children's children thereof: for which reason cities were originally governed by kings, as the barbarian states now are, which are composed of those who had before submitted to kingly government; for every family is governed by the elder, as are the branches thereof, on account of their relationship thereunto, which is what Homer says, " Each one ruled his wife and child; " and in this scattered manner they formerly lived. And the opinion which universally prevails, that the gods themselves are subject to kingly government, arises from hence, that all men formerly were, and many are so now; and as they imagined themselves to be made in the likeness of the gods, so they supposed their manner of life must needs be the same. And when many villages so entirely join themselves together as in every respect to form but one society, that society is a city, and contains in itself, if I may so speak, the end and perfection of government: first founded that we might live, but continued that we may live happily. For which reason every city must be allowed to be the work of nature, if we admit that the original society between male and female is; for to this as their end all subordinate societies tend, and the end of everything is the nature of it. For what every being is in its most perfect state, that certainly is the nature of that being, whether it be a man, a horse, or a house: besides, whatsoever produces the final cause and the end which we

1253a desire, must be best; but a government complete in itself is that final cause and what is best. Hence it is evident that a city is a natural production, and that man is naturally a political animal, and that whosoever is naturally and not accidentally unfit for society, must be either inferior or superior to man: thus the man in Homer, who is reviled for being "without society, without law, without family." Such a one must naturally be of a quarrelsome disposition, and as solitary as the birds. The gift of speech also evidently proves that man is a more social animal than the bees, or any of the herding cattle: for nature, as we say, does nothing in vain, and man is the only animal who enjoys it. Voice indeed, as being the token of pleasure and pain, is imparted to others also, and thus much their nature is capable of, to perceive pleasure and pain, and to impart these sensations to others; but it is by speech that we are enabled to express what is useful for us, and what is hurtful, and of course what is just and what is unjust: for in this particular man differs from other animals, that he alone has a perception of good and evil, of just and unjust, and it is a participation of these common sentiments which forms a family and a city. Besides, the notion of a city naturally precedes that of a family or an individual, for the whole must necessarily be prior to the parts; for if you take away the whole man, you cannot say a foot or a hand remains, unless by equivocation, as supposing a hand of stone to be made, but that would only be a dead one; but everything is understood to be this or that by its energic qualities and powers, so that when these no longer remain, neither can that be said to be the same, but something of the same name. That a city then precedes an individual is plain, for if an individual is not in himself sufficient to compose a perfect government, he is to a city as other parts are to a whole; but he that is incapable of society, or so complete in himself as not to want it, makes no part of a city, as a beast or a god. There is then in all persons a natural impetus to associate with each other in this manner, and he who first founded civil society was the cause of the greatest good; for as by the completion of it man is the most excellent of all living beings, so without law and justice he would be the worst of all, for nothing is so difficult to subdue as injustice in arms: but these arms man is born with, namely, prudence and valour, which he may apply to the most opposite purposes, for he who abuses them will be the most wicked, the most cruel, the most lustful, and most gluttonous being imaginable; for justice is a political virtue, by the rules of it the state is regulated, and these rules are the criterion of what is right.

CHAPTER III

SINCE it is now evident of what parts a city is composed, it will be necessary to treat first of family government, for every city is made up of families, and every family 1253*b* has again its separate parts of which it is composed. When a family is complete, it consists of freemen and slaves; but as in every subject we should begin with examining into the smallest parts of which it consists, and as the first and smallest parts of a family are the master and slave, the husband and wife, the father and child, let us first inquire into these three, what each of them may be, and what they ought to be; that is to say, the herile, the nuptial, and the paternal. Let these then be considered as the three distinct parts of a family: some think that the providing what is necessary for the family is something different from the government of it, others that this is the greatest part of it; it shall be considered separately; but we will first speak of a master and a slave, that we may both understand the nature of those things which are absolutely necessary, and also try if we can learn anything better on this subject than what is already known. Some persons have thought that the power of the master over his slave originates from his superior knowledge, and that this knowledge is the same in the master, the magistrate, and the king, as we have already said; but others think that herile

government is contrary to nature, and that it is the law
which makes one man a slave and another free, but that
in nature there is no difference; for which reason that
power cannot be founded in justice, but in force.

CHAPTER IV

Since then a subsistence is necessary in every family,
the means of procuring it certainly makes up part of the
management of a family, for without necessaries it is
impossible to live, and to live well. As in all arts which
are brought to perfection it is necessary that they should
have their proper instruments if they would complete
their works, so is it in the art of managing a family: now
of instruments some of them are alive, others inanimate;
thus with respect to the pilot of the ship, the tiller is
without life, the sailor is alive; for a servant is as an
instrument in many arts. Thus property is as an instrument to living; an estate is a multitude of instruments;
so a slave is an animated instrument, but every one that
can minister of himself is more valuable than any other
instrument; for if every instrument, at command, or
from a preconception of its master's will, could accomplish
its work (as the story goes of the statues of Dædalus; or
what the poet tells us of the tripods of Vulcan, " that
they moved of their own accord into the assembly of the
gods "), the shuttle would then weave, and the lyre play
of itself; nor would the architect want servants, or the
1254a master slaves. Now what are generally called instruments are the efficients of something else, but possessions
are what we simply use: thus with a shuttle we make
something else for our use; but we only use a coat, or
a bed: since then making and using differ from each other
in species, and they both require their instruments, it is
necessary that these should be different from each other.
Now life is itself what we use, and not what we employ
as the efficient of something else; for which reason the
services of a slave are for use. A possession may be

considered in the same nature as a part of anything;
now a part is not only a part of something, but also is
nothing else; so is a possession; therefore a master is
only the master of the slave, but no part of him; but
the slave is not only the slave of the master, but nothing
else but that. This fully explains what is the nature of
a slave, and what are his capacities; for that being who
by nature is nothing of himself, but totally another's,
and is a man, is a slave by nature; and that man who
is the property of another, is his mere chattel, though he
continues a man; but a chattel is an instrument for use,
separate from the body.

CHAPTER V

BUT whether any person is such by nature, and whether
it is advantageous and just for any one to be a slave or
no, or whether all slavery is contrary to nature, shall be
considered hereafter; not that it is difficult to determine
it upon general principles, or to understand it from
matters of fact; for that some should govern, and others
be governed, is not only necessary but useful, and from
the hour of their birth some are marked out for those
purposes, and others for the other, and there are many
species of both sorts. And the better those are who are
governed the better also is the government, as for instance
of man, rather than the brute creation: for the more
excellent the materials are with which the work is finished,
the more excellent certainly is the work; and wherever
there is a governor and a governed, there certainly is some
work produced; for whatsoever is composed of many
parts, which jointly become one, whether conjunct or
separate, evidently show the marks of governing and
governed; and this is true of every living thing in all
nature; nay, even in some things which partake not of
life, as in music; but this probably would be a disquisition
too foreign to our present purpose. Every living thing
in the first place is composed of soul and body, of these

the one is by nature the governor, the other the governed; now if we would know what is natural, we ought to search for it in those subjects in which nature appears most perfect, and not in those which are corrupted; we should therefore examine into a man who is most perfectly formed both in soul and body, in whom this is evident, for in the depraved and vicious the body seems 1254*b* to rule rather than the soul, on account of their being corrupt and contrary to nature. We may then, as we affirm, perceive in an animal the first principles of herile and political government; for the soul governs the body as the master governs his slave; the mind governs the appetite with a political or a kingly power, which shows that it is both natural and advantageous that the body should be governed by the soul, and the pathetic part by the mind, and that part which is possessed of reason; but to have no ruling power, or an improper one, is hurtful to all; and this holds true not only of man, but of other animals also, for tame animals are naturally better than wild ones, and it is advantageous that both should be under subjection to man; for this is productive of their common safety: so is it naturally with the male and the female; the one is superior, the other inferior; the one governs, the other is governed; and the same rule must necessarily hold good with respect to all mankind. Those men therefore who are as much inferior to others as the body is to the soul, are to be thus disposed of, as the proper use of them is their bodies, in which their excellence consists; and if what I have said be true, they are slaves by nature, and it is advantageous to them to be always under government. He then is by nature formed a slave who is qualified to become the chattel of another person, and on that account is so, and who has just reason enough to know that there is such a faculty, without being indued with the use of it; for other animals have no perception of reason, but are entirely guided by appetite, and indeed they vary very little in their use from each other; for the advantage which we receive, both from slaves and tame animals, arises from their bodily strength administering to our necessities; for it is the intention of nature to make the bodies of slaves and freemen different from each other, that the one should be robust for their necessary purposes, the others erect, useless indeed for what slaves are employed in, but fit for civil life, which is divided into the duties of war and peace; though these rules do not always take place, for slaves have sometimes the bodies of freemen, sometimes the souls; if then it is evident that if some bodies are as much more excellent than others as the statues of the gods excel the human form, every one will allow that the inferior ought to be slaves to the superior; and if this is true with respect to the body, it is still juster to determine in the same manner, when we consider the soul; though it is not so easy to perceive the beauty of 1255a the soul as it is of the body. Since then some men are slaves by nature, and others are freemen, it is clear that where slavery is advantageous to any one, then it is just to make him a slave.

CHAPTER VI

BUT it is not difficult to perceive that those who maintain the contrary opinion have some reason on their side; for a man may become a slave two different ways; for he may be so by law also, and this law is a certain compact, by which whatsoever is taken in battle is adjudged to be the property of the conquerors: but many persons who are conversant in law call in question this pretended right, and say that it would be hard that a man should be compelled by violence to be the slave and subject of another who had the power to compel him, and was his superior in strength; and upon this subject, even of those who are wise, some think one way and some another; but the cause of this doubt and variety of opinions arises from hence, that great abilities, when accompanied with proper means, are generally able to succeed by force: for victory is always owing to a superiority in some advantageous circumstances; so that it seems that force never prevails but in consequence of great abilities. But still the dispute concerning the justice of it remains; for some persons think, that justice consists in benevolence, others think it just that the powerful should govern: in the midst of these contrary opinions, there are no reasons sufficient to convince us, that the right of being master and governor ought not to be placed with those who have the greatest abilities. Some persons, entirely resting upon the right which the law gives (for that which is legal is in some respects just), insist upon it that slavery occasioned by war is just, not that they say it is wholly so, for it may happen that the principle upon which the wars were commenced is unjust; moreover no one will say that a man who is unworthily in slavery is therefore a slave; for if so, men of the noblest families might happen to be slaves, and the descendants of slaves, if they should chance to be taken prisoners in war and sold: to avoid this difficulty they say that such persons should not be called slaves, but barbarians only should; but when they say this, they do nothing more than inquire who is a slave by nature, which was what we at first said; for we must acknowledge that there are some persons who, wherever they are, must necessarily be slaves, but others in no situation; thus also it is with those of noble descent: it is not only in their own country that they are esteemed as such, but everywhere, but the barbarians are respected on this account at home only; as if nobility and freedom were of two sorts, the one universal, the other not so. Thus says the Helen of Theodectes:

" Who dares reproach me with the name of slave?
When from the immortal gods, on either side,
I draw my lineage."

Those who express sentiments like these, shew only that they distinguish the slave and the freeman, the noble and the ignoble from each other by their virtues and their 1255*b* vices; for they think it reasonable, that as a man begets a man, and a beast a beast, so from a good man, a good man should be descended; and this is what nature desires to do, but frequently cannot accomplish it. It is evident then that this doubt has some reason in it, and that these persons are not slaves, and those freemen, by the appointment of nature; and also that in some instances it is sufficiently clear, that it is advantageous to both parties for this man to be a slave, and that to be a master, and that it is right and just, that some should be governed, and others govern, in the manner that nature intended; of which sort of government is that which a master exercises over a slave. But to govern ill is disadvantageous to both; for the same thing is useful to the part and to the whole, to the body and to the soul; but the slave is as it were a part of the master, as if he were an animated part of his body, though separate. For which reason a mutual utility and friendship may subsist between the master and the slave, I mean when they are placed by nature in that relation to each other, for the contrary takes place amongst those who are reduced to slavery by the law, or by conquest.

CHAPTER VII

It is evident from what has been said, that a herile and a political government are not the same, or that all governments are alike to each other, as some affirm; for one is adapted to the nature of freemen, the other to that of slaves. Domestic government is a monarchy, for that is what prevails in every house; but a political state is the government of free men and equals. The master is not so called from his knowing how to manage his slave, but because he is so; for the same reason a slave and a freeman have their respective appellations. There is also one sort of knowledge proper for a master, another for a slave; the slave's is of the nature of that which was taught by a slave at Syracuse; for he for a stipulated sum instructed the boys in all the business of a household slave, of which there are various sorts to be learnt, as the art of cookery, and other such-like services, of which some are allotted to some, and others to others; some employments being more honourable, others more necessary;

according to the proverb, " One slave excels another, one master excels another: " in such-like things the knowledge of a slave consists. The knowledge of the master is to be able properly to employ his slaves, for the mastership of slaves is the employment, not the mere possession of them; not that this knowledge contains anything great or respectable; for what a slave ought to know how to do, that a master ought to know how to order; for which reason, those who have it in their power to be free from these low attentions, employ a steward for this business, and apply themselves either to public affairs or philosophy: the knowledge of procuring what is necessary for a family is different from that which belongs either to the master or the slave: and to do this justly must be either by war or hunting. And thus much of the difference between a master and a slave.

CHAPTER VIII

1256a As a slave is a particular species of property, let us by all means inquire into the nature of property in general, and the acquisition of money, according to the manner we have proposed. In the first place then, some one may doubt whether the getting of money is the same thing as economy, or whether it is a part of it, or something subservient to it; and if so, whether it is as the art of making shuttles is to the art of weaving, or the art of making brass to that of statue founding, for they are not of the same service; for the one supplies the tools, the other the matter: by the matter I mean the subject out of which the work is finished, as wool for the cloth and brass for the statue. It is evident then that the getting of money is not the same thing as economy, for the business of the one is to furnish the means of the other to use them; and what art is there employed in the management of a family but economy, but whether this is a part of it, or something of a different species, is a doubt; for if it is the business of him who is to get money to find out how riches and possessions may be procured, and both these arise from various causes, we must first inquire whether the art of husbandry is part of money-getting or something different, and in general, whether the same is not true of every acquisition and every attention which relates to provision. But as there are many sorts of provision, so are the methods of living both of man and the brute creation very various; and as it is impossible to live without food, the difference in that particular makes the lives of animals so different from each other. Of beasts, some live in herds, others separate, as is most convenient for procuring themselves food; as some of them live upon flesh, others on fruit, and others on whatsoever they light on, nature having so distinguished their course of life, that they can very easily procure themselves subsistence; and as the same things are not agreeable to all, but one animal likes one thing and another another, it follows that the lives of those beasts who live upon flesh must be different from the lives of those who live on fruits; so is it with men, their lives differ greatly from each other; and of all these the shepherd's is the idlest, for they live upon the flesh of tame animals, without any trouble, while they are obliged to change their habitations on account of their flocks, which they are compelled to follow, cultivating, as it were, a living farm. Others live exercising violence over living creatures, one pursuing this thing, another that, these preying upon men; those who live near lakes and marshes and rivers, or the sea itself, on fishing, while others are fowlers, or hunters of wild beasts; but the greater part of mankind live upon the produce of the earth and its cultivated fruits; and the manner in which all those live who follow the direction of nature, and labour for their own subsistence, is nearly the same, without ever thinking to procure any provision by way of exchange or merchandise, such are shepherds, husband- 1256b men, robbers, fishermen, and hunters: some join different employments together, and thus live very agreeably; supplying those deficiencies which were wanting to make their subsistence depend upon themselves only: thus, for instance, the same person shall be a shepherd and a

robber, or a husbandman and a hunter; and so with
respect to the rest, they pursue that mode of life which
necessity points out. This provision then nature herself
seems to have furnished all animals with, as well immediately upon their first origin as also when they are
arrived at a state of maturity; for at the first of these
periods some of them are provided in the womb with
proper nourishment, which continues till that which is
born can get food for itself, as is the case with worms and
birds; and as to those which bring forth their young alive,
they have the means for their subsistence for a certain
time within themselves, namely milk. It is evident then
that we may conclude of those things that are, that
plants are created for the sake of animals, and animals
for the sake of men; the tame for our use and provision;
the wild, at least the greater part, for our provision also,
or for some other advantageous purpose, as furnishing us
with clothes, and the like. As nature therefore makes
nothing either imperfect or in vain, it necessarily follows
that she has made all these things for men: for which
reason what we gain in war is in a certain degree a natural
acquisition; for hunting is a part of it, which it is necessary for us to employ against wild beasts; and those
men who being intended by nature for slavery are unwilling to submit to it, on which occasion such a war is
by nature just: that species of acquisition then only
which is according to nature is part of economy; and this
ought to be at hand, or if not, immediately procured,
namely, what is necessary to be kept in store to live upon,
and which are useful as well for the state as the family.
And true riches seem to consist in these; and the acquisition of those possessions which are necessary for a happy
life is not infinite; though Solon says otherwise in this
verse:

" No bounds to riches can be fixed for man; "

for they may be fixed as in other arts; for the instruments
of no art whatsoever are infinite, either in their number
or their magnitude; but riches are a number of instruments in domestic and civil economy; it is therefore

evident that the acquisition of certain things according
to nature is a part both of domestic and civil economy,
and for what reason.

CHAPTER IX

THERE is also another species of acquisition which they 1257a
particularly call pecuniary, and with great propriety; and
by this indeed it seems that there are no bounds to
riches and wealth.   Now many persons suppose, from their
near relation to each other, that this is one and the same
with that we have just mentioned, but it is not the same
as that, though not very different; one of these is natural,
the other is not, but rather owing to some art and skill;
we will enter into a particular examination of this subject.
   The uses of every possession are two, both dependent
upon the thing itself, but not in the same manner, the
one supposing an inseparable connection with it, the other
not; as a shoe, for instance, which may be either worn,
or exchanged for something else, both these are the uses
of the shoe; for he who exchanges a shoe with some man
who wants one, for money or provisions, uses the shoe
as a shoe, but not according to the original intention, for
shoes were not at first made to be exchanged.   The same
thing holds true of all other possessions; for barter, in
general, had its original beginning in nature, some men
having a surplus, others too little of what was necessary
for them: hence it is evident, that the selling provisions
for money is not according to the natural use of things;
for they were obliged to use barter for those things which
they wanted; but it is plain that barter could have no
place in the first, that is to say, in family society; but
must have begun when the number of those who composed the community was enlarged: for the first of these
had all things in common; but when they came to be
separated they were obliged to exchange with each other
many different things which both parties wanted.   Which
custom of barter is still preserved amongst many bar-

barous nations, who procure one necessary with another, but never sell anything; as giving and receiving wine for corn and the like. This sort of barter is not contradictory to nature, nor is it any species of money-getting; but is necessary in procuring that subsistence which is so consonant thereunto. But this barter introduced the use of money, as might be expected; for a convenient place from whence to import what you wanted, or to export what you had a surplus of, being often at a great distance, money necessarily made its way into commerce; for it is not everything which is naturally most useful that is easiest of carriage; for which reason they invented something to exchange with each other which they should mutually give and take, that being really valuable itself, should have the additional advantage of being of easy conveyance, for the purposes of life, as iron and silver, or anything else of the same nature: and this at first passed in value simply according to its weight or size; but in process of time it had a certain stamp, to save the trouble of weighing, which stamp expressed its value.

1257b Money then being established as the necessary medium of exchange, another species of money-getting soon took place, namely, by buying and selling, at probably first in a simple manner, afterwards with more skill and experience, where and how the greatest profits might be made. For which reason the art of money-getting seems to be chiefly conversant about trade, and the business of it to be able to tell where the greatest profits can be made, being the means of procuring abundance of wealth and possessions: and thus wealth is very often supposed to consist in the quantity of money which any one possesses, as this is the medium by which all trade is conducted and a fortune made, others again regard it as of no value, as being of none by nature, but arbitrarily made so by compact; so that if those who use it should alter their sentiments, it would be worth nothing, as being of no service for any necessary purpose. Besides, he who abounds in money often wants necessary food; and it is impossible to say that any person is in good circumstances when with all his possessions he may perish with hunger.

Like Midas in the fable, who from his insatiable wish had everything he touched turned into gold. For which reason others endeavour to procure other riches and other property, and rightly, for there are other riches and property in nature; and these are the proper objects of economy: while trade only procures money, not by all means, but by the exchange of it, and for that purpose it is this which it is chiefly employed about, for money is the first principle and the end of trade; nor are there any bounds to be set to what is thereby acquired.

Thus also there are no limits to the art of medicine, with respect to the health which it attempts to procure; the same also is true of all other arts; no line can be drawn to terminate their bounds, the several professors of them being desirous to extend them as far as possible. (But still the means to be employed for that purpose are limited; and these are the limits beyond which the art cannot proceed.) Thus in the art of acquiring riches there are no limits, for the object of that is money and possessions; but economy has a boundary, though this has not: for acquiring riches is not the business of that, for which reason it should seem that some boundary should be set to riches, though we see the contrary to this is what is practised; for all those who get riches add to their money without end; the cause of which is the near connection of these two arts with each other, which sometimes occasions the one to change employments with the other, as getting of money is their common object: for economy requires the possession of wealth, but not on its own account but with another view, to purchase things necessary therewith; but the other procures it merely to increase it: so that some persons are confirmed in their belief, that this is the proper object of economy, and think that for this purpose money should be saved and hoarded up without end; the reason for which disposition is, that 1258a they are intent upon living, but not upon living well; and this desire being boundless in its extent, the means which they aim at for that purpose are boundless also; and those who propose to live well, often confine that to the enjoyment of the pleasures of sense; so that as this also

seems to depend upon what a man has, all their care is
to get money, and hence arises the other cause for this
art; for as this enjoyment is excessive in its degree, they
endeavour to procure means proportionate to supply it;
and if they cannot do this merely by the art of dealing
in money, they will endeavour to do it by other ways,
and apply all their powers to a purpose they were not
by nature intended for. Thus, for instance, courage was
intended to inspire fortitude, not to get money by; neither
is this the end of the soldier's or the physician's art, but
victory and health. But such persons make everything
subservient to money-getting, as if this was the only end;
and to the end everything ought to refer.

We have now considered that art of money-getting which
is not necessary, and have seen in what manner we became
in want of it; and also that which is necessary, which is
different from it; for that economy which is natural, and
whose object is to provide food, is not like this unlimited
in its extent, but has its bounds.

CHAPTER X

We have now determined what was before doubtful,
whether or no the art of getting money is his business who
is at the head of a family or a state, and though not strictly
so, it is however very necessary; for as a politician does not
make men, but receiving them from the hand of nature
employs them to proper purposes; thus the earth, or the
sea, or something else ought to supply them with provisions, and this it is the business of the master of the
family to manage properly; for it is not the weaver's
business to make yarn, but to use it, and to distinguish
what is good and useful from what is bad and of no
service; and indeed some one may inquire why getting
money should be a part of economy when the art of
healing is not, as it is as requisite that the family should
be in health as that they should eat, or have anything
else which is necessary; and as it is indeed in some

particulars the business both of the master of the family, and he to whom the government of the state is entrusted, to see after the health of those under their care, but in others not, but the physician's; so also as to money; in some respects it is the business of the master of the family, in others not, but of the servant; but as we have already said, it is chiefly nature's, for it is her part to supply her offspring with food; for everything finds nourishment left for it in what produced it; for which reason the natural riches of all men arise from fruits and animals. Now money-making, as we say, being twofold, it may be applied to two purposes, the service of the house or retail trade; of which the first is necessary and commendable, the other justly censurable; for it has not its origin in 1258*b* nature, but by it men gain from each other; for usury is most reasonably detested, as it is increasing our fortune by money itself, and not employing it for the purpose it was originally intended, namely exchange.

And this is the explanation of the name (τόκος), which means the breeding of money. For as offspring resemble their parents, so usury is money bred of money. Whence of all forms of money-making it is most against nature.

CHAPTER XI

HAVING already sufficiently considered the general principles of this subject, let us now go into the practical part thereof; the one is a liberal employment for the mind, the other necessary. These things are useful in the management of one's affairs; to be skilful in the nature of cattle, which are most profitable, and where, and how; as for instance, what advantage will arise from keeping horses, or oxen, or sheep, or any other live stock; it is also necessary to be acquainted with the comparative value of these things, and which of them in particular places are worth most; for some do better in one place, some in another. Agriculture also should be understood, and the management of arable grounds and orchards;

and also the care of bees, and fish, and birds, from whence
any profit may arise; these are the first and most proper
parts of domestic management.

With respect to gaining money by exchange, the
principal method of doing this is by merchandise, which
is carried on in three different ways, either by sending
the commodity for sale by sea or by land, or else selling
it on the place where it grows; and these differ from each
other in this, that the one is more profitable, the other
safer. The second method is by usury. The third by
receiving wages for work done, and this either by being
employed in some mean art, or else in mere bodily labour.
There is also a third species of improving a fortune, that
is something between this and the first; for it partly
depends upon nature, partly upon exchange; the subject
of which is, things that are immediately from the earth,
or their produce, which, though they bear no fruit, are
yet useful, such as selling of timber and the whole art
of metallurgy, which includes many different species, for
there are various sorts of things dug out of the earth.

These we have now mentioned in general, but to enter
into particulars concerning each of them, though it might
be useful to the artist, would be tiresome to dwell on.
Now of all the works of art, those are the most excellent
wherein chance has the least to do, and those are the
meanest which deprave the body, those the most servile in
which bodily strength alone is chiefly wanted, those most
illiberal which require least skill; but as there are books
written on these subjects by some persons, as by Chares
the Panian, and Apollodorus the Lemnian, upon husbandry and planting; and by others on other matters,
1259a let those who have occasion consult them thereon; besides,
every person should collect together whatsoever he hears
occasionally mentioned, by means of which many of those
who aimed at making a fortune have succeeded in their
intentions; for all these are useful to those who make
a point of getting money, as in the contrivance of Thales
the Milesian (which was certainly a gainful one, but as it
was his it was attributed to his wisdom, though the
method he used was a general one, and would universally

succeed), when they reviled him for his poverty, as if the study of philosophy was useless: for they say that he, perceiving by his skill in astrology that there would be great plenty of olives that year, while it was yet winter, having got a little money, he gave earnest for all the oil works that were in Miletus and Chios, which he hired at a low price, there being no one to bid against him; but when the season came for making oil, many persons wanting them, he all at once let them upon what terms he pleased; and raising a large sum of money by that means, convinced them that it was easy for philosophers to be rich if they chose it, but that that was not what they aimed at; in this manner is Thales said to have shown his wisdom.   It indeed is, as we have said, generally gainful for a person to contrive to make a monopoly of anything; for which reason some cities also take this method when they want money, and monopolise their commodities. There was a certain person in Sicily who laid out a sum of money which was deposited in his hand in buying up all the iron from the iron merchants; so that when the dealers came from the markets to purchase, there was no one had any to sell but himself; and though he put no great advance upon it, yet by laying out fifty talents he made an hundred.   When Dionysius heard this he permitted him to take his money with him, but forbid him to continue any longer in Sicily, as being one who contrived means for getting money inconsistent with his affairs.   This man's view and Thales's was exactly the same; both of them contrived to procure a monopoly for themselves: it is useful also for politicians to understand these things, for many states want to raise money and by such means, as well as private families, nay more so; for which reason some persons who are employed in the management of public affairs confine themselves to this province only.

CHAPTER XII

THERE are then three parts of domestic government, the masters, of which we have already treated, the fathers, and the husbands; now the government of the wife and children should both be that of free persons, but not the 1259*b* same; for the wife should be treated as a citizen of a free state, the children should be under kingly power; for the male is by nature superior to the female, except when something happens contrary to the usual course of nature, as is the elder and perfect to the younger and imperfect. Now in the generality of free states, the governors and the governed alternately change place; for an equality without any preference is what nature chooses; 'however, when one governs and another is governed, she endeavours that there should be a distinction between them in forms, expressions, and honours; according to what Amasis said of his laver. This then should be the established rule between the man and the woman. The government of children should be kingly; for the power of the father over the child is founded in affection and seniority, which is a species of kingly government; for which reason Homer very properly calls Jupiter " the father of gods and men," who was king of both these; for nature requires that a king should be of the same species with those whom he governs, though superior in some particulars, as is the case between the elder and the younger, the father and the son.

CHAPTER XIII

IT is evident then that in the due government of a family, greater attention should be paid to the several members of it and their virtues than to the possessions or riches of it; and greater to the freemen than the slaves: but here some one may doubt whether there is any other

virtue in a slave than his organic services, and of higher
estimation than these, as temperance, fortitude, justice,
and such-like habits, or whether they possess only bodily
qualities: each side of the question has its difficulties;
for if they possess these virtues, wherein do they differ
from freemen? and that they do not, since they are men,
and partakers of reason, is absurd. Nearly the same
inquiry may be made concerning a woman and a child,
whether these also have their proper virtues; whether
a woman ought to be temperate, brave, and just, and
whether a child is temperate or no; and indeed this
inquiry ought to be general, whether the virtues of those
who, by nature, either govern or are governed, are the
same or different; for if it is necessary that both of them
should partake of the fair and good, why is it also necessary that, without exception, the one should govern, the
other always be governed? for this cannot arise from
their possessing these qualities in different degrees; for
to govern, and to be governed, are things different in
species, but *more* or *less* are not.   And yet it is wonderful
that one party ought to have them, and the other not;
for if he who is to govern should not be temperate and
just, how can he govern well? or if he is to be governed,
how can he be governed well? for he who is intemperate 1260*a*
and a coward will never do what he ought: it is evident
then that both parties ought to be virtuous; but there
is a difference between them, as there is between those
who by nature command and who by nature obey, and
this originates in the soul; for in this nature has planted
the governing and submitting principle, the virtues of
which we say are different, as are those of a rational and
an irrational being.   It is plain then that the same
principle may be extended farther, and that there are in
nature a variety of things which govern and are governed;
for a freeman is governed in a different manner from
a slave, a male from a female, and a man from a child:
and all these have parts of mind within them, but in
a different manner.   Thus a slave can have no power of
determination, a woman but a weak one, a child an
imperfect one.   Thus also must it necessarily be with

respect to moral virtues; all must be supposed to possess them, but not in the same manner, but as is best suited to every one's employment; on which account he who is to govern ought to be perfect in moral virtue, for his business is entirely that of an architect, and reason is the architect; while others want only that portion of it which may be sufficient for their station; from whence it is evident, that although moral virtue is common to all those we have spoken of, yet the temperance of a man and a woman are not the same, nor their courage, nor their justice, though Socrates thought otherwise; for the courage of the man consists in commanding, the woman's in obeying; and the same is true in other particulars: and this will be evident to those who will examine different virtues separately; for those who use general terms deceive themselves when they say, that virtue consists in a good disposition of mind, or doing what is right, or something of this sort. They do much better who enumerate the different virtues as Georgias did, than those who thus define them; and as Sophocles speaks of a woman, we think of all persons, that their virtues should be applicable to their characters, for says he,

" Silence is a woman's ornament,"

but it is not a man's; and as a child is incomplete, it is evident that his virtue is not to be referred to himself in his present situation, but to that in which he will be complete, and his preceptor. In like manner the virtue of a slave is to be referred to his master; for we laid it down as a maxim, that the use of a slave was to employ him in what you wanted; so that it is clear enough that few virtues are wanted in his station, only that he may not neglect his work through idleness or fear: some person may question if what I have said is true, whether virtue is not necessary for artificers in their calling, for they often through idleness neglect their work, but the difference between them is very great; for a slave is connected with you for life, but the artificer not so nearly: as near therefore as the artificer approaches to

the situation of a slave, just so much ought he to have
of the virtues of one; for a mean artificer is to a certain
point a slave; but then a slave is one of those things
which are by nature what they are, but this is not true 1260b
of a shoemaker, or any other artist. It is evident then
that a slave ought to be trained to those virtues which
are proper for his situation by his master; and not by
him who has the power of a master, to teach him any
particular art. Those therefore are in the wrong who
would deprive slaves of reason, and say that they have
only to follow their orders; for slaves want more instruction than children, and thus we determine this matter.
It is necessary, I am sensible, for every one who treats
upon government, to enter particularly into the relations
of husband and wife, and of parent and child, and to show
what are the virtues of each and their respective connections with each other; what is right and what is wrong;
and how the one ought to be followed, and the other
avoided. Since then every family is part of a city, and
each of those individuals is part of a family, and the
virtue of the parts ought to correspond to the virtue of
the whole; it is necessary, that both the wives and children
of the community should be instructed correspondent
to the nature thereof, if it is of consequence to the virtue
of the state, that the wives and children therein should
be virtuous, and of consequence it certainly is, for the
wives are one half of the free persons; and of the children
the succeeding citizens are to be formed. As then we
have determined these points, we will leave the rest to be
spoken to in another place, as if the subject was now
finished; and beginning again anew, first consider the
sentiments of those who have treated of the most perfect
forms of government.

BOOK II

CHAPTER I

SINCE then we propose to inquire what civil society is of all others best for those who have it in their power to live entirely as they wish, it is necessary to examine into the polity of those states which are allowed to be well governed; and if there should be any others which some persons have described, and which appear properly regulated, to note what is right and useful in them; and when we point out wherein they have failed, let not this be imputed to an affectation of wisdom, for it is because there are great defects in all those which are already established, that I have been induced to undertake this work. We will begin with that part of the subject which naturally presents itself first to our consideration. The members of every state must of necessity have all things in common, or some things common, and not others, or nothing at all common. To have nothing in common is evidently impossible, for society itself is one species of 1261a community; and the first thing necessary thereunto is a common place of habitation, namely the city, which must be one, and this every citizen must have a share in. But in a government which is to be well founded, will it be best to admit of a community in everything which is capable thereof, or only in some particulars, but in others not? for it is possible that the citizens may have their wives, and children, and goods in common, as in Plato's *Commonwealth;* for in that Socrates affirms that all these particulars ought to be so. Which then shall we prefer? the custom which is already established, or the laws which are proposed in that treatise?

CHAPTER II

Now as a community of wives is attended with many other difficulties, so neither does the cause for which he would frame his government in this manner seem agree-able to reason, nor is it capable of producing that end which he has proposed, and for which he says it ought to take place; nor has he given any particular directions for putting it in practice. Now I also am willing to agree with Socrates in the principle which he proceeds upon, and admit that the city ought to be one as much as possible; and yet it is evident that if it is contracted too much, it will be no longer a city, for that necessarily supposes a multitude; so that if we proceed in this manner, we shall reduce a city to a family, and a family to a single person: for we admit that a family is one in a greater degree than a city, and a single person than a family; so that if this end could be obtained, it should never be put in practice, as it would annihilate the city; for a city does not only consist of a large number of inhabitants, but there must also be different sorts; for were they all alike, there could be no city; for a confederacy and a city are two different things; for a confederacy is valuable from its numbers, although all those who compose it are men of the same calling; for this is entered into for the sake of mutual defence, as we add an additional weight to make the scale go down. The same distinction prevails between a city and a nation when the people are not collected into separate villages, but live as the Arcadians. Now those things in which a city should be one are of different sorts, and in preserving an alternate reciprocation of power between these, the safety thereof consists (as I have already mentioned in my treatise on Morals), for amongst freemen and equals this is absolutely necessary; for all cannot govern at the same time, but either by the year, or according to some other regulation or time, by which means every one in his turn will be in office; as if the shoemakers and carpenters should exchange occupations, and not always be employed in the same calling. But as it is evidently better, that these should continue to exercise their respective trades; so also in civil society, where it is possible, it would be better that the government should continue in the same hands; but where it 1261*b* is not (as nature has made all men equal, and therefore it is just, be the administration good or bad, that all should partake of it), there it is best to observe a rotation, and let those who are their equals by turns submit to those who are at that time magistrates, as they will, in their turns, alternately be governors and governed, as if they were different men: by the same method different persons will execute different offices. From hence it is evident, that a city cannot be one in the manner that some persons propose; and that what has been said to be the greatest good which it could enjoy, is absolutely its destruction, which cannot be: for the good of anything is that which preserves it. For another reason also it is clear, that it is not for the best to endeavour to make a city too much one, because a family is more sufficient in itself than a single person, a city than a family; and indeed Plato supposes that a city owes its existence to that sufficiency in themselves which the members of it enjoy. If then this sufficiency is so desirable, the less the city is one the better.

CHAPTER III

But admitting that it is most advantageous for a city to be one as much as possible, it does not seem to follow that this will take place by permitting all at once to say this is mine, and this is not mine (though this is what Socrates regards as a proof that a city is entirely one), for the word *All* is used in two senses; if it means *each individual*, what Socrates proposes will nearly take place; for each person will say, this is his own son, and his own wife, and his own property, and of everything else that may happen to belong to him, that it is his own. But those who have their wives and children in common will not say so, but all will say so, though not as individuals; therefore, to use the word all is evidently a fallacious mode of speech; for this word is sometimes used distributively, and sometimes collectively, on account of its double meaning, and is the cause of inconclusive syllogisms in reasoning. Therefore for all persons to say the same thing was their own, using the word all in its distributive sense, would be well, but is impossible: in its collective sense it would by no means contribute to the concord of the state. Besides, there would be another inconvenience attending this proposal, for what is common to many is taken least care of; for all men regard more what is their own than what others share with them in, to which they pay less attention than is incumbent on every one: let me add also, that every one is more negligent of what another is to see to, as well as himself, than of his own private business; as in a family one is often worse served by many servants than by a few. Let each citizen then in the state have a thousand children, but let none of them be considered as the children of that individual, but let the relation of father and child be common to them all, and they will all be neglected. Besides, in consequence of this, 1262a whenever any citizen behaved well or ill, every person, be the number what it would, might say, this is my son, or this man's or that; and in this manner would they speak, and thus would they doubt of the whole thousand, or of whatever number the city consisted; and it would be uncertain to whom each child belonged, and when it was born, who was to take care of it: and which do you think is better, for every one to say this is mine, while they may apply it equally to two thousand or ten thousand; or as we say, this is mine in our present forms of government, where one man calls another his son, another calls that same person his brother, another nephew, or some other relation, either by blood or marriage, and first extends his care to him and his, while another regards him as one of the same parish and the same tribe; and

it is better for any one to be a nephew in his private
capacity than a son after that manner. Besides, it will
be impossible to prevent some persons from suspecting
that they are brothers and sisters, fathers and mothers
to each other; for, from the mutual likeness there is
between the sire and the offspring, they will necessarily
conclude in what relation they stand to each other, which
circumstance, we are informed by those writers who
describe different parts of the world, does sometimes
happen; for in Upper Africa there are wives in common
who yet deliver their children to their respective fathers,
being guided by their likeness to them. There are also
some mares and cows which naturally bring forth their
young so like the male, that we can easily distinguish by
which of them they were impregnated: such was the
mare called Just, in Pharsalia.

CHAPTER IV

BESIDES, those who contrive this plan of community
cannot easily avoid the following evils; namely, blows,
murders involuntary or voluntary, quarrels, and re-
proaches, all which it would be impious indeed to be guilty
of towards our fathers and mothers, or those who are
nearly related to us; though not to those who are not
connected to us by any tie of affinity: and certainly these
mischiefs must necessarily happen oftener amongst those
who do not know how they are connected to each other
than those who do; and when they do happen, if it is
among the first of these, they admit of a legal expiation,
but amongst the latter that cannot be done. It is also
absurd for those who promote a community of children
to forbid those who love each other from indulging themselves in the last excesses of that passion, while they do
not restrain them from the passion itself, or those inter-
courses which are of all things most improper, between
a Father and a son, a brother and a brother, and indeed
the thing itself is most absurd. It is also ridiculous to

prevent this intercourse between the nearest relations, for no other reason than the violence of the pleasure, while they think that the relation of father and daughter, the brother and sister, is of no consequence at all. It seems also more advantageous for the state, that the husbandmen should have their wives and children in common than the military, for there will be less affection 1262b among them in that case than when otherwise; for such persons ought to be under subjection, that they may obey the laws, and not seek after innovations. Upon the whole, the consequences of such a law as this would be directly contrary to those things which good laws ought to establish, and which Socrates endeavoured to establish by his regulations concerning women and children: for we think that friendship is the greatest good which can happen to any city, as nothing so much prevents seditions: and amity in a city is what Socrates commends above all things, which appears to be, as indeed he says, the effect of friendship; as we learn from Aristophanes in the *Erotics*, who says, that those who love one another from the excess of that passion, desire to breathe the same soul, and from being two to be blended into one: from whence it would necessarily follow, that both or one of them must be destroyed. But now in a city which admits of this community, the tie of friendship must, from that very cause, be extremely weak, when no father can say, this is my son; or son, this is my father; for as a very little of what is sweet, being mixed with a great deal of water is imperceptible after the mixture, so must all family connections, and the names they go by, be necessarily disregarded in such a community, it being then by no means necessary that the father should have any regard for him he called a son, or the brothers for those they call brothers. There are two things which principally inspire mankind with care and love of their offspring, knowing it is their own, and what ought to be the object of their affection, neither of which can take place in this sort of community. As for exchanging the children of the artificers and husbandmen with those of the military, and theirs reciprocally with these, it will occasion great confusion in whatever manner it shall be done; for of necessity, those who carry the children must know from whom they took and to whom they gave them; and by this means those evils which I have already mentioned will necessarily be the more likely to happen, as blows, incestuous love, murders, and the like; for those who are given from their own parents to other citizens, the military, for instance, will not call them brothers, sons, fathers, or mothers. The same thing would happen to those of the military who were placed among the other citizens; so that by this means every one would be in fear how to act in consequence of consanguinity. And thus let us determine concerning a community of wives and children.

CHAPTER V

WE proceed next to consider in what manner property should be regulated in a state which is formed after the most perfect mode of government, whether it should be common or not; for this may be considered as a separate question from what had been determined concerning 1263a wives and children; I mean, whether it is better that these should be held separate, as they now everywhere are, or that not only possessions but also the usufruct of them should be in common; or that the soil should have a particular owner, but that the produce should be brought together and used as one common stock, as some nations at present do; or on the contrary, should the soil be common, and should it also be cultivated in common, while the produce is divided amongst the individuals for their particular use, which is said to be practised by some barbarians; or shall both the soil and the fruit be common? When the business of the husbandman devolves not on the citizen, the matter is much easier settled; but when those labour together who have a common right of possession, this may occasion several difficulties; for there may not be an equal proportion between their labour and what they consume; and those who labour hard and have but a small proportion of the produce, will certainly complain of those who take a large share of it and do but little for that. Upon the whole, as a community between man and man so entire as to include everything possible, and thus to have all things that man can possess in common, is very difficult, so is it particularly so with respect to property; and this is evident from that community which takes place between those who go out to settle a colony; for they frequently have disputes with each other upon the most common occasions, and come to blows upon trifles: we find, too, that we oftenest correct those slaves who are generally employed in the common offices of the family: a community of property then has these and other inconveniences attending it.

But the manner of life which is now established, more particularly when embellished with good morals and a system of equal laws, is far superior to it, for it will have the advantage of both; by both I mean properties being common, and divided also; for in some respects it ought to be in a manner common, but upon the whole private: for every man's attention being employed on his own particular concerns, will prevent mutual complaints against each other; nay, by this means industry will be increased, as each person will labour to improve his own private property; and it will then be, that from a principle of virtue they will mutually perform good offices to each other, according to the proverb, " All things are common amongst friends; " and in some cities there are traces of this custom to be seen, so that it is not impracticable, and particularly in those which are best governed; some things are by this means in a manner common, and others might be so; for there, every person enjoying his own private property, some things he assists his friend with, others are considered as in common; as in Lacedæmon, where they use each other's slaves, as if they were, so to speak, their own, as they do their horses and dogs, or even any provision they may want in a journey.

It is evident then that it is best to have property

private, but to make the use of it common; but how the citizens are to be brought to it is the particular business of the legislator. And also with respect to pleasure, it is unspeakable how advantageous it is, that a man should think he has something which he may call his own; for it is by no means to no purpose, that each person should have an affection for himself, for that is natural, and yet to be a self-lover is justly censured; for we mean by that, not one that simply loves himself, but one that loves himself more than he ought; in like manner we blame a money-lover, and yet both money and self is what all men love. Besides, it is very pleasing to us to oblige and assist our friends and companions, as well as those whom we are connected with by the rights of hospitality; and this cannot be done without the establishment of private property, which cannot take place with those who make a city too much one; besides, they prevent every opportunity of exercising two principal virtues, modesty and liberality. Modesty with respect to the female sex, for this virtue requires you to abstain from her who is another's; liberality, which depends upon private property, for without that no one can appear liberal, or do any generous action; for liberality consists in imparting to others what is our own.

This system of polity does indeed recommend itself by its good appearance and specious pretences to humanity; and when first proposed to any one, must give him great pleasure, as he will conclude it to be a wonderful bond of friendship, connecting all to all; particularly when any one censures the evils which are now to be found in society, as arising from properties not being common, I mean the disputes which happen between man and man, upon their different contracts with each other; those judgments which are passed in court in consequence of fraud, and perjury, and flattering the rich, none of which arise from properties being private, but from the vices of mankind. Besides, those who live in one general community, and have all things in common, oftener dispute with each other than those who have their property separate; from the very small number indeed of those who have their property in common, compared with those where it is appropriated, the instances of their quarrels are but few. It is also but right to mention, not only the inconveniences they are preserved from who live in a communion of goods, but also the advantages they are deprived of; for when the whole comes to be considered, this manner of life will be found impracticable.

We must suppose, then, that Socrates's mistake arose from the principle he set out with being false; we admit, indeed, that both a family and a city ought to be one in some particulars, but not entirely; for there is a point beyond which if a city proceeds in reducing itself to one, it will be no longer a city.

There is also another point at which it will still continue to be a city, but it will approach so near to not being one, that it will be worse than none; as if any one should reduce the voices of those who sing in concert to one, or a verse to a foot. But the people ought to be made one, and a community, as I have already said, by education; as property at Lacedæmon, and their public tables at Crete, were made common by their legislators. But yet, whosoever shall introduce any education, and think thereby to make his city excellent and respectable, will be absurd, while he expects to form it by such regulations, and not by manners, philosophy, and laws. And who- 1264a ever would establish a government upon a community of goods, ought to know that he should consult the experience of many years, which would plainly enough inform him whether such a scheme is useful; for almost all things have already been found out, but some have been neglected, and others which have been known have not been put in practice. But this would be most evident, if any one could see such a government really established: for it would be impossible to frame such a city without dividing and separating it into its distinct parts, as public tables, wards, and tribes; so that here the laws will do nothing more than forbid the military to engage in agriculture, which is what the Lacedæmonians are at present endeavouring to do.

Nor has Socrates told us (nor is it easy to say) what plan of government should be pursued with respect to the individuals in the state where there is a community of goods established; for though the majority of his citizens will in general consist of a multitude of persons of different occupations, of those he has determined nothing; whether the property of the husbandman ought to be in common, or whether each person should have his share to himself; and also, whether their wives and children ought to be in common: for if all things are to be alike common to all, where will be the difference between them and the military, or what would they get by submitting to their government? and upon what principles would they do it, unless they should establish the wise practice of the Cretans? for they, allowing everything else to their slaves, forbid them only gymnastic exercises and the use of arms. And if they are not, but these should be in the same situation with respect to their property which they are in other cities, what sort of a community will there be? in one city there must of necessity be two, and those contrary to each other; for he makes the military the guardians of the state, and the husbandman, artisans, and others, citizens; and all those quarrels, accusations, and things of the like sort, which he says are the bane of other cities, will be found in his also: notwithstanding Socrates says they will not want many laws in consequence of their education, but such only as may be necessary for regulating the streets, the markets, and the like, while at the same time it is the education of the military only that he has taken any care of. Besides, he makes the husbandmen masters of property upon paying a tribute; but this would be likely to make them far more troublesome and high-spirited than the Helots, the Penestiæ, or the slaves which others employ; nor has he ever determined whether it is necessary to give any attention to them in these particulars, nor thought of what is connected therewith, their polity, their education, their laws; besides, it is of no little consequence, nor is it easy to determine, how these should be framed so as to preserve the community of the military.

Besides, if he makes the wives common, while the property 1264*b* continues separate, who shall manage the domestic concerns with the same care which the man bestows upon his fields? nor will the inconvenience be remedied by making property as well as wives common; and it is absurd to draw a comparison from the brute creation, and say, that the same principle should regulate the connection of a man and a woman which regulates theirs amongst whom there is no family association.

It is also very hazardous to settle the magistracy as Socrates has done; for he would have persons of the same rank always in office, which becomes the cause of sedition even amongst those who are of no account, but more particularly amongst those who are of a courageous and warlike disposition; it is indeed evidently necessary that he should frame his community in this manner; for that golden particle which God has mixed up in the soul of man flies not from one to the other, but always continues with the same; for he says, that some of our species have gold, and others silver, blended in their composition from the moment of their birth: but those who are to be husbandmen and artists, brass and iron; besides, though he deprives the military of happiness, he says, that the legislator ought to make all the citizens happy; but it is impossible that the whole city can be happy, without all, or the greater, or some part of it be happy. For happiness is not like that numerical equality which arises from certain numbers when added together, although neither of them may separately contain it; for happiness cannot be thus added together, but must exist in every individual, as some properties belong to every integral; and if the military are not happy, who else are so? for the artisans are not, nor the multitude of those who are employed in inferior offices. The state which Socrates has described has all these defects, and others which are not of less consequence.

CHAPTER VI

It is also nearly the same in the treatise upon *Laws* which was writ afterwards, for which reason it will be proper in this place to consider briefly what he has there said upon government, for Socrates has thoroughly settled but very few parts of it; as for instance, in what manner the community of wives and children ought to be regulated, how property should be established, and government conducted.

Now he divides the inhabitants into two parts, husbandmen and soldiers, and from these he selects a third part who are to be senators and govern the city; but he has not said whether or no the husbandman and artificer shall have any or what share in the government, or whether they shall have arms, and join with the others in war, or not. He thinks also that the women ought to go to war, and have the same education as the soldiers; as to other particulars, he has filled his treatise with matter foreign to the purpose; and with respect to education, he has only said what that of the guards ought to be.

1265a As to his book of *Laws*, laws are the principal thing which that contains, for he has there said but little concerning government; and this government, which he was so desirous of framing in such a manner as to impart to its members a more entire community of goods than is to be found in other cities, he almost brings round again to be the same as that other government which he had first proposed; for except the community of wives and goods, he has framed both his governments alike, for the education of the citizens is to be the same in both; they are in both to live without any servile employ, and their common tables are to be the same, excepting that in *that* he says the women should have common tables, and that there should be a thousand men-at-arms, in *this*, that there should be five thousand.

All the discourses of Socrates are masterly, noble, new,

and inquisitive; but that they are all true it may probably be too much to say. For now with respect to the number just spoken of, it must be acknowledged that he would want the country of Babylonia for them, or some one like it, of an immeasurable extent, to support five thousand idle persons, besides a much greater number of women and servants. Every one, it is true, may frame an hypothesis as he pleases, but yet it ought to be possible. It has been said, that a legislator should have two things in view when he frames his laws, the country and the people. He will also do well, if he has some regard to the neighbouring states, if he intends that his community should maintain any political intercourse with them, for it is not only necessary that they should understand that practice of war which is adapted to their own country, but to others also; for admitting that any one chooses not this life either in public or private, yet there is not the less occasion for their being formidable to their enemies, not only when they invade their country, but also when they retire out of it.

It may also be considered whether the quantity of each person's property may not be settled in a different manner from what he has done it in, by making it more determinate; for he says, that every one ought to have enough whereon to live moderately, as if any one had said to live well, which is the most comprehensive expression. Besides, a man may live moderately and miserably at the same time; he had therefore better have proposed, that they should live both moderately and liberally; for unless these two conspire, luxury will come in on the one hand, or wretchedness on the other, since these two modes of living are the only ones applicable to the employment of our substance; for we cannot say with respect to a man's fortune, that he is mild or courageous, but we may say that he is prudent and liberal, which are the only qualities connected therewith.

It is also absurd to render property equal, and not to provide for the increasing number of the citizens; but to leave that circumstance uncertain, as if it would regulate itself according to the number of women who

1265*b* should happen to be childless, let that be what it would, because this seems to take place in other cities; but the case would not be the same in such a state which he proposes and those which now actually unite; for in these no one actually wants, as the property is divided amongst the whole community, be their numbers what they will; but as it could not then be divided, the super-numeraries, whether they were many or few, would have nothing at all. But it is more necessary than even to regulate property, to take care that the increase of the people should not exceed a certain number; and in deter-mining that, to take into consideration those children who will die, and also those women who will be barren; and to neglect this, as is done in several cities, is to bring certain poverty on the citizens; and poverty is the cause of sedition and evil. Now Phidon the Corinthian, one of the oldest legislators, thought the families and the number of the citizens should continue the same; although it should happen that all should have allotments at the first, disproportionate to their numbers.

In Plato's *Laws* it is however different; we shall mention hereafter what we think would be best in these particulars. He has also neglected in that treatise to point out how the governors are to be distinguished from the governed; for he says, that as of one sort of wool the warp ought to be made, and of another the woof, so ought some to govern, and others to be governed. But since he admits, that all their property may be increased fivefold, why should he not allow the same increase to the country? he ought also to consider whether his allotment of the houses will be useful to the community, for he appoints two houses to each person, separate from each other; but it is inconvenient for a person to inhabit two houses. Now he is desirous to have his whole plan of government neither a democracy nor an oligarchy, but something between both, which he calls a polity, for it is to be composed of men-at-arms. If Plato intended to frame a state in which more than in any other everything should be common, he has certainly given it a right name; but if he intended it to be the next in perfection to that which he had already framed, it is not so; for perhaps some persons will give the preference to the Lacedæmonian form of government, or some other which may more completely have attained to the aristocratic form.

Some persons say, that the most perfect government should be composed of all others blended together, for which reason they commend that of Lacedæmon; for they say, that this is composed of an oligarchy, a monarchy, and a democracy, their kings representing the monarchical part, the senate the oligarchical; and, that in the ephori may be found the democratical, as these are taken from the people. But some say, that in the ephori is absolute power, and that it is their common meal and daily course of life, in which the democratical form is represented. It is also said in this treatise of 1266*a* *Laws*, that the best form of government must be one composed of a democracy and a tyranny; though such a mixture no one else would ever allow to be any government at all, or if it is, the worst possible; those propose what is much better who blend many governments together; for the most perfect is that which is formed of many parts. But now in this government of Plato's there are no traces of a monarchy, only of an oligarchy and democracy; though he seems to choose that it should rather incline to an oligarchy, as is evident from the appointment of the magistrates; for to choose them by lot is common to both; but that a man of fortune must necessarily be a member of the assembly, or to elect the magistrates, or take part in the management of public affairs, while others are passed over, makes the state incline to an oligarchy; as does the endeavouring that the greater part of the rich may be in office, and that the rank of their appointments may correspond with their fortunes.

The same principle prevails also in the choice of their senate; the manner of electing which is favourable also to an oligarchy; for all are obliged to vote for those who are senators of the first class, afterwards they vote for the same number out of the second, and then out of the third; but this compulsion to vote at the election of senators does not extend to the third and fourth classes, and the first and second class only are obliged to vote for the fourth. By this means he says he shall necessarily have an equal number of each rank, but he is mistaken; for the majority will always consist of those of the first rank, and the most considerable people; and for this reason, that many of the commonalty not being obliged to it, will not attend the elections. From hence it is evident, that such a state will not consist of a democracy and a monarchy, and this will be further proved by what we shall say when we come particularly to consider this form of government.

There will also great danger arise from the manner of electing the senate, when those who are elected themselves are afterwards to elect others; for by this means, if a certain number choose to combine together, though not very considerable, the election will always fall according to their pleasure. Such are the things which Plato proposes concerning government in his book of *Laws*.

CHAPTER VII

THERE are also some other forms of government, which have been proposed either by private persons, or philosophers, or politicians, all of which come much nearer to those which have been really established, or now exist, than these two of Plato's; for neither have they introduced the innovation of a community of wives and children, and public tables for the women, but have been contented to set out with establishing such rules as are absolutely necessary.

There are some persons who think, that the first object of government should be to regulate well everything relating to private property; for they say, that a neglect herein is the source of all seditions whatsoever. For this reason, Phaleas the Chalcedonian first proposed, that the fortunes of the citizens should be equal, which he thought 1266b was not difficult to accomplish when a community was first settled, but that it was a work of greater difficulty in one that had been long established; but yet that it might be effected, and an equality of circumstances introduced by these means, that the rich should give marriage portions, but never receive any, while the poor should always receive, but never give.

But Plato, in his treatise of *Laws*, thinks that a difference in circumstances should be permitted to a certain degree; but that no citizen should be allowed to possess more than five times as much as the lowest census, as we have already mentioned. But legislators who would establish this principle are apt to overlook what they ought to consider; that while they regulate the quantity of provisions which each individual shall possess, they ought also to regulate the number of his children; for if these exceed the allotted quantity of provision, the law must necessarily be repealed; and yet, in spite of the repeal, it will have the bad effect of reducing many from wealth to poverty, so difficult is it for innovators not to fall into such mistakes. That an equality of goods was in some degree serviceable to strengthen the bands of society, seems to have been known to some of the ancients; for Solon made a law, as did some others also, to restrain persons from possessing as much land as they pleased. And upon the same principle there are laws which forbid men to sell their property, as among the Locrians, unless they can prove that some notorious misfortuue has befallen them. They were also to preserve their ancient patrimony, which custom being broken through by the Leucadians, made their government too democratic; for by that means it was no longer necessary to be possessed of a certain fortune to be qualified to be a magistrate. But if an equality of goods is established, this may be either too much, when it enables the people to live luxuriously, or too little, when it obliges them to live hard. Hence it is evident, that it is not proper for the legislator to establish an equality of circumstances, but to fix a proper medium. Besides, if any one should regulate the division of property in such a manner that there should be a moderate sufficiency for all, it would be of no use; for it is of more consequence that the citizens should entertain a şimilarity of sentiments than an equality of circumstances; but this can never be attained unless they are properly educated under the direction of the law. But probably Phaleas may say, that this is what he himself mentions; for he both proposes an equality of property and one plan of education in his city. But he should have said particularly what education he intended, nor is it of any service to have this too much one; for this education may be one, and yet such as will make the citizens over-greedy to grasp after honours, or riches, or both. Besides, not only an inequality of possessions, but also of honours, will occasion 1267a seditions, but this upon contrary grounds; for the vulgar will be seditious if there be an inequality of goods, but those of more elevated sentiments, if there is an equality of honours.

" When good and bad do equal honours share."

For men are not guilty of crimes for necessaries only (for which he thinks an equality of goods would be a sufficient remedy, as they would then have no occasion to steal for cold or hunger), but that they may enjoy what they desire, and not wish for it in vain; for if their desires extend beyond the common necessaries of life, they will be wicked to gratify them; and not only so, but if their wishes point that way, they will do the same to enjoy those pleasures which are free from the alloy of pain. What remedy then shall we find for these three disorders? and first, to prevent stealing from necessity, let every one be supplied with a moderate subsistence, which may make the addition of his own industry necessary; secondly, to prevent stealing to procure the luxuries of life, let temperance be enjoined; and thirdly, let those who wish for pleasure in itself seek for it only in philosophy, for all others want the assistance of men.

Since then men are guilty of the greatest crimes from ambition, and not from necessity, no one, for instance, aims at being a tyrant to keep him from the cold, hence great honour is due to him who kills not a thief, but a tyrant; so that polity which Phaleas establishes would only be salutary to prevent little crimes. He has also been very desirous to establish such rules as will conduce to perfect the internal policy of his state, and he ought also to have done the same with respect to its neighbours and all foreign nations; for the considerations of the military establishment should take place in planning every government, that it may not be unprovided in case of a war, of which he has said nothing; so also with respect to property, it ought not only to be adapted to the exigencies of the state, but also to such dangers as may arise from without.

Thus it should not be so much as to tempt those who are near, and more powerful to invade it, while those who possess it are not able to drive out the invaders, nor so little as that the state should not be able to go to war with those who are quite equal to itself, and of this he has determined nothing; it must indeed be allowed that it is advantageous to a community to be rather rich than poor; probably the proper boundary is this, not to possess enough to make it worth while for a more powerful neighbour to attack you, any more than he would those who had not so much as yourself; thus when Autophradatus proposed to besiege Atarneus, Eubulus advised him to consider what time it would require to take the city, and then would have him determine whether it would answer, for that he should choose, if it would even take less than he proposed, to quit the place; his saying this made Autophradatus reflect upon the business and give over the siege. There is, indeed, some advantage in an equality of goods amongst the citizens to prevent seditions; and yet, to say truth, no very great one; for men of great abilities will stomach their being put upon a level with the rest of the community. For 1267*b* which reason they will very often appear ready for every commotion and sedition; for the wickedness of mankind is insatiable. For though at first two oboli might be sufficient, yet when once it is become customary, they continually want something more, until they set no limits to their expectations; for it is the nature of our desires to be boundless, and many live only to gratify them. But for this purpose the first object is, not so much to establish an equality of fortune, as to prevent those who are of a good disposition from desiring more than their own, and those who are of a bad one from being able to acquire it; and this may be done if they are kept in an inferior station, and not exposed to injustice. Nor has he treated well the equality of goods, for he has extended his regulation only to land; whereas a man's substance consists not only in this, but also in slaves, cattle, money, and all that variety of things which fall under the name of chattels; now there must be either an equality established in all these, or some certain rule, or they must be left entirely at large. It appears too by his laws, that he intends to establish only a small state, as all the artificers are to belong to the public, and add nothing to the complement of citizens; but if all those who are to be employed in public works are to be the slaves of the public, it should be done in the same manner as it is at Epidamnum, and as Diophantus formerly regulated it at Athens. From these particulars any one may nearly judge whether Phaleas's community is well or ill established.

CHAPTER VIII

Hippodamus, the son of Euruphon a Milesian, contrived the art of laying out towns, and separated the Pireus. This man was in other respects too eager after notice, and seemed to many to live in a very affected manner, with his flowing locks and his expensive ornaments, and a coarse warm vest which he wore, not only in the winter, but also in the hot weather. As he was very desirous of the character of a universal scholar, he was the first who, not being actually engaged in the management of public affairs, sat himself to inquire what sort of government was best; and he planned a state, consisting of ten thousand persons, divided into three parts, one consisting of artisans, another of husbandmen, and the third of

soldiers; he also divided the lands into three parts, and
allotted one to sacred purposes, another to the public,
and the third to individuals.   The first of these was to
supply what was necessary for the established worship
of the gods; the second was to be allotted to the support
of the soldiery; and the third was to be the property of
the husbandman.   He thought also that there need only
be three sorts of laws, corresponding to the three sorts of
actions which can be brought, namely, for assault, tres-
passes, or death.   He ordered also that there should be
a particular court of appeal, into which all causes might
be removed which were supposed to have been unjustly
determined elsewhere; which court should be composed
of old men chosen for that purpose.   He thought also 1268a
that they should not pass sentence by votes; but that
every one should bring with him a tablet, on which he
should write, that he found the party guilty, if it was so,
but if not, he should bring a plain tablet; but if he
acquitted him of one part of the indictment but not of
the other, he should express that also on the tablet;
for he disapproved of that general custom already established, as it obliges the judges to be guilty of perjury if
they determined positively either on the one side or the
other.   He also made a law, that those should be re-
warded who found out anything for the good of the city,
and that the children of those who fell in battle should
be educated at the public expense; which law had never
been proposed by any other legislator, though it is at
present in use at Athens as well as in other cities, he
would have the magistrates chosen out of the people in
general, by whom he meant the three parts before spoken
of; and that those who were so elected should be the
particular guardians of what belonged to the public, to
strangers, and to orphans.

These are the principal parts and most worthy of notice
in Hippodamus's plan.   But some persons might doubt
the propriety of his division of the citizens into three
parts; for the artisans, the husbandmen, and the soldiers
are to compose one community, where the husbandmen
are to have no arms, and the artisans neither arms nor

land, which would in a manner render them slaves to the
soldiery. It is also impossible that the whole community
should partake of all the honourable employments in it;
for the generals and the guardians of the state must
necessarily be appointed out of the soldiery, and indeed
the most honourable magistrates; but as the two other
parts will not have their share in the government, how
can they be expected to have any affection for it? But
it is necessary that the soldiery should be superior to the
other two parts, and this superiority will not be easily
gained without they are very numerous; and if they are
so, why should the community consist of any other
members? why should any others have a right to elect
the magistrates? Besides, of what use are the husbandmen to this community? Artisans, 'tis true, are necessary, for these every city wants, and they can live upon
their business. If the husbandmen indeed furnished the
soldiers with provisions, they would be properly part of
the community; but these are supposed to have their
private property, and to cultivate it for their own use.
Moreover, if the soldiers themselves are to cultivate that
common land which is appropriated for their support,
there will be no distinction between the soldier and the
husbandman, which the legislator intended there should
be; and if there should be any others who are to cultivate
the private property of the husbandman and the common
lands of the military, there will be a fourth order in the
state which will have no share in it, and always entertain
hostile sentiments towards it. If any one should propose
that the same persons should cultivate their own lands
and the public ones also, then there would be a deficiency
1268b of provisions to supply two families, as the lands would
not immediately yield enough for themselves and the
soldiers also; and all these things would occasion great
confusion.

Nor do I approve of his method of determining causes,
when he would have the judge split the case which comes
simply before him; and thus, instead of being a judge,
become an arbitrator. Now when any matter is brought
to arbitration, it is customary for many persons to confer

together upon the business that is before them; but when a cause is brought before judges it is not so; and many legislators take care that the judges shall not have it in their power to communicate their sentiments to each other. Besides, what can prevent confusion on the bench when one judge thinks a fine should be different from what another has set it at; one proposing twenty minæ, another ten, or be it more or less, another four, and another five; and it is evident, that in this manner they will differ from each other, while some will give the whole damages sued for, and others nothing; in this situation, how shall their determinations be settled? Besides, a judge cannot be obliged to perjure himself who simply acquits or condemns, if the action is fairly and justly brought; for he who acquits the party does not say that he ought not to pay any fine at all, but that he ought not to pay a fine of twenty minæ. But he that condemns him is guilty of perjury if he sentences him to pay twenty minæ while he believes the damages ought not to be so much.

Now with respect to these honours which he proposes to bestow on those who can give any information useful to the community, this, though very pleasing in speculation, is what the legislator should not settle, for it would encourage informers, and probably occasion commotions in the state. And this proposal of his gives rise also to further conjectures and inquiries; for some persons have doubted whether it is useful or hurtful to alter the established law of any country, if even for the better; for which reason one cannot immediately determine upon what he here says, whether it is advantageous to alter the law or not. We know, indeed, that it is possible to propose to new model both the laws and government as a common good; and since we have mentioned this subject, it may be very proper to enter into a few particulars concerning it, for it contains some difficulties, as I have already said, and it may appear better to alter them, since it has been found useful in other sciences.

Thus the science of physic is extended beyond its ancient bounds; so is the gymnastic, and indeed all other arts and powers; so that one may lay it down for certain, that the same thing will necessarily hold good in the art of government. And it may also be affirmed, that experience itself gives a proof of this; for the ancient laws are too simple and barbarous; which allowed the Greeks to wear swords in the city, and to buy their wives of each 1269a other. And indeed all the remains of old laws which we have are very simple; for instance, a law in Cuma relative to murder. If any person who prosecutes another for murder can produce a certain number of witnesses to it of his own relations, the accused person shall be held guilty.

Upon the whole, all persons ought to endeavour to follow what is right, and not what is established; and it is probable that the first men, whether they sprung out of the earth, or were saved from some general calamity, had very little understanding or knowledge, as is affirmed of these aborigines; so that it would be absurd to continue in the practice of their rules. Nor is it, moreover, right to permit written laws always to remain without alteration; for as in all other sciences, so in politics, it is impossible to express everything in writing with perfect exactness; for when we commit anything to writing we must use general terms, but in every action there is something particular to itself, which these may not comprehend; from whence it is evident, that certain laws will at certain times admit of alterations. But if we consider this matter in another point of view, it will appear to require great caution; for when the advantage proposed is trifling, as the accustoming the people easily to abolish their laws is of bad consequence, it is evidently better to pass over some faults which either the legislator or the magistrates may have committed; for the alterations will not be of so much service as a habit of disobeying the magistrates will be of disservice. Besides, the instance brought from the arts is fallacious; for it is not the same thing to alter the one as the other. For a law derives all its strength from custom, and this requires long time to establish; so that, to make it an easy matter to pass from the established laws to other new ones, is to weaken the power of laws. Besides, here is another question; if the laws are to be

altered, are they all to be altered, and in every government, or not, and whether at the pleasure of one person
or many? all which particulars will make a great
difference; for which reason we will at present drop the
inquiry, to pursue it at some other time.

CHAPTER IX

THERE are two considerations which offer themselves
with respect to the government established at Lacedæmon
and Crete, and indeed in almost all other states whatsoever; one is whether their laws do or do not promote
the best establishment possible? the other is whether
there is anything, if we consider either the principles upon
which it is founded or the executive part of it, which
prevents the form of government that they had proposed
to follow from being observed; now it is allowed that in
every well-regulated state the members of it should be
free from servile labour; but in what manner this shall
be effected is not so easy to determine; for the Penestæ
have very often attacked the Thessalians, and the Helots
the Lacedæmonians, for they in a manner continually
watch an opportunity for some misfortune befalling them.
But no such thing has ever happened to the Cretans; the 1269b
reason for which probably is, that although they are
engaged in frequent wars with the neighbouring cities,
yet none of these would enter into an alliance with the
revolters, as it would be disadvantageous for them, who
themselves also have their villains. But now there is
perpetual enmity between the Lacedæmonians and all
their neighbours, the Argives, the Messenians, and the
Arcadians. Their slaves also first revolted from the
Thessalians while they were engaged in wars with their
neighbours the Acheans, the Perrabeans, and the Mag-
nesians. It seems to me indeed, if nothing else, yet
something very troublesome to keep upon proper terms
with them; for if you are remiss in your discipline they
grow insolent, and think themselves upon an equality

with their masters; and if they are hardly used they are continually plotting against you and hate you. It is evident, then, that those who employ slaves have not as yet hit upon the right way of managing them.

As to the indulging of women in any particular liberties, it is hurtful to the end of government and the prosperity of the city; for as a man and his wife are the two parts of a family, if we suppose a city to be divided into two parts, we must allow that the number of men and women will be equal.

In whatever city then the women are not under good regulations, we must look upon one half of it as not under the restraint of law, as it there happened; for the legislator, desiring to make his whole city a collection of warriors with respect to the men, he most evidently accomplished his design; but in the meantime the women were quite neglected, for they live without restraint in every improper indulgence and luxury. So that in such a state riches will necessarily be in general esteem, particularly if the men are governed by their wives, which has been the case with many a brave and warlike people except the Celts, and those other nations, if there are any such, who openly practise pederasty. And the first mythologists seem not improperly to have joined Mars and Venus together; for all nations of this character are greatly addicted either to the love of women or of boys, for which reason it was thus at Lacedæmon; and many things in their state were done by the authority of the women. For what is the difference, if the power is in the hands of the women, or in the hands of those whom they themselves govern? it must turn to the same account. As this boldness of the women can be of no use in any common occurrences, if it was ever so, it must be in war; but even here we find that the Lacedæmonian women were of the greatest disservice, as was proved at the time of the Theban invasion, when they were of no use at all, as they are in other cities, but made more disturbance than even the enemy.

The origin of this indulgence which the Lacedæmonian women enjoy is easily accounted for, from the long time

the men were absent from home upon foreign expeditions 1270a
against the Argives, and afterwards the Arcadians and
Messenians, so that, when these wars were at an end,
their military life, in which there is no little virtue, prepared them to obey the precepts of their law-giver; but
we are told, that when Lycurgus endeavoured also to
reduce the women to an obedience to his laws, upon their
refusal he declined it. It may indeed be said that the
women were the causes of these things, and of course all
the fault was theirs. But we are not now considering
where the fault lies, or where it does not lie, but what is
right and what is wrong; and when the manners of the
women are not well regulated, as I have already said, it
must not only occasion faults which are disgraceful to the
state, but also increase the love of money. In the next
place, fault may be found with his unequal division of
property, for some will have far too much, others too
little; by which means the land will come into few hands,
which business is badly regulated by his laws. For he
made it infamous for any one either to buy or sell their
possessions, in which he did right; but he permitted any
one that chose it to give them away, or bequeath them,
although nearly the same consequences will arise from one
practice as from the other. It is supposed that near two
parts in five of the whole country is the property of
women, owing to their being so often sole heirs, and having
such large fortunes in marriage; though it would be better
to allow them none, or a little, or a certain regulated
proportion. Now every one is permitted to make a
woman his heir if he pleases; and if he dies intestate, he
who succeeds as heir at law gives it to whom he pleases.
From whence it happens that although the country is àble
to support fifteen hundred horse and thirty thousand foot,
the number does not amount to one thousand.

And from these facts it is evident, that this particular is
badly regulated; for the city could not support one shock,
but was ruined for want of men. They say, that during
the reigns of their ancient kings they used to present
foreigners with the freedom of their city, to prevent there
being a want of men while they carried on long wars; it

is also affirmed that the number of Spartans was formerly
ten thousand; but be that as it will, an equality of property conduces much to increase the number of the people.
The law, too, which he made to encourage population
was by no means calculated to correct this inequality; for
being willing that the Spartans should be as numerous as
1270b possible, to make them desirous of having large families
he ordered that he who had three children should be
excused the night-watch, and that he who had four should
pay no taxes: though it is very evident, that while the
land was divided in this manner, that if the people
increased there must many of them be very poor.

Nor was he less blamable for the manner in which he
constituted the ephori; for these magistrates take cognisance of things of the last importance, and yet they are
chosen out of the people in general; so that it often
happens that a very poor person is elected to that office,
who, from that circumstance, is easily bought. There
have been many instances of this formerly, as well as in
the late affair at Andros. And these men, being corrupted with money, went as far as they could to ruin the
city: and, because their power was too great and nearly
tyrannical, their kings were obliged to flatter them, which
contributed greatly to hurt the state; so that it altered
from an aristocracy to a democracy. This magistracy is
indeed the great support of the state; for the people are
easy, knowing that they are eligible to the first office in it;
so that, whether it took place by the intention of the
legislator, or whether it happened by chance, this is of
great service to their affairs; for it is necessary that every
member of the state should endeavour that each part of
the government should be preserved, and continue the
same. And upon this principle their kings have always
acted, out of regard to their honour; the wise and good
from their attachment to the senate, a seat wherein they
consider as the reward of virtue; and the common people,
that they may support the ephori, of whom they consist.
And it is proper that these magistrates should be chosen
out of the whole community, not as the custom is at
present, which is very ridiculous. The ephori are the

supreme judges in causes of the last consequence; but as it is quite accidental what sort of persons they may be, it is not right that they should determine according to their own opinion, but by a written law or established custom. Their way of life also is not consistent with the manners of the city, for it is too indulgent; whereas that of others is too severe; so that they cannot support it, but are obliged privately to act contrary to law, that they may enjoy some of the pleasures of sense.   There are also great defects in the institution of their senators.   If indeed they were fitly trained to the practice of every human virtue, every one would readily admit that they would be useful to the government; but still it might be debated whether they should be continued judges for life, to determine points of the greatest moment, since the mind has its old age as well as the body; but as they are so brought up, 1271a that even the legislator could not depend upon them as good men, their power must be inconsistent with the safety of the state: for it is known that the members of that body have been guilty both of bribery and partiality in many public affairs; for which reason it had been much better if they had been made answerable for their conduct, which they are not.   But it may be said the ephori seem to have a check upon all the magistrates.   They have indeed in this particular very great power; but I affirm that they should not be entrusted with this control in the manner they are.   Moreover, the mode of choice which they make use of at the election of their senators is very childish.   Nor is it right for any one to solicit for a place he is desirous of; for every person, whether he chooses it or not, ought to execute any office he is fit for.   But his intention was evidently the same in this as in the other parts of his government.   For making his citizens ambitious after honours, with men of that disposition he has filled his senate, since no others will solicit for that office; and yet the principal part of those crimes which men are deliberately guilty of arise from ambition and avarice.

We will inquire at another time whether the office of a king is useful to the state: thus much is certain, that they should be chosen from a consideration of their conduct, and not as they are now. But that the legislator himself did not expect to make all his citizens honourable and completely virtuous is evident from this, that he distrusts them as not being good men; for he sent those upon the same embassy that were at variance with each other; and thought, that in the dispute of the kings the safety of the state consisted. Neither were their common meals at first well established: for these should rather have been provided at the public expense, as at Crete, where, as at Lacedæmon, every one was obliged to buy his portion, although he might be very poor, and could by no means bear the expense, by which means the contrary happened to what the legislator desired: for he intended that those public meals should strengthen the democratic part of his government: but this regulation had quite the contrary effect, for those who were very poor could not take part in them; and it was an observation of their forefathers, that the not allowing those who could not contribute their proportion to the common tables to partake of them, would be the ruin of the state. Other persons have censured his laws concerning naval affairs, and not without reason, as it gave rise to disputes. For the commander of the fleet is in a manner set up in opposition to the kings, who are generals of the army for life.

1271b   There is also another defect in his laws worthy of censure, which Plato has given in his book of *Laws;* that the whole constitution was calculated only for the business of war: it is indeed excellent to make them conquerors; for which reason the preservation of the state depended thereon. The destruction of it commenced with their victories: for they knew not how to be idle, or engage in any other employment than war. In this particular also they were mistaken, that though they rightly thought, that those things which are the objects of contention amongst mankind are better procured by virtue than vice, yet they wrongfully preferred the things themselves to virtue. Nor was the public revenue well managed at Sparta, for the state was worth nothing

while they were obliged to carry on the most extensive
wars, and the subsidies were very badly raised; for as
the Spartans possessed a large extent of country, they
were not exact upon each other as to what they paid in.
And thus an event contrary to the legislator's intention
took place; for the state was poor, the individuals
avaricious. Enough of the Lacedæmonian government;
for these seem the chief defects in it.

CHAPTER X

THE government of Crete bears a near resemblance to
this, in some few particulars it is not worse, but in general
it is far inferior in its contrivance. For it appears and
is allowed in many particulars the constitution of Lacedæmon was formed in imitation of that of Crete; and in
general most new things are an improvement upon the
old. For they say, that when Lycurgus ceased to be
guardian to King Charilles he went abroad and spent
a long time with his relations in Crete, for the Lycians
are a colony of the Lacedæmonians; and those who first
settled there adopted that body of laws which they
found already established by the inhabitants; in like
manner also those who now live near them have the very
laws which Minos first drew up.

This island seems formed by nature to be the mistress
of Greece, for it is entirely surrounded by a navigable
ocean which washes almost all the maritime parts of that
country, and is not far distant on the one side from
Peloponnesus, on the other, which looks towards Asia,
from Triopium and Rhodes. By means of this situation
Minos acquired the empire of the sea and the islands;
some of which he subdued, in others planted colonies:
at last he died at Camicus while he was attacking Sicily.
There is this analogy between the customs of the Lacedæmonians and the Cretans, the Helots cultivate the grounds 1272a
for the one, the domestic slaves for the other. Both
states have their common meals, and the Lacedæmonians
called these formerly not φιδιτια but ανδρια, as the

Cretans do; which proves from whence the custom arose. In this particular their governments are also alike: the ephori have the same power with those of Crete, who are called κοσμοι; with this difference only, that the number of the one is five, of the other ten. The senators are the same as those whom the Cretans call the council. There was formerly also a kingly power in Crete; but it was afterwards dissolved, and the command of their armies was given to the κοσμοι. Every one also has a vote in their public assembly; but this has only the power of confirming what has already passed the council and the κοσμοι.

The Cretans conducted their public meals better than the Lacedæmonians, for at Lacedæmon each individual was obliged to furnish what was assessed upon him; which if he could not do, there was a law which deprived him of the rights of a citizen, as has been already mentioned: but in Crete they were furnished by the community; for all the corn and cattle, taxes and contributions, which the domestic slaves were obliged to furnish, were divided into parts and allotted to the gods, the exigencies of the state, and these public meals; so that all the men, women, and children were maintained from a common stock. The legislator gave great attention to encourage a habit of eating sparingly, as very useful to the citizens. He also endeavoured, that his community might not be too populous, to lessen the connection with women, by introducing the love of boys: whether in this he did well or ill we shall have some other opportunity of considering. But that the public meals were better ordered at Crete than at Lacedæmon is very evident.

The institution of the κοσμοι was still worse than that of the ephori: for it contained all the faults incident to that magistracy and some peculiar to itself; for in both cases it is uncertain who will be elected: but the Lacedæmonians have this advantage which the others have not, that as all are eligible, the whole community have a share in the highest honours, and therefore all desire to preserve the state: whereas among the Cretans the κοσμοι are not chosen out of the people in general, but out of some certain families, and the senate out of the κοσμοι. And the same observations which may be made on the senate at Lacedæmon may be applied to these; for their being under no control, and their continuing for life, is an honour greater than they merit; and to have their proceedings not regulated by a written law, but left to their own discretion, is dangerous. (As to there being no insurrections, although the people share not in the management of public affairs, this is no proof of a well-constituted government, as the κοσμοι have no opportunity of being bribed like the ephori, as they live in an 1272*b* island far from those who would corrupt them.)   But the method they take to correct that fault is absurd, impolitic, and tyrannical: for very often either their fellow - magistrates or some private persons conspire together and turn out the κοσμοι.   They are also permitted to resign their office before their time is elapsed, and if all this was done by law it would be well, and not at the pleasure of the individuals, which is a bad rule to follow.   But what is worst of all is, that general confusion which those who are in power introduce to impede the ordinary course of justice; which sufficiently shows what is the nature of the government, or rather lawless force: for it is usual with the principal persons amongst them to collect together some of the common people and their friends, and then revolt and set up for themselves, and come to blows with each other.   And what is the difference, if a state is dissolved at once by such violent means, or if it gradually so alters in process of time as to be no longer the same constitution?   A state like this would ever be exposed to the invasions of those who were powerful and inclined to attack it; but, as has been already mentioned, its situation preserves it, as it is free from the inroads of foreigners; and for this reason the family slaves still remain quiet at Crete, while the Helots are perpetually revolting: for the Cretans take no part in foreign affairs, and it is but lately that any foreign troops have made an attack upon the island; and their ravages soon proved the ineffectualness of their laws. And thus much for the government of Crete.

CHAPTER XI

THE government of Carthage seems well established, and in many respects superior to others; in some particulars it bears a near resemblance to the Lacedæmonians; and indeed these three states, the Cretans, the Lacedæmonians, and the Carthaginians are in some things very like each other, in others they differ greatly. Amongst many excellent constitutions this may show how well their government is framed, that although the people are admitted to a share in the administration, the form of it remains unaltered, without any popular insurrections, worth notice, on the one hand, or degenerating into a tyranny on the other. Now the Carthaginians have these things in common with the Lacedæmonians: public tables for those who are connected together by the tie of mutual friendship, after the manner of their *Phiditia*: they have also a magistracy, consisting of an hundred and four persons, similar to the ephori, or rather selected with more judgment; for amongst the Lacedæmonians, all the citizens are eligible, but amongst the Carthaginians, they are chosen out of those of the better sort: there is also some analogy between the king and the senate in both these governments, though the Carthaginian method of appointing their kings is best, for they do not confine themselves to one family; nor do they permit the election to be at large, nor have they any regard to seniority; for if amongst the candidates there are any of greater merit than the rest, these they prefer to those who may be older; for as their power is very extensive, if they are 1273*a* persons of no account, they may be very hurtful to the state, as they have always been to the Lacedæmonians; also the greater part of those things which become reprehensible by their excess are common to all those governments which we have described.

Now of those principles on which the Carthaginians have established their mixed form of government, composed of an aristocracy and democracy, some incline to produce a democracy, others an oligarchy: for instance, if the kings and the senate are unanimous upon any point in debate, they can choose whether they will bring it before the people or no; but if they disagree, it is to these they must appeal, who are not only to hear what has been approved of by the senate, but are finally to determine upon it; and whosoever chooses it, has a right to speak against any matter whatsoever that may be proposed, which is not permitted in other cases. The five, who elect each other, have very great and extensive powers; and these choose the hundred, who are magistrates of the highest rank: their power also continues longer than any other magistrates, for it commences before they come into office, and is prolonged after they are out of it; and in this particular the state inclines to an oligarchy: but as they are not elected by lot, but by suffrage, and are not permitted to take money, they are the greatest supporters imaginable of an aristocracy.

The determining all causes by the same magistrates, and not one in one court and another in another, as at Lacedæmon, has the same influence. The constitution of Carthage is now shifting from an aristocracy to an oligarchy, in consequence of an opinion which is favourably entertained by many, who think that the magistrates in the community ought not to be persons of family only, but of fortune also; as it is impossible for those who are in bad circumstances to support the dignity of their office, or to be at leisure to apply to public business. As choosing men of fortune to be magistrates make a state incline to an oligarchy, and men of abilities to an aristocracy, so is there a third method of proceeding which took place in the polity of Carthage; for they have an eye to these two particulars when they elect their officers, particularly those of the highest rank, their kings and their generals. It must be admitted, that it was a great fault in their legislator not to guard against the constitution's degenerating from an aristocracy; for this is a most necessary thing to provide for at first, that those citizens who have the best abilities should never be obliged to do anything unworthy their character, but be always at leisure to serve the public, not only when in office, but also when private persons; for if once you are obliged to look among the wealthy, that you may have men at leisure to serve you, your greatest offices, of king and general, will soon become venal; in consequence of which, riches will be more honourable than virtue, and a love of money be the ruling principle in the city; for what those who have the chief power regard as honourable will necessarily be the object which the 1273*b* citizens in general will aim at; and where the first honours are not paid to virtue, there the aristocratic form of government cannot flourish: for it is reasonable to conclude, that those who bought their places should generally make an advantage of what they laid out their money for; as it is absurd to suppose, that if a man of probity who is poor should be desirous of gaining something, a bad man should not endeavour to do the same, especially to reimburse himself; for which reason the magistracy should be formed of those who are most able to support an aristocracy. It would have been better for the legislature to have passed over the poverty of men of merit, and only to have taken care to have ensured them sufficient leisure, when in office, to attend to public affairs.

It seems also improper, that one person should execute several offices, which was approved of at Carthage; for one business is best done by one person; and it is the duty of the legislator to look to this, and not make the same person a musician and a shoemaker: so that where the state is not small it is more politic and more popular to admit many persons to have a share in the government; for, as I just now said, it is not only more usual, but everything is better and sooner done, when one thing only is allotted to one person: and this is evident both in the army and navy, where almost every one, in his turn, both commands and is under command. But as their government inclines to an oligarchy, they avoid the ill effects of it by always appointing some of the popular party to the government of cities to make their fortunes. Thus they consult this fault in their constitution and render it stable; but this is depending on chance; whereas

the legislator ought to frame his government, that there
be no room for insurrections. But now, if there should
be any general calamity, and the people should revolt
from their rulers, there is no remedy for reducing them to
obedience by the laws. And these are the particulars
of the Lacedæmonian, the Cretan, and the Carthaginian
governments which seem worthy of commendation.

CHAPTER XII

SOME of those persons who have written upon government
had never any share in public affairs, but always led
a private life. Everything worthy of notice in their
works we have already spoke to.   Others were legislators,
some in their own cities, others were employed in regulating the governments of foreign states. Some of them
only composed a body of laws; others formed the constitution also, as Lycurgus; and Solon, who did both.
The Lacedæmonians have been already mentioned.
Some persons think that Solon was an excellent legislator,
who could dissolve a pure oligarchy, and save the people
from that slavery which hung over them, and establish
the ancient democratic form of government in his country;
wherein every part of it was so framed as to be well
adapted to the whole. In the senate of Areopagus an
oligarchy was preserved; by the manner of electing their 1274a
magistrates, an aristocracy; and in their courts of justice,
a democracy.
Solon seems not to have altered the established form
of government, either with respect to the senate or the
mode of electing their magistrates; but to have raised
the people to great consideration in the state by allotting
the supreme judicial department to them; and for this
some persons blame him, as having done what would soon
overturn that balance of power he intended to establish;
for by trying all causes whatsoever before the people,
who were chosen by lot to determine them, it was necessary to flatter a tyrannical populace who had got this

power; which contributed to bring the government to that pure democracy it now is.

Both Ephialtes and Pericles abridged the power of the Areopagites, the latter of whom introduced the method of paying those who attended the courts of justice: and thus every one who aimed at being popular proceeded increasing the power of the people to what we now see it. But it is evident that this was not Solon's intention, but that it arose from accident; for the people being the cause of the naval victory over the Medes, assumed greatly upon it, and enlisted themselves under factious demagogues, although opposed by the better part of the citizens. He thought it indeed most necessary to entrust the people with the choice of their magistrates and the power of calling them to account; for without that they must have been slaves and enemies to the other citizens: but he ordered them to elect those only who were persons of good account and property, either out of those who were worth five hundred medimns, or those who were called ζευγιται, or those of the third census, who were called horsemen.

As for those of the fourth, which consisted of mechanics, they were incapable of any office. Zaleucus was the legislator of the Western Locrians, as was Charondas, the Catanean, of his own cities, and those also in Italy and Sicily which belonged to the Calcidians. Some persons endeavour to prove that Onomacritus, the Locrian, was the first person of note who drew up laws; and that he employed himself in that business while he was at Crete, where he continued some time to learn the prophetic art: and they say, that Thales was his companion; and that Lycurgus and Zaleucus were the scholars of Thales, and Charondas of Zaleucus; but those who advance this, advance what is repugnant to chronology. Philolaus also, of the family of the Bacchiades, was a Theban legislator. This man was very fond of Diocles, a victor in the Olympic games, and when he left his country from a disgust at an improper passion which his mother Alithoè had entertained for him, and settled at Thebes, Philolaus followed him, where they both died, and where they still show their tombs placed in view of each other, but so disposed, that one of them looks towards Corinth, the other does not; the reason they give for this is, that Diocles, from his detestation of his mother's passion, would have his tomb so placed that no one could see Corinth from it; but Philolaus chose that it might be seen from his: and this was the cause of their living at Thebes. 1274*b*

As Philolaus gave them laws concerning many other things, so did he upon adoption, which they call adoptive laws; and this he in particular did to preserve the number of families. Charondas did nothing new, except in actions for perjury, which he was the first person who took into particular consideration. He also drew up his laws with greater elegance and accuracy than even any of our present legislators. Philolaus introduced the law for the equal distribution of goods; Plato that for the community of women, children, and goods, and also for public tables for the women; and one concerning drunkenness, that they might observe sobriety in their sunposiums. He also made a law concerning their warlike exercises; that they should acquire a habit of using both hands alike, as it was necessary that one hand should be as useful as the other.

As for Draco's laws, they were published when the government was already established, and they have nothing particular in them worth mentioning, except their severity on account of the enormity of their punishments. Pittacus was the author of some laws, but never drew up any form of government; one of which was this, that if a drunken man beat any person he should be punished more than if he did it when sober; for as people are more apt to be abusive when drunk than sober, he paid no consideration to the excuse which drunkenness might claim, but regarded only the common benefit. Andromadas Reginus was also a lawgiver to the Thracian Calcidians. There are some laws of his concerning murders and heiresses extant, but these contain nothing that any one can say is new and his own. And thus much for different sorts of governments, as well those which really exist as those which different persons have proposed.

BOOK III

CHAPTER I

EVERY one who inquires into the nature of government, and what are its different forms, should make this almost his first question, What is a city? For upon this there is a dispute: for some persons say the city did this or that, while others say, not the city, but the oligarchy, or the tyranny. We see that the city is the only object which both the politician and legislator have in view in all they do: but government is a certain ordering of those who inhabit a city. As a city is a collective body, and, like other wholes, composed of many parts, it is evident our first inquiry must be, what a citizen is: for a city is a certain number of citizens. So that we must consider whom we ought to call citizen, and who is one; 1275a for this is often doubtful: for every one will not allow that this character is applicable to the same person; for that man who would be a citizen in a republic would very often not be one in an oligarchy.. We do not include in this inquiry many of those who acquire this appellation out of the ordinary way, as honorary persons, for instance, but those only who have a natural right to it.

Now it is not residence which constitutes a man a citizen; for in this sojourners and slaves are upon an equality with him; nor will it be sufficient for this purpose, that you have the privilege of the laws, and may plead or be impleaded, for this all those of different nations, between whom there is a mutual agreement for that purpose, are allowed; although it very often happens, that sojourners have not a perfect right therein without the protection of a patron, to whom they are obliged to apply, which shows that their share in the community is incomplete. In like manner, with respect to boys who are not

66

yet enrolled, or old men who are past war, we admit
that they are in some respects citizens, but not completely
so, but with some exceptions, for these are not yet arrived
to years of maturity, and those are past service; nor is
there any difference between them. But what we mean
is sufficiently intelligible and clear, we want a complete
citizen, one in whom there is no deficiency to be corrected
to make him so. As to those who are banished, or
infamous, there may be the same objections made and
the same answer given. There is nothing that more
characterises a complete citizen than having a share in
the judicial and executive part of the government.

With respect to offices, some are fixed to a particular
time, so that no person is, on any account, permitted to
fill them twice; or else not till some certain period has
intervened; others are not fixed, as a juryman's, and a
member of the general assembly: but probably some one
may say these are not offices, nor have the citizens in
these capacities any share in the government; though
surely it is ridiculous to say that those who have the
principal power in the state bear no office in it. But this
objection is of no weight, for it is only a dispute about
words; as there is no general term which can be applied
both to the office of a juryman and a member of the
assembly. For the sake of distinction, suppose we call
it an indeterminate office: but I lay it down as a maxim,
that those are citizens who could exercise it. Such then
is the description of a citizen who comes nearest to what
all those who are called citizens are. Every one also
should know, that of the component parts of those things
which differ from each other in species, after the first
or second remove, those which follow have either nothing
at all or very little common to each.

Now we see that governments differ from each other
in their form, and that some of them are defective, others 1275*b*
as excellent as possible: for it is evident, that those
which have many deficiencies and degeneracies in them
must be far inferior to those which are without such
faults. What I mean by degeneracies will be hereafter
explained. Hence it is clear that the office of a citizen

must differ as governments do from each other: for
which reason he who is called a citizen has, in a democracy,
every privilege which that station supposes. In other
forms of government he may enjoy them; but not necessarily: for in some states the people have no power; nor
have they any general assembly, but a few select men.

The trial also of different causes is allotted to different
persons; as at Lacedæmon all disputes concerning contracts are brought before some of the ephori: the senate
are the judges in cases of murder, and so on; some being
to be heard by one magistrate, others by another: and
thus at Carthage certain magistrates determine all causes.
But our former description of a citizen will admit of
correction; for in some governments the office of a juryman and a member of the general assembly is not an
indeterminate one; but there are particular persons
appointed for these purposes, some or all of the citizens
being appointed jurymen or members of the general
assembly, and this either for all causes and all public
business whatsoever, or else for some particular one: and
this may be sufficient to show what a citizen is; for he
who has a right to a share in the judicial and executive
part of government in any city, him we call a citizen of
that place; and a city, in one word, is a collective body
of such persons sufficient in themselves to all the purposes
of life.

CHAPTER II

In common use they define a citizen to be one who is
sprung from citizens on both sides, not on the father's or
the mother's only. Others carry the matter still further,
and inquire how many of his ancestors have been citizens,
as his grandfather, great-grandfather, etc., but some
persons have questioned how the first of the family could
prove themselves citizens, according to this popular and
careless definition. Gorgias of Leontium, partly enter-
taining the same doubt, and partly in jest, says, that as

a mortar is made by a mortar-maker, so a citizen is made by a citizen-maker, and a Larissæan by a Larissæan-maker. This is indeed a very simple account of the matter; for if citizens are so, according to this definition, it will be impossible to apply it to the first founders or first inhabitants of states, who cannot possibly claim in right either of their father or mother. It is probably a matter of still more difficulty to determine their rights as citizens who are admitted to their freedom after any revolution in the state. As, for instance, at Athens, after the expulsion of the tyrants, when Clisthenes enrolled many foreigners and city-slaves amongst the tribes; and the doubt with respect to them was, not whether they were citizens or no, but whether they were legally so or not. Though indeed some persons may have this further 1276a doubt, whether a citizen can be a citizen when he is illegally made; as if an illegal citizen, and one who is no citizen at all, were in the same predicament: but since we see some persons govern unjustly, whom yet we admit to govern, though not justly, and the definition of a citizen is one who exercises certain offices, for such a one we have defined a citizen to be, it is evident, that a citizen illegally created yet continues to be a citizen, but whether justly or unjustly so belongs to the former inquiry.

CHAPTER III

It has also been doubted what was and what was not the act of the city; as, for instance, when a democracy arises out of an aristocracy or a tyranny; for some persons then refuse to fulfil their contracts; as if the right to receive the money was in the tyrant and not in the state, and many other things of the same nature; as if any covenant was founded for violence and not for the common good. So in like manner, if anything is done by those who have the management of public affairs where a democracy is established, their actions are to be considered as the actions of the state, as well as in the oligarchy or tyranny.

And here it seems very proper to consider this question,
When shall we say that a city is the same, and when shall
we say that it is different?

It is but a superficial mode of examining into this
question to begin with the place and the people; for it
may happen that these may be divided from that, or that
some one of them may live in one place, and some in
another (but this question may be regarded as no very
knotty one; for, as a city may acquire that appellation
on many accounts, it may be solved many ways); and
in like manner, when men inhabit one common place,
when shall we say that they inhabit the same city, or that
the city is the same? for it does not depend upon the
walls; for I can suppose Peloponnesus itself surrounded
with a wall, as Babylon was, and every other place, which
rather encircles many nations than one city, and that
they say was taken three days when some of the inhabitants knew nothing of it: but we shall find a proper
time to determine this question; for the extent of a city,
how large it should be, and whether it should consist of
more than one people, these are particulars that the
politician should by no means be unacquainted with.
This, too, is a matter of inquiry, whether we shall say
that a city is the same while it is inhabited by the same
race of men, though some of them are perpetually dying,
others coming into the world, as we say that a river or a
fountain is the same, though the waters are continually
changing; or when a revolution takes place shall we
1276b say the men are the same, but the city is different: for
if a city is a community, it is a community of citizens,
but if the mode of government should alter, and become
of another sort, it would seem a necessary consequence
that the city is not the same; as we regard the tragic
chorus as different from the comic, though it may
probably consist of the same performers: thus every other
community or composition is said to be different if the
species of composition is different; as in music the same
hands produce different harmony, as the Doric and
Phrygian.   If this is true, it is evident, that when we speak
of a city as being the same we refer to the government

there established; and this, whether it is called by the same name or any other, or inhabited by the same men or different. But whether or no it is right to dissolve the community when the constitution is altered is another question.

CHAPTER IV

AFTER what has been said, it follows that we should consider whether the same virtues which constitute a good man make a valuable citizen, or different; and if a particular inquiry is necessary for this matter we must first give a general description of the virtues of a good citizen; for as a sailor is one of those who make up a community, so is a citizen, although the province of one sailor may be different from another's (for one is a rower, another a steersman, a third a boatswain, and so on, each having their several appointments), it is evident that the most accurate description of any one good sailor must refer to his peculiar abilities, yet there are some things in which the same description may be applied to the whole crew, as the safety of the ship is the common business of all of them, for this is the general centre of all their cares: so also with respect to citizens, although they may in a few particulars be very different, yet there is one care common to them all, the safety of the community, for the community of the citizens composes the state; for which reason the virtue of a citizen has necessarily a reference to the state. But if there are different sorts of governments, it is evident that those actions which constitute the virtue of an excellent citizen in one community will not constitute it in another; wherefore the virtue of such a one cannot be perfect: but we say, a man is good when his virtues are perfect; from whence it follows, that an excellent citizen does not possess that virtue which constitutes a good man. Those who are any ways doubtful concerning this question may be convinced of the truth of it by examining into the best formed states: for, if it is impossible that a city should consist entirely of excellent citizens (while it is necessary that every one should do well in his calling, in which consists his excellence, as it is impossible that all the citizens should have the same 1277a qualifications) it is impossible that the virtue of a citizen and a good man should be the same; for all should possess the virtue of an excellent citizen: for from hence necessarily arise the perfection of the city: but that every one should possess the virtue of a good man is impossible, without all the citizens in a well-regulated state were necessarily virtuous. Besides, as a city is composed of dissimilar parts, as an animal is of life and body; the soul of reason and appetite; a family of a man and his wife; property of a master and a slave; in the same manner, as a city is composed of all these and many other very different parts, it necessarily follows that the virtue of all the citizens cannot be the same; as the business of him who leads the band is different from the other dancers. From all which proofs it is evident that the virtues of a citizen cannot be one and the same. But do we never find those virtues united which constitute a good man and excellent citizen? for we say, such a one is an excellent magistrate and a prudent and good man; but prudence is a necessary qualification for all those who engage in public affairs. Nay, some persons affirm that the education of those who are intended to command should, from the beginning, be different from other citizens, as the children of kings are generally instructed in riding and warlike exercises; and thus Euripides says:

> " . . . No showy arts
> Be mine, but teach me what the state requires."

As if those who are to rule were to have an education peculiar to themselves. But if we allow, that the virtues of a good man and a good magistrate may be the same, and a citizen is one who obeys the magistrate, it follows that the virtue of the one cannot in general be the same as the virtue of the other, although it may be true of some particular citizen; for the virtue of the magistrate must be different from the virtue of the citizen. For which reason Jason declared that was he deprived of his kingdom he should pine away with regret, as not knowing how to live a private man. But it is a great recommendation to know how to command as well as to obey; and to do both these things well is the virtue of an accomplished citizen. If then the virtue of a good man consists only in being able to command, but the virtue of a good citizen renders him equally fit for the one as well as the other, the commendation of both of them is not the same. It appears, then, that both he who commands and he who obeys should each of them learn their separate business: but that the citizen should be master of and take part in both these, as any one may easily perceive; in a family government there is no occasion for the master to know how to perform the necessary offices, but rather to enjoy the labour of others; for to do the other is a servile part. I mean by the other, the common family business of the slave.

There are many sorts of slaves; for their employments are various: of these the handicraftsmen are one, who, as their name imports, get their living by the labour of their hands, and amongst these all mechanics are in- 1277*b* cluded; for which reasons such workmen, in some states, were not formerly admitted into any share in the government; till at length democracies were established: it is not therefore proper for any man of honour, or any citizen, or any one who engages in public affairs, to learn these servile employments without they have occasion for them for their own use; for without this was observed the distinction between a master and a slave would be lost. But there is a government of another sort, in which men govern those who are their equals in rank, and freemen, which we call a political government, in which men learn to command by first submitting to obey, as a good general of horse, or a commander-in-chief, must acquire a knowledge of their duty by having been long under the command of another, and the like in every appointment in the army: for well is it said, no one knows how to command who has not himself been under command of another. The virtues of those are indeed different, but a good citizen must necessarily be endowed with them;

he ought also to know in what manner freemen ought to
govern, as well as be governed: and this, too, is the duty
of a good man. And if the temperance and justice of him
who commands is different from his who, though a freeman, is under command, it is evident that the virtues of
a good citizen cannot be the same as justice, for instance,
but must be of a different species in these two different
situations, as the temperance and courage of a man and
a woman are different from each other; for a man
would appear a coward who had only that courage which
would be graceful in a woman, and a woman would be
thought a talker who should take as large a part in the
conversation as would become a man of consequence.

The domestic employments of each of them are also
different; it is the man's business to acquire subsistence,
the woman's to take care of it. But direction and knowledge of public affairs is a virtue peculiar to those who
govern, while all others seem to be equally requisite for
both parties; but with this the governed have no concern,
it is theirs to entertain just notions: they indeed are like
flute-makers, while those who govern are the musicians
who play on them. And thus much to show whether the
virtue of a good man and an excellent citizen is the same,
or if it is different, and also how far it is the same, and
how far different.

CHAPTER V

But with respect to citizens there is a doubt remaining,
whether those only are truly so who are allowed to share
in the government, or whether the mechanics also are to
be considered as such? for if those who are not permitted
to rule are to be reckoned among them, it is impossible that
the virtue of all the citizens should be the same, for these
also are citizens; and if none of them are admitted to be
citizens, where shall they be ranked? for they are neither
1278a sojourners nor foreigners? or shall we say that there will
no inconvenience arise from their not being citizens, as

they are neither slaves nor freedmen: for this is certainly true, that all those are not citizens who are necessary to the existence of a city, as boys are not citizens in the same manner that men are, for those are perfectly so, the others under some conditions; for they are citizens, though imperfect ones: for in former times among some people the mechanics were either slaves or foreigners, for which reason many of them are so now: and indeed the best regulated states will not permit a mechanic to be a citizen; but if it be allowed them, we cannot then attribute the virtue we have described to every citizen or freeman, but to those only who are disengaged from servile offices. Now those who are employed by one person in them are slaves; those who do them for money are mechanics and hired servants: hence it is evident on the least reflection what is their situation, for what I have said is fully explained by appearances. Since the number of communities is very great, it follows necessarily that there will be many different sorts of citizens, particularly of those who are governed by others, so that in one state it may be necessary to admit mechanics and hired servants to be citizens, but in others it may be impossible; as particularly in an aristocracy, where honours are bestowed on virtue and dignity: for it is impossible for one who lives the life of a mechanic or hired servant to acquire the practice of virtue. In an oligarchy also hired servants are not admitted to be citizens; because there a man's right to bear any office is regulated by his fortune; but mechanics are, for many citizens are very rich.

There was a law at Thebes that no one could have a share in the government till he had been ten years out of trade. In many states the law invites strangers to accept the freedom of the city; and in some democracies the son of a free-woman is himself free. The same is also observed in many others with respect to natural children; but it is through want of citizens regularly born that they admit such: for these laws are always made in consequence of a scarcity of inhabitants; so, as their numbers increase, they first deprive the children of a male or female slave of this privilege, next the child of a free-woman, and last of all they will admit none but those whose fathers and mothers were both free.

That there are many sorts of citizens, and that he may be said to be as completely who shares the honours of the state, is evident from what has been already said. Thus Achilles, in Homer, complains of Agamemnon's treating him like an unhonoured stranger; for a stranger or sojourner is one who does not partake of the honours of the state: and whenever the right to the freedom of the city is kept obscure, it is for the sake of the inhabitants. 1278b From what has been said it is plain whether the virtue of a good man and an excellent citizen is the same or different: and we find that in some states it is the same, in others not; and also that this is not true of each citizen, but of those only who take the lead, or are capable of taking the lead, in public affairs, either alone or in conjunction with others.

CHAPTER VI

HAVING established these points, we proceed next tc consider whether one form of government only should be established, or more than one; and if more, how many, and of what sort, and what are the differences between them. The form of government is the ordering and regulating of the city, and all the offices in it, particularly those wherein the supreme power is lodged; and this power is always possessed by the administration; but the administration itself is that particular form of government which is established in any state: thus in a democracy the supreme power is lodged in the whole people; on the contrary, in an oligarchy it is in the hands of a few. We say then, that the form of government in these states is different, and we shall find the same thing hold good in others. Let us first determine for whose sake a city is established, and point out the different species of rule which man may submit to in social life.

I have already mentioned in my treatise on the management of a family, and the power of the master, that man

is an animal naturally formed for society, and that therefore, when he does not want any foreign assistance, he
will of his own accord desire to live with others; not but
that mutual advantage induces them to it, as far as it
enables each person to live more agreeably; and this is
indeed the great object not only to all in general, but
also to each individual: but it is not merely matter of
choice, but they join in society also, even that they may
be able to live, which probably is not without some share
of merit, and they also support civil society, even for the
sake of preserving life, without they are grievously over-
whelmed with the miseries of it: for it is very evident
that men will endure many calamities for the sake of
living, as being something naturally sweet and desirable.
It is easy to point out the different modes of government,
and we have already settled them in our exoteric discourses. The power of the master, though by nature
equally serviceable, both to the master and to the slave,
yet nevertheless has for its object the benefit of the
master, while the benefit of the slave arises accidentally;
for if the slave is destroyed, the power of the master is
at an end: but the authority which a man has over his
wife, and children, and his family, which we call domestic
government, is either for the benefit of those who are
under subjection, or else for the common benefit of the
whole: but its particular object is the benefit of the
governed, as we see in other arts; in physic, for instance,
and the gymnastic exercises, wherein, if any benefit 1279a
arise to the master, it is accidental; for nothing forbids
the master of the exercises from sometimes being himself
one of those who exercises, as the steersman is always
one of the sailors; but both the master of the exercises
and the steersman consider the good of those who are
under their government. Whatever good may happen
to the steersman when he is a sailor, or to the master of
the exercises when he himself makes one at the games,
is not intentional, or the object of their power; thus in
all political governments which are established to preserve
and defend the equality of the citizens it is held right
to rule by turns. Formerly, as was natural, every one

expected that each of his fellow-citizens should in his turn serve the public, and thus administer to his private good, as he himself when in office had done for others; but now every one is desirous of being continually in power, that he may enjoy the advantage which he makes of public business and being in office; as if places were a never-failing remedy for every complaint, and were on that account so eagerly sought after.

It is evident, then, that all those governments which have a common good in view are rightly established and strictly just, but those who have in view only the good of the rulers are all founded on wrong principles, and are widely different from what a government ought to be, for they are tyranny over slaves, whereas a city is a community of freemen.

CHAPTER VII

HAVING established these particulars, we come to consider next the different number of governments which there are, and what they are; and first, what are their excellencies: for when we have determined this, their defects will be evident enough.

It is evident that every form of government or administration, for the words are of the same import, must contain a supreme power over the whole state, and this supreme power must necessarily be in the hands of one person, or a few, or many; and when either of these apply their power for the common good, such states are well governed; but when the interest of the one, the few, or the many who enjoy this power is alone consulted, then ill; for you must either affirm that those who make up the community are not citizens, or else let these share in the advantages of government. We usually call a state which is governed by one person for the common good, a kingdom; one that is governed by more than one, but by a few only, an aristocracy; either because the government is in the hands of the most worthy citizens, or because it is the best form for the city and its inhabitants. When the citizens at large govern for the public good, it is called a state; which is also a common name for all other governments, and these distinctions are consonant to reason; for it will not be difficult to find one person, or a very few, of very distinguished abilities, but almost impossible to meet with the majority 1279b of a people eminent for every virtue; but if there is one common to a whole nation it is valour; for this is created and supported by numbers: for which reason in such a state the profession of arms will always have the greatest share in the government.

Now the corruptions attending each of these governments are these; a kingdom may degenerate into a tyranny, an aristocracy into an oligarchy, and a state into a democracy. Now a tyranny is a monarchy where the good of one man only is the object of government, an oligarchy considers only the rich, and a democracy only the poor; but neither of them have a common good in view.

CHAPTER VIII

It will be necessary to enlarge a little more upon the nature of each of these states, which is not without some difficulty, for he who would enter into a philosophical inquiry into the principles of them, and not content himself with a superficial view of their outward conduct, must pass over and omit nothing, but explain the true spirit of each of them. A tyranny then is, as has been said, a monarchy, where one person has an absolute and despotic power over the whole community and every member therein: an oligarchy, where the supreme power of the state is lodged with the rich: a democracy, on the contrary, is where those have it who are worth little or nothing. But the first difficulty that arises from the distinctions which we have laid down is this, should it happen that the majority of the inhabitants who possess the power of the state (for this is a democracy) should be rich, the question is, how does this agree with what we have said? the same difficulty occurs, should it ever happen that the poor compose a smaller part of the people than the rich, but from their superior abilities acquire the supreme power; for this is what they call an oligarchy: it should seem then that our definition of the different states was not correct: nay, moreover, could any one suppose that the majority of the people were poor, and the minority rich, and then describe the state in this manner, that an oligarchy was a government in which the rich, being few in number, possessed the supreme power, and that a democracy was a state in which the poor, being many in number, possessed it, still there will be another difficulty; for what name shall we give to those states we have been describing? I mean, that in which the greater number are rich, and that in which the lesser number are poor (where each of these possess the supreme power), if there are no other states than those we have described. It seems therefore evident to reason, that whether the supreme power is vested in the hands of many or few may be a matter of accident; but that it is clear enough, that when it is in the hands of the few, it will be a government of the rich; when in the hands of the many, it will be a government of the poor; since in all countries there are many poor and few rich: it is not therefore the cause that has been already assigned (namely, the number of people in power) that makes the difference between the two governments; but an oligarchy and democracy differ in this from each other, in the poverty of those who govern in the one, and the riches 1280a of those who govern in the other; for when the government is in the hands of the rich, be they few or be they more, it is an oligarchy; when it is in the hands of the poor, it is a democracy: but, as we have already said, the one will be always few, the other numerous, but both will enjoy liberty; and from the claims of wealth and liberty will arise continual disputes with each other for the lead in public affairs.

CHAPTER IX

LET us first determine what are the proper limits of an oligarchy and a democracy, and what is just in each of these states; for all men have some natural inclination to justice; but they proceed therein only to a certain degree; nor can they universally point out what is absolutely just; as, for instance, what is equal appears just, and is so; but not to all; only among those who are equals: and what is unequal appears just, and is so; but not to all, only amongst those who are unequals; which circumstance some people neglect, and therefore judge ill; the reason for which is, they judge for themselves, and every one almost is the worst judge in his own cause. Since then justice has reference to persons, the same distinctions must be made with respect to persons which are made with respect to things, in the manner that I have already described in my *Ethics*.

As to the equality of the things, these they agree in; but their dispute is concerning the equality of the persons, and chiefly for the reason above assigned; because they judge ill in their own cause; and also because each party thinks, that if they admit what is right in some particulars, they have done justice on the whole: thus, for instance, if some persons are unequal in riches, they suppose them unequal in the whole; or, on the contrary, if they are equal in liberty, they suppose them equal in the whole: but what is absolutely just they omit; for if civil society was founded for the sake of preserving and increasing property, every one's right in the city would be equal to his fortune; and then the reasoning of those who insist upon an oligarchy would be valid; for it would not be right that he who contributed one mina should have an equal share in the hundred along with him who brought in all the rest, either of the original money or what was afterwards acquired.

Nor was civil society founded merely to preserve the lives of its members; but that they might live well: for otherwise a state might be composed of slaves, or the animal creation: but this is not so; for these have no share in the happiness of it; nor do they live after their own choice; nor is it an alliance mutually to defend each other from injuries, or for a commercial intercourse: for then the Tyrrhenians and Carthaginians, and all other nations between whom treaties of commerce subsist, would be citizens of one city; for they have articles to regulate their exports and imports, and engagements for mutual protection, and alliances for mutual defence; but 1280b yet they have not all the same magistrates established among them, but they are different among the different people; nor does the one take any care, that the morals of the other should be as they ought, or that none of those who have entered into the common agreements should be unjust, or in any degree vicious, only that they do not injure any member of the confederacy. But whosoever endeavours to establish wholesome laws in a state, attends to the virtues and the vices of each individual who composes it; from whence it is evident, that the first care of him who would found a city, truly deserving that name, and not nominally so, must be to have his citizens virtuous; for otherwise it is merely an alliance for self-defence; differing from those of the same cast which are made between different people only in place: for law is an agreement and a pledge, as the sophist Lycophron says, between the citizens of their intending to do justice to each other, though not sufficient to make all the citizens just and good: and that this is fact is evident, for could any one bring different places together, as, for instance, enclose Megara and Corinth in a wall, yet they would not be one city, not even if the inhabitants intermarried with each other, though this inter-community contributes much to make a place one city. Besides, could we suppose a set of people to live separate from each other, but within such a distance as would admit of an intercourse, and that there were laws subsisting between each party, to prevent their injuring one another in their mutual dealings, supposing one a carpenter, another a husbandman, shoemaker, and the like, and that their

numbers were ten thousand, still all that they would
have together in common would be a tariff for trade, or
an alliance for mutual defence, but not the same city.
And why? not because their mutual intercourse is not
near enough, for even if persons so situated should come
to one place, and every one should live in his own house
as in his native city, and there should be alliances subsisting between each party to mutually assist and prevent
any injury being done to the other, still they would not
be admitted to be a city by those who think correctly,
if they preserved the same customs when they were
together as when they were separate.

It is evident, then, that a city is not a community of
place; nor established for the sake of mutual safety or
traffic with each other; but that these things are the
necessary consequences of a city, although they may all
exist where there is no city: but a city is a society of
people joining together with their families and their
children to live agreeably for the sake of having their
lives as happy and as independent as possible: and for
this purpose it is necessary that they should live in one
place and intermarry with each other: hence in all
cities there are family-meetings, clubs, sacrifices, and
public entertainments to promote friendship; for a love
of sociability is friendship itself; so that the end then
for which a city is established is, that the inhabitants of
it may live happy, and these things are conducive to that
end: for it is a community of families and villages for
the sake of a perfect independent life; that is, as we have
already said, for the sake of living well and happily.   It
is not therefore founded for the purpose of men's merely 1281a
living together, but for their living as men ought; for
which reason those who contribute most to this end
deserve to have greater power in the city than those who
are their equals in family and freedom, but their inferiors
in civil virtue, or those who excel them in wealth but are
below them in worth.   It is evident from what has been
said, that in all disputes upon government each party
says something that is just.

CHAPTER X

IT may also be a doubt where the supreme power ought
to be lodged. Shall it be with the majority, or the
wealthy, with a number of proper persons, or one better
than the rest, or with a tyrant? But whichever of these
we prefer some difficulty will arise. For what? shall the
poor have it because they are the majority? they may
then divide among themselves what belongs to the rich:
nor is this unjust; because truly it has been so judged by
the supreme power. But what avails it to point out
what is the height of injustice if this is not? Again, if
the many seize into their own hands everything which
belongs to the few, it is evident that the city will be at
an end. But virtue will never destroy what is virtuous;
nor can what is right be the ruin of the state: therefore
such a law can never be right, nor can the acts of a tyrant
ever be wrong, for of necessity they must all be just;
for he, from his unlimited power, compels every one to
obey his command, as the multitude oppress the rich. Is
it right then that the rich, the few, should have the
supreme power? and what if they be guilty of the same
rapine and plunder the possessions of the majority, that
will be as right as the other: but that all things of this
sort are wrong and unjust is evident. Well then, these
of the better sort shall have it: but must not then all the
other citizens live unhonoured, without sharing the offices
of the city; for the offices of a city are its honours, and
if one set of men are always in power, it is evident that
the rest must be without honour. Well then, let it be
with one person of all others the fittest for it: but by
this means the power will be still more contracted, and
a greater number than before continue unhonoured. But
some one may say, that it is wrong to let man have the
supreme power and not the law, as his soul is subject to
so many passions. But if this law appoints an aristocracy,
or a democracy, how will it help us in our present doubts?
for those things will happen which we have already
mentioned.

CHAPTER XI

OTHER particulars we will consider separately; but it seems proper to prove, that the supreme power ought to be lodged with the many, rather than with those of the better sort, who are few; and also to explain what doubts (and probably just ones) may arise: now, though not one individual of the many may himself be fit for the supreme power, yet when these many are joined together, it does not follow but they may be better qualified for it than 1281*b* those; and this not separately, but as a collective body; as the public suppers exceed those which are given at one person's private expense: for, as they are many, each person brings in his share of virtue and wisdom; and thus, coming together, they are like one man made up of a multitude, with many feet, many hands, and many intelligences: thus is it with respect to the manners and understandings of the multitude taken together; for which reason the public are the best judges of music and poetry; for some understand one part, some another, and all collectively the whole; and in this particular men of consequence differ from each of the many; as they say those who are beautiful do from those who are not so, and as fine pictures excel any natural objects, by collecting the several beautiful parts which were dispersed among different originals into one, although the separate parts, as the eye or any other, might be handsomer than in the picture.

But if this distinction is to be made between every people and every general assembly, and some few men of consequence, it may be doubtful whether it is true; nay, it is clear enough that, with respect to a few, it is not; since the same conclusion might be applied even to brutes: and indeed wherein do some men differ from brutes? Not but that nothing prevents what I have said being true of the people in some states. The doubt then which we have lately proposed, with all its consequences, may be settled in this manner; it is necessary that the freemen who compose the bulk of the people should have absolute power in some things; but as they are neither men of property, nor act uniformly upon principles of virtue, it is not safe to trust them with the first offices in the state, both on account of their iniquity and their ignorance; from the one of which they will do what is wrong, from the other they will mistake: and yet it is dangerous to allow them no power or share in the government; for when there are many poor people who are incapable of acquiring the honours of their country, the state must necessarily have many enemies in it; let them then be permitted to vote in the public assemblies and to determine causes; for which reason Socrates, and some other legislators, gave them the power of electing the officers of the state, and also of inquiring into their conduct when they came out of office, and only prevented their being magistrates by themselves; for the multitude when they are collected together have all of them sufficient understanding for these purposes, and, mixing among those of higher rank, are serviceable to the city, as some things, which alone are improper for food, when mixed with others make the whole more wholesome than a few of them would be.

But there is a difficulty attending this form of government, for it seems, that the person who himself was capable of curing any one who was then sick, must be the best judge whom to employ as a physician; but such a one must be himself a physician; and the same holds true in every other practice and art: and as a physician ought 1282a to give an account of his practice to a physician, so ought it to be in other arts: those whose business is physic may be divided into three sorts, the first of these is he who makes up the medicines; the second prescribes, and is to the other as the architect is to the mason; the third is he who understands the science, but never practises it: now these three distinctions may be found in those who understand all other arts; nor have we less opinion of their judgment who are only instructed in the principles of the art than of those who practise it: and with respect to elections the same method of proceeding seems right;

for to elect a proper person in any science is the business
of those who are skilful therein; as in geometry, of
geometricians; in steering, of steersmen: but if some
individuals should know something of particular arts and
works, they do not know more than the professors of
them: so that even upon this principle neither the election
of magistrates, nor the censure of their conduct, should
be entrusted to the many.

But probably all that has been here said may not be
right; for, to resume the argument I lately used, if the
people are not very brutal indeed, although we allow that
each individual knows less of these affairs than those who
have given particular attention to them, yet when they
come together they will know them better, or at least
not worse; besides, in some particular arts it is not the
workman only who is the best judge; namely, in those
the works of which are understood by those who do not
profess them: thus he who builds a house is not the only
judge of it, for the master of the family who inhabits it
is a better; thus also a steersman is a better judge of a
tiller than he who made it; and he who gives an entertainment than the cook. What has been said seems a
sufficient solution of this difficulty; but there is another
that follows: for it seems absurd that the power of the
state should be lodged with those who are but of indifferent morals, instead of those who are of excellent
characters. Now the power of election and censure are
of the utmost consequence, and this, as has been said, in
some states they entrust to the people; for the general
assembly is the supreme court of all, and they have a
voice in this, and deliberate in all public affairs, and try
all causes, without any objection to the meanness of their
circumstances, and at any age: but their treasurers,
generals, and other great officers of state are taken from
men of great fortune and worth. This difficulty also
may be solved upon the same principle; and here too they
may be right, for the power is not in the man who is
member of the assembly, or council, but the assembly
itself, and the council, and the people, of which each
individual of the whole community are the parts, I mean

as senator, adviser, or judge; for which reason it is very right, that the many should have the greatest powers in their own hands; for the people, the council, and the judges are composed of them, and the property of all these collectively is more than the property of any person, or a few who fill the great offices of the state: and thus I determine these points.

The first question that we stated shows plainly, that the supreme power should be lodged in laws duly made, 1282b and that the magistrate or magistrates, either one or more, should be authorised to determine those cases which the laws cannot particularly speak to, as it is impossible for them, in general language, to explain themselves upon everything that may arise: but what these laws are which are established upon the best foundations has not been yet explained, but still remains a matter of some question: but the laws of every state will necessarily be like every state, either trifling or excellent, just or unjust; for it is evident, that the laws must be framed correspondent to the constitution of the government; and, if so, it is plain, that a well-formed government will have good laws, a bad one, bad ones.

CHAPTER XII

Since in every art and science the end aimed at is always good, so particularly in this, which is the most excellent of all, the founding of civil society, the good wherein aimed at is justice; for it is this which is for the benefit of all. Now, it is the common opinion, that justice is a certain equality; and in this point all the philosophers are agreed when they treat of morals: for they say what is just, and to whom; and that equals ought to receive equal: but we should know how we are to determine what things are equal and what unequal; and in this there is some difficulty, which calls for the philosophy of the politician. Some persons will probably say, that the employments of the state ought to be given according to every particular excellence of each citizen, if there is no other difference between them and the rest of the community, but they are in every respect else alike: for justice attributes different things to persons differing from each other in their character, according to their respective merits. But if this is admitted to be true, complexion, or height, or any such advantage will be a claim for a greater share of the public rights. But that this is evidently absurd is clear from other arts and sciences; for with respect to musicians who play on the flute together, the best flute is not given to him who is of the best family, for he will play never the better for that, but the best instrument ought to be given to him who is the best artist.

If what is now said does not make this clear, we will explain it still further: if there should be any one, a very excellent player on the flute, but very deficient in family and beauty, though each of them are more valuable endowments than a skill in music, and excel this art in a higher degree than that player excels others, yet the best flutes ought to be given to him; for the superiority 1283a in beauty and fortune should have a reference to the business in hand; but these have none. Moreover, according to this reasoning, every possible excellence might come in comparison with every other; for if bodily strength might dispute the point with riches or liberty, even any bodily strength might do it; so that if one person excelled in size more than another did in virtue, and his size was to qualify him to take place of the other's virtue, everything must then admit of a comparison with each other; for if such a size is greater than virtue by so much, it is evident another must be equal to it: but, since this is impossible, it is plain that it would be contrary to common sense to dispute a right to any office in the state from every superiority whatsoever: for if one person is slow and the other swift, neither is the one better qualified nor the other worse on that account, though in the gymnastic races a difference in these particulars would gain the prize; but a pretension to the offices of the state should be founded on a superiority in those qualifications which are useful to it: for which reason those of family, independency, and fortune, with great propriety, contend with each other for them; for these are the fit persons to fill them: for a city can no more consist of all poor men than it can of all slaves. But if such persons are requisite, it is evident that those also who are just and valiant are equally so; for without justice and valour no state can be supported, the former being necessary for its existence, the latter for its happiness.

CHAPTER XIII

It seems, then, requisite for the establishment of a state, that all, or at least many of these particulars should be well canvassed and inquired into; and that virtue and education may most justly claim the right of being considered as the necessary means of making the citizens happy, as we have already said. As those who are equal in one particular are not therefore equal in all, and those who are unequal in one particular are not therefore unequal in all, it follows that all those governments which are established upon a principle which supposes they are, are erroneous.

We have already said, that all the members of the community will dispute with each other for the offices of the state; and in some particulars justly, but not so in general; the rich, for instance, because they have the greatest landed property, and the ultimate right to the soil is vested in the community; and also because their fidelity is in general most to be depended on. The freemen and men of family will dispute the point with each other, as nearly on an equality; for these latter have a right to a higher regard as citizens than obscure persons, for honourable descent is everywhere of great esteem: nor is it an improper conclusion, that the descendants of men of worth will be men of worth themselves; for noble birth is the fountain of virtue to men of family:

for the same reason also we justly say, that virtue has
a right to put in her pretensions. Justice, for instance,
is a virtue, and so necessary to society, that all others
must yield her the precedence.

Let us now see what the many have to urge on their
side against the few; and they may say, that if, when
collectively taken, they are compared with them, they
are stronger, richer, and better than they are. But
should it ever happen that all these should inhabit the 1283b
same city, I mean the good, the rich, the noble, as well
as the many, such as usually make up the community,
I ask, will there then be any reason to dispute concerning
who shall govern, or will there not? for in every community which we have mentioned there is no dispute
where the supreme power should be placed; for as these
differ from each other, so do those in whom that is placed;
for in one state the rich enjoy it, in others the meritorious,
and thus each according to their separate manners.
Let us however consider what is to be done when all
these happen at the same time to inhabit the same city.
If the virtuous should be very few in number, how then
shall we act? shall we prefer the virtuous on account
of their abilities, if they are capable of governing the city?
or should they be so many as almost entirely to compose
the state?

There is also a doubt concerning the pretensions of all
those who claim the honours of government: for those
who found them either on fortune or family have nothing
which they can justly say in their defence; since it is
evident upon their principle, that if any one person can
be found richer than all the rest, the right of governing
all these will be justly vested in this one person. In the
same manner, one man who is of the best family will
claim it from those who dispute the point upon family
merit: and probably in an aristocracy the same dispute
might arise on the score of virtue, if there is one man
better than all the other men of worth who are in the
same community; it seems just, by the same reasoning,
that he should enjoy the supreme power. And upon this
principle also, while the many suppose they ought to have

the supreme command, as being more powerful than the few, if one or more than one, though a small number, should be found stronger than themselves, these ought rather to have it than they.

All these things seem to make it plain, that none of these principles are justly founded on which these persons would establish their right to the supreme power; and that all men whatsoever ought to obey them: for with respect to those who claim it as due to their virtue or their fortune, they might have justly some objection to make; for nothing hinders but that it may sometimes happen, that the many may be better or richer than the few, not as individuals, but in their collective capacity.

As to the doubt which some persons have proposed and objected, we may answer it in this manner; it is this, whether a legislator, who would establish the most perfect system of laws, should calculate them for the use of the better part of the citizens, or the many, in the circumstances we have already mentioned? The rectitude of anything consists in its equality; that therefore which is equally right will be advantageous to the whole state, and to every member of it in common.

Now, in general, a citizen is one who both shares in the government and also in his turn submits to be governed; 1284a their condition, it is true, is different in different states: the best is that in which a man is enabled to choose and to persevere in a course of virtue during his whole life, both in his public and private state. But should there be one person, or a very few, eminent for an uncommon degree of virtue, though not enough to make up a civil state, so that the virtue of the many, or their political abilities, should be too inferior to come in comparison with theirs, if more than one; or if but one, with his only; such are not to be considered as part of the city; for it would be doing them injustice to rate them on a level with those who are so far their inferiors in virtue and political abilities, that they appear to them like a god amongst men. From whence it is evident, that a system of laws must be calculated for those who are equal to each other in nature and power. Such men, therefore, are not the object of law; for they are themselves a law: and it would be ridiculous in any one to endeavour to include them in the penalties of a law: for probably they might say what Antisthenes tells us the lions did to the hares when they demanded to be admitted to an equal share with them in the government. And it is on this account that democratic states have established the ostracism; for an equality seems the principal object of their government. For which reason they compel all those who are very eminent for their power, their fortune, their friendships, or any other cause which may give them too great weight in the government, to submit to the ostracism, and leave the city for a stated time; as the fabulous histories relate the Argonauts served Hercules, for they refused to take him with them in the ship *Argo* on account of his superior valour. For which reason those who hate a tyranny and find fault with the advice which Periander gave to Thrasybulus, must not think there was nothing to be said in its defence; for the story goes, that Periander said nothing to the messenger in answer to the business he was consulted about, but striking off those ears of corn which were higher than the rest, reduced the whole crop to a level; so that the messenger, without knowing the cause of what was done, related the fact to Thrasybulus, who understood by it that he must take off all the principal men in the city. Nor is this serviceable to tyrants only; nor is it tyrants only who do it; for the same thing is practised both in oligarchies and democracies: for the ostracism has in a manner nearly the same power, by restraining and banishing those who are too great; and what is done in one city is done also by those who have the supreme power in separate states; as the Athenians with respect to the Samians, the Chians, and the Lesbians; for when they suddenly acquired the superiority over all Greece, they brought the other states into subjection, contrary to the treaties which subsisted between them. The King of Persia also very often reduces the Medes and Babylonians when they assume upon their former power: 1284*b* and this is a principle which all governments whatsoever keep in their eye; even those which are best administered, as well as those which are not, do it; these for the sake of private utility, the others for the public good.

The same thing is to be perceived in the other arts and sciences; for a painter would not represent an animal with a foot disproportionally large, though he had drawn it remarkably beautiful; nor would the shipwright make the prow or any other part of the vessel larger than it ought to be; nor will the master of the band permit any who sings louder and better than the rest to sing in concert with them. There is therefore no reason that a monarch should not act in agreement with free states, to support his own power, if they do the same thing for the benefit of their respective communities; upon which account when there is any acknowledged difference in the power of the citizens, the reason upon which the ostracism is founded will be politically just; but it is better for the legislator so to establish his state at the beginning as not to want this remedy: but if in course of time such an inconvenience should arise, to endeavour to amend it by some such correction. Not that this was the use it was put to: for many did not regard the benefit of their respective communities, but made the ostracism a weapon in the hand of sedition.

It is evident, then, that in corrupt governments it is partly just and useful to the individual, though probably it is as clear that it is not entirely just: for in a well-governed state there may be great doubts about the use of it, not on account of the pre-eminence which one may have in strength, riches, or connection: but when the pre-eminence is virtue, what then is to be done? for it seems not right to turn out and banish such a one; neither does it seem right to govern him, for that would be like desiring to share the power with Jupiter and to govern him: nothing then remains but what indeed seems natural, and that is for all persons quietly to submit to the government of those who are thus eminently virtuous, and let them be perpetually kings in the separate states.

CHAPTER XIV

AFTER what has been now said, it seems proper to change our subject and to inquire into the nature of monarchies; for we have already admitted them to be one of those species of government which are properly founded. And here let us consider whether a kingly government is proper for a city or a country whose principal object is the happiness of the inhabitants, or rather some other. But let us first determine whether this is of one kind only, or more; 1285a and it is easy to know that it consists of many different species, and that the forms of government are not the same in all: for at Sparta the kingly power seems chiefly regulated by the laws; for it is not supreme in all circumstances; but when the king quits the territories of the state he is their general in war; and all religious affairs are entrusted to him: indeed the kingly power with them is chiefly that of a general who cannot be called to an account for his conduct, and whose command is for life: for he has not the power of life and death, except as a general; as they frequently had in their expeditions by martial law, which we learn from Homer; for when Agamemnon is affronted in council, he restrains his resentment, but when he is in the field and armed with this power, he tells the Greeks:

> " Whoe'er I know shall shun th' impending fight,
> To dogs and vultures soon shall be a prey;
> For death is mine. . . ."

This, then, is one species of monarchical government in which the kingly power is in a general for life; and is sometimes hereditary, sometimes elective: besides, there is also another, which is to be met with among some of the barbarians, in which the kings are invested with powers nearly equal to a tyranny, yet are, in some respects, bound by the laws and the customs of their country; for as the barbarians are by nature more prone to slavery than the Greeks, and those in Asia more than those in Europe, they endure without murmuring a

despotic government; for this reason their governments
are tyrannies; but yet not liable to be overthrown, as
being customary and according to law. Their guards
also are such as are used in a kingly government, not a
despotic one; for the guards of their kings are his citizens,
but a tyrant's are foreigners. The one commands, in the
manner the law directs, those who willingly obey; the
other, arbitrarily, those who consent not. The one,
therefore, is guarded by the citizens, the other against
them.

These, then, are the two different sorts of these monarchies, and another is that which in ancient Greece
they called æsumnetes; which is nothing more than an
elective tyranny; and its difference from that which is
to be found amongst the barbarians consists not in its
not being according to law, but only in its not being
according to the ancient customs of the country. Some
persons possessed this power for life, others only for a
particular time or particular purpose, as the people of
Mitylene elected Pittacus to oppose the exiles, who were
headed by Antimenides and Alcæus the poet, as we
learn from a poem of his; for he upbraids the Mitylenians
for having chosen Pittacus for their tyrant, and with one
1285b voice extolling him to the skies who was the ruin of a
rash and devoted people. These sorts of government
then are, and ever were, despotic, on account of their
being tyrannies; but inasmuch as they are elective, and
over a free people, they are also kingly.

A fourth species of kingly government is that which
was in use in the heroic times, when a free people submitted to a kingly government, according to the laws and
customs of their country. For those who were at first
of benefit to mankind, either in arts or arms, or by collecting them into civil society, or procuring them an
establishment, became the kings of a willing people, and
established an hereditary monarchy. They were particularly their generals in war, and presided over their
sacrifices, excepting such only as belonged to the priests:
they were also the supreme judges over the people; and
in this case some of them took an oath, others did not;

when they did, the form of swearing was by their sceptre held out.

In ancient times the power of the kings extended to everything whatsoever, both civil, domestic, and foreign; but in after-times they relinquished some of their privileges, and others the people assumed, so that, in some states, they left their kings only the right of presiding over the sacrifices; and even those whom it were worth while to call by that name had only the right of being commander-in-chief in their foreign wars.

These, then, are the four sorts of kingdoms: the first is that of the heroic times; which was a government over a free people, with its rights in some particulars marked out; for the king was their general, their judge, and their high priest. The second, that of the barbarians; which is an hereditary despotic government regulated by laws: the third is that which they call æsumnetic, which is an elective tyranny. The fourth is the Lacedæmonian; and this, in few words, is nothing more than an hereditary generalship: and in these particulars they differ from each other. There is a fifth species of kingly government, which is when one person has a supreme power over all things whatsoever, in the manner that every state and every city has over those things which belong to the public: for as the master of a family is king in his own house, so such a king is master of a family in his own city or state.

CHAPTER XV

But the different sorts of kingly governments may, if I may so say, be reduced to two; which we will consider more particularly. The last spoken of, and the Lacedæmonian, for the chief of the others are placed between these, which are as it were at the extremities, they having less power than an absolute government, and yet more than the Lacedæmonians; so that the whole matter in question may be reduced to these two points; the one is, whether it is advantageous to the citizens to have the office of general continue in one person for life, and whether it should be confined to any particular families, or whether every one should be eligible: the other, whether 1286a it is advantageous for one person to have the supreme power over everything or not. But to enter into the particulars concerning the office of a Lacedæmonian general would be rather to frame laws for a state than to consider the nature and utility of its constitution, since we know that the appointing of a general is what is done in every state. Passing over this question then, we will proceed to consider the other part of their government, which is the polity of the state; and this it will be necessary to examine particularly into, and to go through such questions as may arise.

Now the first thing which presents itself to our consideration is this, whether it is best to be governed by a good man, or by good laws? Those who prefer a kingly government think that laws can only speak a general language, but cannot adapt themselves to particular circumstances; for which reason it is absurd in any science to follow written rule; and even in Egypt the physician was allowed to alter the mode of cure which the law prescribed to him, after the fourth day; but if he did it sooner it was at his own peril: from whence it is evident, on the very same account, that a government of written laws is not the best; and yet general reasoning is necessary to all those who are to govern, and it will be much more perfect in those who are entirely free from passions than in those to whom they are natural. But now this is a quality which laws possess; while the other is natural to the human soul. But some one will say in answer to this, that man will be a better judge of particulars. It will be necessary, then, for a king to be a lawgiver, and that his laws should be published, but that those should have no authority which are absurd, as those which are not, should. But whether is it better for the community that those things which cannot possibly come under the cognisance of the law either at all or properly should be under the government of every worthy citizen, as the present method is, when the public community, in their general assemblies, act as judges and counsellors, where all their determinations are upon particular cases. For one individual, be he who he will, will be found, upon comparison, inferior to a whole people taken collectively: but this is what a city is, as a public entertainment is better than one man's portion: for this reason the multitude judge of many things better than any one single person. They are also less liable to corruption from their numbers, as water is from its quantity: besides, the judgment of an individual must necessarily be perverted if he is overcome by anger or any other passion; but it would be hard indeed if the whole community should be misled by anger. Moreover, let the people be free, and they will do nothing but in conformity to the law, except only in those cases which the law cannot speak to. But though what I am going to propose may not easily be met with, yet if the majority of the state should happen to be good men, should they prefer one uncorrupt governor or many equally good, is it not evident that they should choose the many? But there may be divisions among 1286*b* these which cannot happen when there is but one. In answer to this it may be replied that all their souls will be as much animated with virtue as this one man's.

If then a government of many, and all of them good men, compose an aristocracy, and the government of one a kingly power, it is evident that the people should rather choose the first than the last; and this whether the state is powerful or not, if many such persons so alike can be met with: and for this reason probable it was, that the first governments were generally monarchies; because it was difficult to find a number of persons eminently virtuous, more particularly as the world was then divided into small communities; besides, kings were appointed in return for the benefits they had conferred on mankind; but such actions are peculiar to good men: but when many persons equal in virtue appeared at the time, they brooked not a superiority, but sought after an equality and established a free state; but after this, when they degenerated, they made a property of the public; which probably gave rise to oligarchies; for they made wealth meritorious, and the honours of government were reserved for the rich: and these afterwards turned to tyrannies, and these in their turn gave rise to democracies; for the power of the tyrants continually decreasing, on account of their rapacious avarice, the people grew powerful enough to frame and establish democracies: and as cities after that happened to increase, probably it was not easy for them to be under any other government than a democracy.   But if any person prefers a kingly government in a state, what is to be done with the king's children? Is the family also to reign?   But should they have such children as some persons usually have, it will be very detrimental.   It may be said, that then the king who has it in his power will never permit such children to succeed to his kingdom.   But it is not easy to trust to that; for it is very hard and requires greater virtue than is to be met with in human nature.   There is also a doubt concerning the power with which a king should be entrusted: whether he should be allowed force sufficient to compel those who do not choose to be obedient to the laws, and how he is to support his government? for if he is to govern according to law and do nothing of his own will which is contrary thereunto, at the same time it will be necessary to protect that power with which he guards the law. This matter however may not be very difficult to determine; for he ought to have a proper power, and such a one is that which will be sufficient to make the king superior to any one person or even a large part of the community, but inferior to the whole, as the ancients always appointed guards for that person whom they created æsumnetes or tyrant; and some one advised the Syracusians, when Dionysius asked for guards, to allow him such.

CHAPTER XVI

1287a WE will next consider the absolute monarch that we have just mentioned, who does everything according to his own will: for a king governing under the direction of laws which he is obliged to follow does not of himself create any particular species of government, as we have already said: for in every state whatsoever, either aristocracy or democracy, it is easy to appoint a general for life; and there are many who entrust the administration of affairs to one person only; such is the government at Dyrrachium, and nearly the same at Opus. As for an absolute monarchy as it is called, that is to say, when the whole state is wholly subject to the will of one person, namely the king, it seems to many that it is unnatural that one man should have the entire rule over his fellow-citizens when the state consists of equals: for nature requires that the same right and the same rank should necessarily take place amongst all those who are equal by nature: for as it would be hurtful to the body for those who are of different constitutions to observe the same regimen, either of diet or clothing, so is it with respect to the honours of the state as hurtful, that those who are equal in merit should be unequal in rank; for which reason it is as much a man's duty to submit to command as to assume it, and this also by rotation; for this is law, for order is law; and it is more proper that law should govern than any one of the citizens: upon the same principle, if it is advantageous to place the supreme power in some particular persons, they should be appointed to be only guardians, and the servants of the laws, for the supreme power must be placed somewhere; but they say, that it is unjust that where all are equal one person should continually enjoy it. But it seems unlikely that man should be able to adjust that which the law cannot determine; it may be replied, that the law having laid down the best rules possible, leaves the adjustment and application of particulars to the discretion of the magistrate; besides, it allows anything to be altered which experience proves may be better established. Moreover, he who would place the supreme power in mind, would place it in God and the laws; but he who entrusts man with it, gives it to a wild beast, for such his appetites sometimes make him; for passion influences those who are in power, even the very best of men: for which reason law is reason without desire.

The instance taken from the arts seems fallacious: wherein it is said to be wrong for a sick person to apply for a remedy to books, but that it would be far more eligible to employ those who are skilful in physic; for these do nothing contrary to reason from motives of friendship, but earn their money by curing the sick, whereas those who have the management of public affairs do many things through hatred or favour. And, as a proof of what we have advanced, it may be observed, that whenever a sick person suspects that his physician has been persuaded by his enemies to be guilty of any foul practice to him in his profession, he then rather chooses to apply to books for his cure: and not only this, 1287b but even physicians themselves when they are ill call in other physicians: and those who teach others the gymnastic exercises, exercise with those of the same profession, as being incapable from self-partiality to form a proper judgment of what concerns themselves. From whence it is evident, that those who seek for what is just, seek for a mean; now law is a mean. Moreover, the moral law is far superior and conversant with far superior objects than the written law; for the supreme magistrate is safer to be trusted to than the one, though he is inferior to the other. But as it is impossible that one person should have an eye to everything himself, it will be necessary that the supreme magistrate should employ several subordinate ones under him; why then should not this be done at first, instead of appointing one person in this manner? Besides, if, according to what has been already said, the man of worth is on that account fit to govern, two men of worth are certainly better than one: as, for instance, in Homer, " Let two together go: " and also Agamemnon's wish; " Were ten such faithful counsel mine! " Not but that there are even now some particular magistrates invested with supreme power to decide, as judges, those things which the law cannot, as being one of those cases which comes not properly under its jurisdiction; for of those which can there is no doubt: since then laws comprehend some things, but not all, it is necessary to enquire and consider which of the two

is preferable, that the best man or the best law should
govern; for to reduce every subject which can come
under the deliberation of man into a law is impossible.

No one then denies, that it is necessary that there should
be some person to decide those cases which cannot come
under the cognisance of a written law: but we say, that
it is better to have many than one; for though every one
who decides according to the principles of the law decides
justly; yet surely it seems absurd to suppose, that one
person can see better with two eyes, and hear better with
two ears, or do better with two hands and two feet, than
many can do with many: for we see that absolute
monarchs now furnish themselves with many eyes and
ears and hands and feet; for they entrust those who are
friends to them and their government with part of their
power; for if they are not friends to the monarch, they
will not do what he chooses; but if they are friends to
him, they are friends also to his government: but a friend
is an equal and like his friend: if then he thinks that such
should govern, he thinks that his equal also should govern.
These are nearly the objections which are usually made
to a kingly power.

CHAPTER XVII

PROBABLY what we have said may be true of some persons,
but not of others; for some men are by nature formed
to be under the government of a master; others, of a
king; others, to be the citizens of a free state, just and
useful; but a tyranny is not according to nature, nor
the other perverted forms of government; for they are
contrary to it. But it is evident from what has been
said, that among equals it is neither advantageous nor **1288a**
right that one person should be lord over all where there
are no established laws, but his will is the law; or
where there are; nor is it right that one who is good
should have it over those who are good; or one who is
not good over those who are not good; nor one who is

superior to the rest in worth, except in a particular manner, which shall be described, though indeed it has been already mentioned. But let us next determine what people are best qualified for a kingly government, what for an aristocratic, and what for a democratic. And, first, for a kingly; and it should be those who are accustomed by nature to submit the civil government of themselves to a family eminent for virtue: for an aristocracy, those who are naturally framed to bear the rule of free men, whose superior virtue makes them worthy of the management of others: for a free state, a war-like people, formed by nature both to govern and be governed by laws which admit the poorest citizen to share the honours of the commonwealth according to his worth. But whenever a whole family or any one of another shall happen so far to excel in virtue as to exceed all other persons in the community, then it is right that the kingly power should be in them, or if it is an individual who does so, that he should be king and lord of all; for this, as we have just mentioned, is not only correspondent to that principle of right which all founders of all states, whether aristocracies, oligarchies, or democracies, have a regard to (for in placing the supreme power they all think it right to fix it to excellence, though not the same); but it is also agreeable to what has been already said; as it would not be right to kill, or banish, or ostracise such a one for his superior merit. Nor would it be proper to let him have the supreme power only in turn; for it is contrary to nature that what is highest should ever be lowest: but this would be the case should such a one ever be governed by others. So that there can nothing else be done but to submit, and permit him continually to enjoy the supreme power. And thus much with respect to kingly power in different states, and whether it is or is not advantageous to them, and to what, and in what manner.

CHAPTER XVIII

SINCE then we have said that there are three sorts of regular governments, and of these the best must necessarily be that which is administered by the best men (and this must be that which happens to have one man, or one family, or a number of persons excelling all the rest in virtue, who are able to govern and be governed in such a manner as will make life most agreeable, and we have already shown that the virtue of a good man and of a citizen in the most perfect government will be the same), it is evident, that in the same manner, and for those very qualities which would procure a man the character of good, any one would say, that the government of a state was a well-established aristocracy or kingdom; so that it will be found to be education and 1288*b* morals that are almost the whole which go to make a good man, and the same qualities will make a good citizen or good king.

These particulars being treated of, we will now proceed to consider what sort of government is best, how it naturally arises, and how it is established; for it is necessary to make a proper inquiry concerning this.

BOOK IV

CHAPTER I

IN every art and science which is not conversant in parts, but in some one genus in which it is complete, it is the business of that art alone to determine what is fitted to its particular genus; as what particular exercise is fitted to a certain particular body, and suits it best: for that body which is formed by nature the most perfect and superior to others necessarily requires the best exercise; and also of what one kind that must be which will suit the generality; and this is the business of the gymnastic arts: and although any one should not desire to acquire an exact knowledge and skill in these exercises, yet it is not, on that account, the less necessary that he who professes to be a master and instruct the youth in them should be perfect therein: and we see that this is what equally befalls the healing, shipbuilding, cloth-making, and indeed all other arts; so that it evidently belongs to the same art to find out what kind of government is best, and would of all others be most correspondent to our wish, while it received no molestation from without: and what particular species of it is adapted to particular persons; for there are many who probably are incapable of enjoying the best form: so that the legislator, and he who is truly a politician, ought to be acquainted not only with that which is most perfect imaginable, but also that which is the best suited to any given circumstances. There is, moreover, a third sort, an imaginary one, and he ought, if such a one should be presented to his consideration, to be able to discern what sort of one it would be at the beginning; and, when once established, what would be the proper means to preserve it a long time. I mean, for instance, if a state should happen not to have the best form of government, or be deficient in what was necessary, or not receive every advantage possible, but something less. And, besides all this, it is necessary to know what sort of government is best fitting for all cities: for most of those writers who have treated this subject, however speciously they may handle other parts of it, have failed in describing the practical parts: for it is not enough to be able to perceive what is best without it is what can be put in practice. It should also be simple, and easy for all to attain to. But some seek only the most subtile forms of government. Others again, choosing **1289a** rather to treat of what is common, censure those under which they live, and extol the excellence of a particular state, as the Lacedæmonian, or some other: but every legislator ought to establish such a form of government as from the present state and disposition of the people who are to receive it they will most readily submit to and persuade the community to partake of: for it is not a business of less trouble to correct the mistakes of an established government than to form a new one; as it is as difficult to recover what we have forgot as to learn anything afresh. He, therefore, who aspires to the character of a legislator, ought, besides all we have already said, to be able to correct the mistakes of a government already established, as we have before mentioned. But this is impossible to be done by him who does not know how many different forms of government there are: some persons think that there is only one species both of democracy and oligarchy; but this is not true: so that every one should be acquainted with the difference of these governments, how great they are, and whence they arise; and should have equal knowledge to perceive what laws are best, and what are most suitable to each particular government: for all laws are, and ought to be, framed agreeable to the state that is to be governed by them, and not the state to the laws: for government is a certain ordering in a state which particularly respects the magistrates in what manner they shall be regulated, and where the supreme power shall be placed; and what shall be the final object which each community shall have in view; but the laws are something different from what regulates and expresses the form of the constitution; it is their office to direct the conduct of the magistrate in the execution of his office and the punishment of offenders. From whence it is evident, that the founders of laws should attend both to the number and the different sorts of government; for it is impossible that the same laws should be calculated for all sorts of oligarchies and all sorts of democracies, for of both these governments there are many species, not one only.

CHAPTER II

SINCE, then, according to our first method in treating of the different forms of government, we have divided those which are regular into three sorts, the kingly, the aristocratical, the free states, and shown the three excesses which these are liable to: the kingly, of becoming tyrannical; the aristocratical, oligarchical; and the free state, democratical: and as we have already treated of the aristocratical and kingly; for to enter into an inquiry what sort of government is best is the same thing as to treat of these two expressly; for each of them desires to be established upon the principles of virtue: and as, moreover, we have already determined wherein a kingly power and an aristocracy differ from each other, and when a state may be said to be governed by a king, it now remains that we examine into a free state, and also these other governments, an oligarchy, a democracy, and a 1289b tyranny; and it is evident of these three excesses which must be the worst of all, and which next to it; for, of course, the excesses of the best and most holy must be the worst; for it must necessarily happen either that the name of king only will remain, or else that the king will assume more power than belongs to him, from whence tyranny will arise, the worst excess imaginable, a government the most contrary possible to a free state. The excess next hurtful is an oligarchy; for an aristocracy differs much from this sort of government: that which is least so is a democracy. This subject has been already treated of by one of those writers who have gone before me, though his sentiments are not the same as mine: for he thought, that of all excellent constitutions, as a good oligarchy or the like, a democracy was the worst, but of all bad ones, the best.

Now I affirm, that all these states have, without exception, fallen into excess; and also that he should not have said that one oligarchy was better than another, but that it was not quite so bad. But this question we shall not enter into at present. We shall first inquire how many different sorts of free states there are; since there are many species of democracies and oligarchies; and which of them is the most comprehensive, and most desirable after the best form of government; or if there is any other like an aristocracy, well established; and also which of these is best adapted to most cities, and which of them is preferable for particular persons: for, probably, some may suit better with an oligarchy than a democracy, and others better with a democracy than an oligarchy; and afterwards in what manner any one ought to proceed who desires to establish either of these states, I mean every species of democracy, and also of oligarchy. And to conclude, when we shall have briefly gone through everything that is necessary, we will endeavour to point out the sources of corruption, and stability, in government, as well those which are common to all as those which are peculiar to each state, and from what causes they chiefly arise.

CHAPTER III

THE reason for there being many different sorts of governments is this, that each state consists of a great number of parts; for, in the first place, we see that all cities are made up of families: and again, of the multitude of these some must be rich, some poor, and others in the middle station; and that, both of the rich and poor, some will be used to arms, others not. We see also, that some of the common people are husbandmen, others attend the market, and others are artificers. There is also a difference between the nobles in their wealth, and the dignity in which they live: for instance, in the number of horses they breed; for this cannot be supported without a large fortune: for which reason, in former times, those cities whose strength consisted in horse became by that means oligarchies; and they used horse in their expeditions against the neighbouring cities; as the Eretrians, the Chalcidians, the Magnetians, who lived near the river Meander, and many others in Asia. Moreover, besides the difference of fortune, there is that which arises from family and merit; or, if there are any other distinctions 1290a which make part of the city, they have been already mentioned in treating of an aristocracy, for there we considered how many parts each city must necessarily be composed of; and sometimes each of these have a share in the government, sometimes a few, sometimes more.

It is evident then, that there must be many forms of government, differing from each other in their particular constitution: for the parts of which they are composed each differ from the other. For government is the ordering of the magistracies of the state; and these the community share between themselves, either as they can attain them by force, or according to some common equality which there is amongst them, as poverty, wealth, or something which they both partake of. There must therefore necessarily be as many different forms of governments as there are different ranks in the society, arising from the superiority of some over others, and their different situations. And these seem chiefly to be two, as they say, of the winds: namely, the north and the south; and all the others are declinations from these. And thus in politics, there is the government of the many and the government of the few; or a democracy and an oligarchy: for an aristocracy may be considered

as a species of oligarchy, as being also a government of
the few; and what we call a free state may be considered
as a democracy: as in the winds they consider the west
as part of the north, and the east as part of the south:
and thus it is in music, according to some, who say
there are only two species of it, the Doric and the Phrygian,
and all other species of composition they call after one
of these names; and many people are accustomed to
consider the nature of government in the same light; but
it is both more convenient and more correspondent to
truth to distinguish governments as I have done, into
two species: one, of those which are established upon
proper principles; of which there may be one or two
sorts: the other, which includes all the different excesses
of these; so that we may compare the best form of
government to the most harmonious piece of music; the
oligarchic and despotic to the more violent tunes; and
the democratic to the soft and gentle airs.

CHAPTER IV

WE ought not to define a democracy as some do, who say
simply, that it is a government where the supreme power
is lodged in the people; for even in oligarchies the supreme
power is in the majority. Nor should they define an
oligarchy a government where the supreme power is in
the hands of a few: for let us suppose the number of
a people to be thirteen hundred, and that of these one
thousand were rich, who would not permit the three
hundred poor to have any share in the government,
although they were free, and their equal in everything
else; no one would say, that this government was a
democracy. In like manner, if the poor, when few in
number, should acquire the power over the rich, though
more than themselves, no one would say, that this was
an oligarchy; nor this, when the rest who are rich have
no share in the administration. We should rather say,
that a democracy is when the supreme power is in the 1290b

hands of the freemen; an oligarchy, when it is in the hands
of the rich: it happens indeed that in the one case the
many will possess it, in the other the few; because there
are many poor and few rich. And if the power of the
state was to be distributed according to the size of the
citizens, as they say it is in Æthiopia, or according to
their beauty, it would be an oligarchy: for the number
of those who are large and beautiful is small.

Nor are those things which we have already mentioned
alone sufficient to describe these states; for since there
are many species both of a democracy and an oligarchy,
the matter requires further consideration; as we cannot
admit, that if a few persons who are free possess the
supreme power over the many who are not free, that this
government is a democracy: as in Apollonia, in Ionia,
and in Thera: for in each of these cities the honours of
the state belong to some few particular families, who
first founded the colonies. Nor would the rich, because
they are superior in numbers, form a democracy, as
formerly at Colophon; for there the majority had large
possessions before the Lydian war: but a democracy is
a state where the freemen and the poor, being the majority,
are invested with the power of the state. An oligarchy
is a state where the rich and those of noble families, being
few, possess it.

We have now proved that there are various forms of
government and have assigned a reason for it; and shall
proceed to show that there are even more than these,
and what they are, and why; setting out with the principle we have already laid down. We admit that every
city consists not of one, but many parts: thus, if we
should endeavour to comprehend the different species
of animals we should first of all note those parts which
every animal must have, as a certain sensorium, and also
what is necessary to acquire and retain food, as a mouth
and a belly; besides certain parts to enable it to move
from place to place. If, then, these are the only parts
of an animal and there are differences between them;
namely, in their various sorts of stomachs, bellies, and
sensoriums: to which we must add their motive powers;

the number of the combinations of all these must necessarily make up the different species of animals. For it is not possible that the same kind of animal should have any very great difference in its mouth or ears; so that when all these are collected, who happen to have these things similar in all, they make up a species of animals of which there are as many as there are of these general combinations of necessary parts.

The same thing is true of what are called states; for a city is not made of one but many parts, as has already been often said; one of which is those who supply it with provisions, called husbandmen, another called mechanics, 1291a whose employment is in the manual arts, without which the city could not be inhabited; of these some are busied about what is absolutely necessary, others in what contribute to the elegancies and pleasures of life; the third sort are your exchange-men, I mean by these your buyers, sellers, merchants, and victuallers; the fourth are your hired labourers or workmen; the fifth are the men-at-arms, a rank not less useful than the other, without you would have the community slaves to every invader; but what cannot defend itself is unworthy of the name of a city; for a city is self-sufficient, a slave not. So that when Socrates, in Plato's *Republic*, says that a city is necessarily composed of four sorts of people, he speaks elegantly but not correctly, and these are, according to him, weavers, husbandmen, shoe-makers, and builders; he then adds, as if these were not sufficient, smiths,.herdsmen for what cattle are necessary, and also merchants and victuallers, and these are by way of appendix to his first list; as if a city was established for necessity, and not happiness, or as if a shoe-maker and a husbandman were equally useful. He reckons not the military a part before the increase of territory and joining to the borders of the neighbouring powers will make war necessary: and even amongst them who compose his four divisions, or whoever have any connection with each other, it will be necessary to have some one to distribute justice, and determine between man and man. If, then, the mind is a more valuable part of man than the body, every one would wish to have those things more regarded in his city which tend to the advantage of these than common matters, such are war and justice; to which may be added council, which is the business of civil wisdom (nor is it of any consequence whether these different employments are filled by different persons or one, as the same man is oftentimes both a soldier and a husbandman): so that if both the judge and the senator are parts of the city, it necessarily follows that the soldier must be so also. The seventh sort are those who serve the public in expensive employments at their own charge: these are called the rich. The eighth are those who execute the different offices of the state, and without these it could not possibly subsist: it is therefore necessary that there should be some persons capable of governing and filling the places in the city; and this either for life or in rotation: the office of senator, and judge, of which we have already sufficiently treated, are the only ones remaining. If, then, these things are necessary for a state, that it may be happy and just, it follows that the citizens who engage in public affairs should be men of abilities therein. 1291*b* Several persons think, that different employments may be allotted to the same person; as a soldier's, a husband-man's, and an artificer's; as also that others may be both senators and judges.

Besides, every one supposes himself a man of political abilities, and that he is qualified for almost every department in the state. But the same person cannot at once be poor and rich: for which reason the most obvious division of the city is into two parts, the poor and rich; moreover, since for the generality the one are few, the other many, they seem of all the parts of a city most contrary to each other; so that as the one or the other prevail they form different states; and these are the democracy and the oligarchy.

But that there are many different states, and from what causes they arise, has been already mentioned: and that there are also different species both of democracies and oligarchies we will now show. Though this indeed is evident from what we have already said: there are also many different sorts of common people, and also of those who are called gentlemen. Of the different sorts of the first are husbandmen, artificers, exchange-men, who are employed in buying and selling, seamen, of which some are engaged in war, some in traffic, some in carrying goods and passengers from place to place, others in fishing, and of each of these there are often many, as fishermen at Tarentum and Byzantium, masters of galleys at Athens, merchants at Ægina and Chios, those who let ships on freight at Tenedos; we may add to these those who live by their manual labour and have but little property; so that they cannot live without some employ: and also those who are not free-born on both sides, and whatever other sort of common people there may be. As for gentlemen, they are such as are distinguished either by their fortune, their birth, their abilities, or their education, or any such-like excellence which is attributed to them.

The most pure democracy is that which is so called principally from that equality which prevails in it: for this is what the law in that state directs; that the poor shall be in no greater subjection than the rich; nor that the supreme power shall be lodged with either of these, but that both shall share it. For if liberty and equality, as some persons suppose, are chiefly to be found in a democracy, it must be most so by every department of government being alike open to all; but as the people are the majority, and what they vote is law, it follows that such a state must be a democracy. This, then, is one species thereof. Another is, when the magistrates are elected by a certain census; but this should be but small, and every one who was included in it should be eligible, but as soon as he was below it should lose that right. 1292a Another sort is, in which every citizen who is not infamous has a share in the government, but where the government is in the laws. Another, where every citizen without exception has this right. Another is like these in other particulars, but there the people govern, and not the law: and this takes place when everything is determined by a majority of votes, and not by a law; which happens when the people are influenced by the demagogues: for where a democracy is governed by stated laws there is no room for them, but men of worth fill the first offices in the state: but where the power is not vested in the laws, there demagogues abound: for there the people rule with kingly power: the whole composing one body; for they are supreme, not as individuals but in their collective capacity.

Homer also discommends the government of many; but whether he means this we are speaking of, or where each person exercises his power separately, is uncertain. When the people possess this power they desire to be altogether absolute, that they may not be under the control of the law, and this is the time when flatterers are held in repute. Nor is there any difference between such a people and monarchs in a tyranny: for their manners are the same, and they both hold a despotic power over better persons than themselves. For their decrees are like the others' edicts; their demagogues like the others' flatterers: but their greatest resemblance consists in the mutual support they give to each other, the flatterer to the tyrant, the demagogue to the people: and to them it is owing that the supreme power is lodged in the votes of the people, and not in the laws; for they bring everything before them, as their influence is owing to their being supreme whose opinions they entirely direct; for these are they whom the multitude obey. Besides, those who accuse the magistrates insist upon it, that the right of determining on their conduct lies in the people, who gladly receive their complaints as the means of destroying all their offices.

Any one, therefore, may with great justice blame such a government as being a democracy, and not a free state; for where the government is not in the laws, then there is no free state, for the law ought to be supreme over all things; and particular incidents which arise should be determined by the magistrates or the state. If, therefore, a democracy is to be reckoned a free state, it is evident that any such establishment which centres all power in the votes of the people cannot, properly speaking, be a

democracy: for their decrees cannot be general in their
extent. Thus, then, we may describe the several species
of democracies.

CHAPTER V

OF the different species of oligarchies one is, when the
right to the offices is regulated by a certain census; so
that the poor, although the majority, have no share in it;
while all those who are included therein take part in the
management of public affairs. Another sort is, when 1292*b*
the magistrates are men of very small fortune, who upon
any vacancy do themselves fill it up: and if they do this
out of the community at large, the state approaches to
an aristocracy; if out of any particular class of people,
it will be an oligarchy. Another sort of oligarchy is,
when the power is an hereditary nobility. The fourth is,
when the power is in the same hands as the other, but
not under the control of law; and this sort of oligarchy
exactly corresponds to a tyranny in monarchies, and to
that particular species of democracies which I last
mentioned in treating of that state: this has the particular name of a dynasty. These are the different sorts
of oligarchies and democracies.

It should also be known, that it often happens that
a free state, where the supreme power is in the laws,
may not be democratic, and yet in consequence of the
established manners and customs of the people, may be
governed as if it was; so, on the other hand, where the
laws may countenance a more democratic form of government, these may make the state inclining to an oligarchy;
and this chiefly happens when there has been any alteration in the government; for the people do not easily
change, but love their own ancient customs; and it is
by small degrees only that one thing takes place of
another; so that the ancient laws will remain, while the
power will be in the hands of those who have brought
about a revolution in the state.

CHAPTER VI

It is evident from what has been said, that there are as
many different sorts of democracies and oligarchies as
I have reckoned up: for, of necessity, either all ranks
of the people which I have enumerated must have a share
in the government, or some only, and others not; for
when the husbandmen, and those only who possess
moderate fortunes, have the supreme power, they will
govern according to law; for as they must get their livings
by their employs, they have but little leisure for public
business: they will therefore establish proper laws, and
never call public assemblies but when there is a necessity
for them; and they will readily let every one partake
with them in the administration of public affairs as soon
as they possess that fortune which the law requires for
their qualification: every one, therefore, who is qualified
will have his share in the government: for to exclude any
would be to make the government an oligarchy, and for
all to have leisure to attend without they had a subsistence would be impossible: for these reasons, therefore,
this government is a species of democracy. Another
species is distinguished by the mode of electing their
magistrates, in which every one is eligible, to whose
birth there are no objections, provided he is supposed to
have leisure to attend: for which reason in such a democracy the supreme power will be vested in the laws, as
there will be nothing paid to those who go to the public
assemblies. A third species is where every freeman has a
right to a share in the government, which he will not accept
for the cause already assigned; for which reason here also
the supreme power will be in the law. The fourth species
1293a of democracy, the last which was established in order
of time, arose when cities were greatly enlarged to what
they were at first, and when the public revenue became
something considerable; for then the populace, on
account of their numbers, were admitted to share in the
management of public affairs, for then even the poorest

people were at leisure to attend to them, as they received wages for so doing; nay, they were more so than others, as they were not hindered by having anything of their own to mind, as the rich had; for which reason these last very often did not frequent the public assemblies and the courts of justice: thus the supreme power was lodged in the poor, and not in the laws. These are the different sorts of democracies, and such are the causes which necessarily gave birth to them.

The first species of oligarchy is, when the generality of the state are men of moderate and not too large property; for this gives them leisure for the management of public affairs: and, as they are a numerous body, it necessarily follows that the supreme power must be in the laws, and not in men; for as they are far removed from a monarchical government, and have not sufficient fortune to neglect their private affairs, while they are too many to be supported by the public, they will of course determine to be governed by the laws, and not by each other. But if the men of property in the state are but few, and their property is large, then an oligarchy of the second sort will take place; for those who have most power will think that they have a right to lord it over the others; and, to accomplish this, they will associate to themselves some who have an inclination for public affairs, and as they are not powerful enough to govern without law, they will make a law for that purpose. And if those few who have large fortunes should acquire still greater power, the oligarchy will then alter into one of the third sort; for they will get all the offices of the state into their own hands by a law which directs the son to succeed upon the death of his father; and, after that, when, by means of their increasing wealth and powerful connections, they extend still further their oppression, a monarchical dynasty will directly succeed wherein men will be supreme, and not the·law; and this is the fourth species of an oligarchy correspondent to the last-mentioned class of democracies.

CHAPTER VII

THERE are besides two other states, a democracy and an oligarchy, one of which all speak of, and it is always esteemed a species of the four sorts; and thus they reckon them up; a monarchy, an oligarchy, a democracy, and this fourth which they call an aristocracy. There is also a fifth, which bears a name that is also common to the other four, namely, a state: but as this is seldom to be met with, it has escaped those who have endeavoured to enumerate the different sorts of governments, which 1293*b* they fix at four only, as does Plato in his *Republic*.

An aristocracy, of which I have already treated in the first book, is rightly called so; for a state governed by the best men, upon the most virtuous principles, and not upon any hypothesis, which even good men may propose, has alone a right to be called an aristocracy, for it is there only that a man is at once a good man and a good citizen; while in other states men are good only relative to those states. Moreover, there are some other states which are called by the same name, that differ both from oligarchies and free states, wherein not only the rich but also the virtuous have a share in the administration; and have therefore acquired the name of aristocracies; for in those governments wherein virtue is not their common care, there are still men of worth and approved goodness. Whatever state, then, like the Carthaginians, favours the rich, the virtuous, and the citizens at large, is a sort of aristocracy: when only the two latter are held in esteem, as at Lacedæmon, and the state is jointly composed of these, it is a virtuous democracy. These are the two species of aristocracies after the first, which is the best of all governments. There is also a third, which is, whenever a free state inclines to the dominion of a few.

CHAPTER VIII

IT now remains for us to treat of that government which is particularly called a free state, and also of a tyranny; and the reason for my choosing to place that free state here is, because this, as well as those aristocracies already mentioned, although they do not seem excesses, yet, to speak true, they have all departed from what a perfect government is. Nay, they are deviations both of them equally from other forms, as I said at the beginning. It is proper to mention a tyranny the last of all governments, for it is of all others the least like one: but as my intention is to treat of all governments in general, for this reason that also, as I have said, will be taken into consideration in its proper place.

I shall now inquire into a free state and show what it is; and we shall the better understand its positive nature as we have already described an oligarchy and a democracy; for a free state is indeed nothing more than a mixture of them, and it has been usual to call those which incline most to a democracy, a free state; those which incline most to an oligarchy, an aristocracy, because those who are rich are generally men of family and education; besides, they enjoy those things which others are often guilty of crimes to procure: for which reason they are regarded as men of worth and honour and note.

Since, then, it is the genius of an aristocracy to allot the larger part of the government to the best citizens, they therefore say, that an oligarchy is chiefly composed of those men who are worthy and honourable: now it 1294a seems impossible that where the government is in the nands of the good, there the laws should not be good, but bad; or, on the contrary, that where the government is in the hands of the bad, there the laws should be good; nor is a government well constituted because the laws are, without at the same time care is taken that they are observed; for to enforce obedience to the laws which

it makes is one proof of a good constitution in the state;
another is, to have laws well calculated for those who
are to abide by them; for if they are improper they must
be obeyed: and this may be done two ways, either by
their being the best relative to the particular state, or
the best absolutely. An aristocracy seems most likely
to confer the honours of the state on the virtuous; for
virtue is the object of an aristocracy, riches of an oligarchy,
and liberty of a democracy; for what is approved of by
the majority will prevail in all or in each of these three
different states; and that which seems good to most of
those who compose the community will prevail: for
what is called a state prevails in many communities,
which aim at a mixture of rich and poor, riches and
liberty: as for the rich, they are usually supposed to
take the place of the worthy and honourable. As there
are three things which claim an equal rank in the state,
freedom, riches, and virtue (for as for the fourth, rank,
it is an attendant on two of the others, for virtue and
riches are the origin of family), it is evident, that the
conjuncture of the rich and the poor make up a free state;
but that all three tend to an aristocracy more than any
other, except that which is truly so, which holds the
first rank.

We have already seen that there are governments
different from a monarchy, a democracy, and an oligarchy;
and what they are, and wherein they differ from each
other; and also aristocracies and states properly so called,
which are derived from them; and it is evident that these
are not much unlike each other.

CHAPTER IX

We shall next proceed to show how that government
which is peculiarly called a state arises alongside of democracy and oligarchy, and how it ought to be established;
and this will at the same time show what are the proper
boundaries of both these governments, for we must

mark out wherein they differ from one another, and then from both these compose a state of such parts of each of them as will show from whence they were taken.

There are three different ways in which two states may be blended and joined together; for, in the first place, all those rules may be adopted which the laws of each of them have ordered; as for instance in the judicial department, for in an oligarchy the rich are fined if they do not come to the court as jurymen, but the poor are not paid for their attendance; but in democracies they are, while the rich are not fined for their neglect. Now these things, as being common to both, are fit to be observed in a free **1294**_b_ state which is composed of both. This, then, is one way in which they may be joined together. In the second place, a medium may be taken between the different methods which each state observes; for instance, in a democracy the right to vote in the public assembly is either confined by no census at all, or limited by a very small one; in an oligarchy none enjoy it but those whose census is high: therefore, as these two practices are contrary to each other, a census between each may be established in such a state. In the third place, different laws of each community may be adopted; as, for instance, as it seems correspondent to the nature of a democracy, that the magistrates should be chosen by lot, but an aristocracy by vote, and in the one state according to a census, but not in the other: let, then, an aristocracy and a free state copy something from each of them; let them follow an oligarchy in choosing their magistrates by vote, but a democracy in not admitting of any census, and thus blend together the different customs of the two governments. But the best proof of a happy mixture of a democracy and an oligarchy is this, when a person may properly call the same state a democracy and an oligarchy. It is evident that those who speak of it in this manner are induced to it because both these governments are there well blended together: and indeed this is common to all mediums, that the extremes of each side should be discerned therein, as at Lacedæmon; for many affirm that it is a democracy from the many particulars in which it follows that form of government; as, for instance, in the first place, in the bringing up of their children, for the rich and poor are brought up in the same manner; and their education is such that the children of the poor may partake of it; and the same rules are observed when they are youths and men, there is no distinction between a rich person and a poor one; and in their public tables the same provision is served to all. The rich also wear only such clothes as the poorest man is able to purchase. Moreover, with respect to two magistracies of the highest rank, one they have a right to elect to, the other to fill; namely, the senate and the ephori. Others consider it as an oligarchy, the principles of which it follows in many things, as in choosing all their officers by vote, and not by lot; in there being but a few who have a right to sit in judgment on capital causes and the like. Indeed, a state which is well composed of two others ought to resemble them both, and neither. Such a state ought to have its means of preservation in itself, and not without; and when I say in itself, I do not mean that it should owe this to the forbearance of their neighbours, for this may happen to a bad government, but to every member of the community's not being willing that there should be the least alteration in their constitution. Such is the method in which a free state or an aristocracy ought to be established.

CHAPTER X

It now remains to treat of a tyranny; not that there is 1295a much to be said on that subject, but as it makes part of our plan, since we enumerated it amongst our different sorts of governments. In the beginning of this work we inquired into the nature of kingly government, and entered into a particular examination of what was most properly called so, and whether it was advantageous to a state or not, and what it should be, and how established; and we divided a tyranny into two pieces when we were upon this subject, because there is something analogous between this and a kingly government, for they are both of them established by law; for among some of the barbarians they elect a monarch with absolute power, and formerly among the Greeks there were some such, whom they called æsumnetes.   Now these differ from each other; for some possess only kingly power regulated by law, and rule those who voluntarily submit to their government; others rule despotically according to their own will.   There is a third species of tyranny, most properly so called, which is the very opposite to kingly power; for this is the government of one who rules over his equals and superiors without being accountable for his conduct, and whose object is his own advantage, and not the advantage of those he governs; for which reason he rules by compulsion, for no freemen will ever willingly submit to such a government.   These are the different species of tyrannies, their principles, and their causes.

CHAPTER XI

We proceed now to inquire what form of government and what manner of life is best for communities in general, not adapting it to that superior virtue which is above the reach of the vulgar, or that education which every advantage of nature and fortune only can furnish, nor to those imaginary plans which may be formed at pleasure; but to that mode of life which the greater part of mankind can attain to, and that government which most cities may establish: for as to those aristocracies which we have now mentioned, they are either too perfect for a state to support, or one so nearly alike to that state we are now going to inquire into, that we shall treat of them both as one.

The opinions which we form upon these subjects must depend upon one common principle: for if what I have said in my treatise on Morals is true, a happy life must arise from an uninterrupted course of virtue; and if

virtue consists in a certain medium, the middle life must
certainly be the happiest; which medium is attainable
1295*b* by every one.   The boundaries of virtue and vice in the
state must also necessarily be the same as in a private
person; for the form of government is the life of the city.
In every city the people are divided into three sorts;
the very rich, the very poor, and those who are between
them.   If this is universally admitted, that the mean
is best, it is evident that even in point of fortune medi-
ocrity is to be preferred; for that state is most submissive
to reason; for those who are very handsome, or very
strong, or very noble, or very rich; or, on the contrary,
those who are very poor, or very weak, or very mean,
with difficulty obey it; for the one are capricious and
greatly flagitious, the other rascally and mean, the crimes
of each arising from their different excesses: nor will they
go through the different offices of the state; which is
detrimental to it: besides, those who excel in strength,
in riches, or friends, or the like, neither know how nor
are willing to submit to command: and this begins at
home when they are boys; for there they are brought up
too delicately to be accustomed to obey their preceptors:
as for the very poor, their general and excessive want of
what the rich enjoy reduces them to a state too mean:
so that the one know not how to command, but to be
commanded as slaves, the others know not how to submit
to any command, nor to command themselves but with
despotic power.

A city composed of such men must therefore consist
of slaves and masters, not freemen; where one party
must hate, and the other despise, where there could be
no possibility of friendship or political community: for
community supposes affection; for we do not even on
the road associate with our enemies.   It is also the genius
of a city to be composed as much as possible of equals;
which will be most so when the inhabitants are in the
middle state: from whence it follows, that that city must
be best framed which is composed of those whom we say
are naturally its proper members.   It is men of this
station also who will be best assured of safety and pro-

tection; for they will neither covet what belongs to others, as the poor do; nor will others covet what is theirs, as the poor do what belongs to the rich; and thus, without plotting against any one, or having any one plot against them, they will live free from danger: for which reason Phocylides wisely wishes for the middle state, as being most productive of happiness. It is plain, then, that the most perfect political community must be amongst those who are in the middle rank, and those states are best instituted wherein these are a larger and more respectable part, if possible, than both the other; or, if that cannot be, at least than either of them separate; so that being thrown into the balance it may prevent either scale from preponderating.

It is therefore the greatest happiness which the citizens can enjoy to possess a moderate and convenient fortune; for when some possess too much, and others nothing at 1296a all, the government must either be in the hands of the meanest rabble or else a pure oligarchy; or, from the excesses of both, a tyranny; for this arises from a headstrong democracy or an oligarchy, but very seldom when the members of the community are nearly on an equality with each other. We will assign a reason for this when we come to treat of the alterations which different states are likely to undergo. The middle state is therefore best, as being least liable to those seditions and insurrections which disturb the community; and for the same reason extensive governments are least liable to these inconveniences; for there those in a middle state are very numerous, whereas in small ones it is easy to pass to the two extremes, so as hardly to have any in a medium remaining, but the one half rich, the other poor: and from the same principle it is that democracies are more firmly established and of longer continuance than oligarchies; but even in those when there is a want of a proper number of men of middling fortune, the poor extend their power too far, abuses arise, and the government is soon at an end.

We ought to consider as a proof of what I now advance, that the best lawgivers themselves were those in the middle rank of life, amongst whom was Solon, as is evident from his poems, and Lycurgus, for he was not a king, and Charondas, and indeed most others. What has been said will show us why of so many free states some have changed to democracies, others to oligarchies: for whenever the number of those in the middle state has been too small, those who were the more numerous, whether the rich or the poor, always overpowered them, and assumed to themselves the administration of public affairs; from hence arose either a democracy or an oligarchy. Moreover, when in consequence of their disputes and quarrels with each other, either the rich get the better of the poor, or the poor of the rich, neither of them will establish a free state; but, as the record of their victory, one which inclines to their own principles, and form either a democracy or an oligarchy.

Those who made conquests in Greece, having all of them an eye to the respective forms of government in their own cities, established either democracies or oligarchies, not considering what was serviceable to the state, but what was similar to their own; for which reason a government has never been established where the supreme power has been placed amongst those of the middling rank, or very seldom; and, amongst a few, one man only of those who have yet been conquerors has been persuaded to give the preference to this order of 1296b men: it is indeed an established custom with the inhabitants of most cities not to desire an equality, but either to aspire to govern, or when they are conquered, to submit.

Thus we have shown what the best state is, and why. It will not be difficult to perceive of the many states which there are, for we have seen that there are various forms both of democracies and oligarchies, to which we should give the first place, to which the second, and in the same manner the next also; and to observe what are the particular excellences and defects of each, after we have first described the best possible; for that must be the best which is nearest to this, that worst which is most distant from the medium, without any one has

a particular plan of his own which he judges by. I mean
by this, that it may happen, that although one form of
government may be better than another, yet there is no
reason to prevent another from being preferable thereunto
in particular circumstances and for particular purposes.

CHAPTER XII

AFTER what has been said, it follows that we should now
show what particular form of government is most suitable
for particular persons; first laying this down as a general
maxim, that that party which desires to support the
actual administration of the state ought always to be
superior to that which would alter it. Every city is
made up of quality and quantity: by quality I mean
liberty, riches, education, and family, and by quantity
its relative populousness: now it may happen that quality
may exist in one of those parts of which the city is composed, and quantity in another; thus the number of the
ignoble may be greater than the number of those of
family, the number of the poor than that of the rich; but
not so that the quantity of the one shall overbalance the
quality of the other; those must be properly adjusted
to each other; for where the number of the poor exceeds
the proportion we have mentioned, there a democracy
will rise up, and if the husbandry should have more power
than others, it will be a democracy of husbandmen; and
the democracy will be a particular species according to
that class of men which may happen to be most numerous:
thus, should these be the husbandmen, it will be of these,
and the best; if of mechanics and those who hire themselves out, the worst possible: in the same manner it may
be of any other set between these two. But when the
rich and the noble prevail more by their quality than
they are deficient in quantity, there an oligarchy ensues;
and this oligarchy may be of different species, according
to the nature of the prevailing party.

Every legislator in framing his constitution ought to

have a particular regard to those in the middle rank of life; and if he intends an oligarchy, these should be the object of his laws; if a democracy, to these they should be entrusted; and whenever their number exceeds that of the two others, or at least one of them, they give 1297a stability to the constitution; for there is no fear that the rich and the poor should agree to conspire together against them, for neither of these will choose to serve the other. If any one would choose to fix the administration on the widest basis, he will find none preferable to this; for to rule by turns is what the rich and the poor will not submit to, on account of their hatred to each other. It is, moreover, allowed that an arbitrator is the most proper person for both parties to trust to; now this arbitrator is the middle rank.

Those who would establish aristocratical governments are mistaken not only in giving too much power to the rich, but also in deceiving the common people; for at last, instead of an imaginary good, they must feel a real evil, for the encroachments of the rich are more destructive to the state than those of the poor.

CHAPTER XIII

THERE are five particulars in which, under fair pretences, the rich craftily endeavour to undermine the rights of the people, these are their public assemblies, their offices of state, their courts of justice, their military power, and their gymnastic exercises. With respect to their public assemblies, in having them open to all, but in fining the rich only, or others very little, for not attending; with respect to offices, in permitting the poor to swear off, but not granting this indulgence to those who are within the census; with respect to their courts of justice, in fining the rich for non-attendance, but the poor not at all, or those a great deal, and these very little, as was done by the laws of Charondas. In some places every citizen who was enrolled had a right to attend the public assemblies

and to try causes; which if they did not do, a very heavy
fine was laid upon them; that through fear of the fine
they might avoid being enrolled, as they were then obliged
to do neither the one nor the other. The same spirit of
legislation prevailed with respect to their bearing arms
and their gymnastic exercises; for the poor are excused
if they have no arms, but the rich are fined; the same
method takes place if they do not attend their gymnastic
exercises, there is no penalty on one, but there is on the
other: the consequence of which is, that the fear of this
penalty induces the rich to keep the one and attend the
other, while the poor do neither. These are the deceitful
contrivances of oligarchical legislators.

The contrary prevails in a democracy; for there they
make the poor a proper allowance for attending the
assemblies and the courts, but give the rich nothing for
doing it: whence it is evident, that if any one would
properly blend these customs together, they must extend
both the pay and the fine to every member of the community, and then every one would share in it, whereas
part only now do. The citizens of a free state ought to 1297*b*
consist of those only who bear arms: with respect to
their census it is not easy to determine exactly what it
ought to be, but the rule that should direct upon this
subject should be to make it as extensive as possible, so
that those who are enrolled in it make up a greater part
of the people than those who are not; for those who are
poor, although they partake not of the offices of the state,
are willing to live quiet, provided that no one disturbs
them in their property: but this is not an easy matter;
for it may not always happen, that those who are at the
head of public affairs are of a humane behaviour. In
time of war the poor are accustomed to show no alacrity
without they have provisions found them; when they
have, then indeed they are willing to fight.

In some governments the power is vested not only in
those who bear arms, but also in those who have borne
them. Among the Malienses the state was composed of
these latter only, for all the officers were soldiers who had
served their time. And the first states in Greece which

succeeded those where kingly power was established, were governed by the military. First of all the horse, for at that time the strength and excellence of the army depended on the horse, for as to the heavy-armed foot they were useless without proper discipline; but the art of tactics was not known to the ancients, for which reason their strength lay in their horse: but when cities grew larger, and they depended more on their foot, greater numbers partook of the freedom of the city; for which reason what we call republics were formerly called democracies. The ancient governments were properly oligarchies or kingdoms; for on account of the few persons in each state, it would have been impossible to have found a sufficient number of the middle rank; so these being but few, and those used to subordination, they more easily submitted to be governed.

We have now shown why there are many sorts of governments, and others different from those we have treated of: for there are more species of democracies than one, and the like is true of other forms, and what are their differences, and whence they arise; and also of all others which is the best, at least in general; and which is best suited for particular people.

CHAPTER XIV

WE will now proceed to make some general reflections upon the governments next in order, and also to consider each of them in particular; beginning with those principles which appertain to each: now there are three things in all states which a careful legislator ought well to consider, which are of great consequence to all, and which properly attended to the state must necessarily be happy; and according to the variation of which the one will differ from the other. The first of these is the
1298a public assembly; the second the officers of the state, that is, who they ought to be, and with what power they should be entrusted, and in what manner they should be appointed; the third, the judicial department.

Now it is the proper business of the public assembly to determine concerning war and peace, making or breaking off alliances, to enact laws, to sentence to death, banishment, or confiscation of goods, and to call the magistrates to account for their behaviour when in office. Now these powers must necessarily be entrusted to the citizens in general, or all of them to some; either to one magistrate or more; or some to one, and some to another, or some to all, but others to some: to entrust all to all is in the spirit of a democracy, for the people aim at equality. There are many methods of delegating these powers to the citizens at large, one of which is to let them execute them by turn, and not altogether, as was done by Tellecles, the Milesian, in his state. In others the supreme council is composed of the different magistrates, and they succeed to the offices of the community by proper divisions of tribes, wards, and other very small proportions, till every one in his turn goes through them: nor does the whole community ever meet together, without it is when new laws are enacted, or some national affair is debated, or to hear what the magistrates have to propose to them. Another method is for the people to meet in a collective body, but only for the purpose of holding the comitia, making laws, determining concerning war or peace, and inquiring into the conduct of their magistrates, while the remaining part of the public business is conducted by the magistrates, who have their separate departments, and are chosen out of the whole community either by vote or ballot. Another method is for the people in general to meet for the choice of the magistrates, and to examine into their conduct; and also to deliberate concerning war and alliances, and to leave other things to the magistrates, whoever happen to be chosen, whose particular employments are such as necessarily require persons well skilled therein. A fourth method is for every person to deliberate upon every subject in public assembly, where the magistrates can determine nothing of themselves, and have only the privilege of giving their opinions first; and this is the method of the most pure democracy, which is analogous to the proceedings in a dynastic oligarchy and a tyrannic monarchy.

These, then, are the methods in which public business is conducted in a democracy. When the power is in the hands of part of the community only, it is an oligarchy, and this also admits of different customs; for whenever the officers of the state are chosen out of those who have a moderate fortune, and these from that circumstance are many, and when they depart not from that line which the law has laid down, but carefully follow it, and when all within the census are eligible, certainly it is then an oligarchy, but founded on true principles of government 1298b from its moderation. When the people in general do not partake of the deliberative power, but certain persons chosen for that purpose, who govern according to law; this also, like the first, is an oligarchy. When those who have the deliberative power elect each other, and the son succeeds to the father, and when they can supersede the laws, such a government is of necessity a strict oligarchy. When some persons determine on one thing, and others on another, as war and peace, and when all inquire into the conduct of their magistrates, and other things are left to different officers, elected either by vote or lot, then the government is an aristocracy or a free state. When some are chosen by vote and others by lot, and these either from the people in general, or from a certain number elected for that purpose, or if both the votes and the lots are open to all, such a state is partly an aristocracy, partly a free government itself. These are the different methods in which the deliberative power is vested in different states, all of whom follow some regulation here laid down.

It is advantageous to a democracy, in the present sense of the word, by which I mean a state wherein the people at large have a supreme power, even over the laws, to hold frequent public assemblies; and it will be best in this particular to imitate the example of oligarchies in their courts of justice; for they fine those who are appointed to try causes if they do not attend, so should they reward the poor for coming to the public assemblies: and their counsels will be best when all advise with each other, the

citizens with the nobles, the nobles with the citizens.   It
is also advisable when the council is to be composed of
part of the citizens, to elect, either by vote or lot, an
equal number of both ranks.   It is also proper, if the
common people in the state are very numerous, either not
to pay every one for his attendance, but such a number
only as will make them equal to the nobles, or to reject
many of them by lot.

In an oligarchy they should either call up some of the
common people to the council, or else establish a court,
as is done in some other states, whom they call pre-
advisers or guardians of the laws, whose business should
be to propose first what they should afterwards enact.
By this means the people would have a place in the
administration of public affairs, without having it in
their power to occasion any disorder in the government.
Moreover, the people may be allowed to have a vote in
whatever bill is proposed, but may not themselves propose
anything contrary thereto; or they may give their advice,
while the power of determining may be with the magistrates only.   It is also necessary to follow a contrary
practice to what is established in democracies, for the
people should be allowed the power of pardoning, but not
of condemning, for the cause should be referred back
again to the magistrates: whereas the contrary takes
place in republics; for the power of pardoning is with the
few, but not of condemning, which is always referred **1299ᵃ**
to the people at large.   And thus we determine concerning
the deliberative power in any state, and in whose hands
it shall be.

CHAPTER XV

WE now proceed to consider the choice of magistrates;
for this branch of public business contains many different
parts, as how many there shall be, what shall be their
particular office, and with respect to time how long each
of them shall continue in place; for some make it six
months, others shorter, others for a year, others for a

much longer time; or whether they should be perpetual, or for a long time, or neither; for the same person may fill the same office several times, or he may not be allowed to enjoy it even twice, but only once: and also with respect to the appointment of magistrates, who are to be eligible, who is to choose them, and in what manner; for in all these particulars we ought properly to distinguish the different ways which may be followed; and then to show which of these is best suited to such and such governments.

Now it is not easy to determine to whom we ought properly to give the name of magistrate, for a government requires many persons in office; but every one of those who is either chosen by vote or lot is not to be reckoned a magistrate. The priests, for instance, in the first place; for these are to be considered as very different from civil magistrates: to these we may add the choregi and heralds; nay, even ambassadors are elected: there are some civil employments which belong to the citizens; and these are either when they are all engaged in one thing, as when as soldiers they obey their general, or when part of them only are, as in governing the women or educating the youth; and also some economic, for they often elect corn-meters: others are servile, and in which, if they are rich, they employ slaves. But indeed they are most properly called magistrates, who are members of the deliberative council, or decide causes, or are in some command, the last more especially, for to command is peculiar to magistrates. But to speak truth, this question is of no great consequence, nor is it the province of the judges to decide between those who dispute about words; it may indeed be an object of speculative inquiry; but to inquire what officers are necessary in a state, and how many, and what, though not most necessary, may yet be advantageous in a well-established government, is a much more useful employment, and this with respect to all states in general, as well as to small cities.

In extensive governments it is proper to allot one employment to one person, as there are many to serve the public in so numerous a society, where some may be

passed over for a long time, and others never be in office
but once; and indeed everything is better done which
has the whole attention of one person, than when that 1299b
attention is divided amongst many; but in small states
it is necessary that a few of the citizens should execute
many employments; for their numbers are so small it
will not be convenient to have many of them in office
at the same time; for where shall we find others to succeed them in turn? Small states will sometimes want
the same magistrates and the same laws as large ones;
but the one will not want to employ them so often as the
other; so that different charges may be intrusted to the
same person without any inconvenience, for they will
not interfere with each other, and for want of sufficient
members in the community it will be necessary. If we
could tell how many magistrates are necessary in every
city, and how many, though not necessary, it is yet
proper to have, we could then the better know how many
different offices one might assign to one magistrate. It
is also necessary to know what tribunals in different
places should have different things under their jurisdiction, and also what things should always come under
the cognisance of the same magistrate; as, for instance,
decency of manners, shall the clerk of the market take
cognisance of that if the cause arises in the market, and
another magistrate in another place, or the same magistrate everywhere: or shall there be a distinction made
of the fact, or the parties? as, for instance, in decency
of manners, shall it be one cause when it relates to a man,
another when it relates to a woman?

In different states shall the magistrates be different or
the same? I mean, whether in a democracy, an oligarchy,
an aristocracy, and a monarchy, the same persons shall
have the same power? or shall it vary according to the
different formation of the government? as in an aristocracy the offices of the state are allotted to those who
are well educated; in an oligarchy to those who are rich;
in a democracy to the freemen? Or shall the magistrates
differ as the communities differ? For it may happen
that the very same may be sometimes proper, sometimes

otherwise: in this state it may be necessary that the magistrate have great powers, in that but small. There are also certain magistrates peculiar to certain states; as the pre-advisers are not proper in a democracy, but a senate is; for one such order is necessary, whose business shall be to consider beforehand and prepare those bills which shall be brought before the people that they may have leisure to attend to their own affairs; and when these are few in number the state inclines to an oligarchy. The pre-advisers indeed must always be few; for they are peculiar to an oligarchy: and where there are both these offices in the same state, the pre-adviser's is superior to the senator's, the one having only a democratical power, the other an oligarchical: and indeed the 1300a power of the senate is lost in those democracies, in which the people, meeting in one public assembly, take all the business into their own hands; and this is likely to happen either when the community in general are in easy circumstances, or when they are paid for their attendance; for they are then at leisure often to meet together and determine everything for themselves. A magistrate whose business is to control the manners of the boys, or women, or who takes any department similar to this, is to be found in an aristocracy, not in a democracy; for who can forbid the wives of the poor from appearing in public? neither is such a one to be met with in an oligarchy; for the women there are too delicate to bear control. And thus much for this subject. Let us endeavour to treat at large of the establishment of magistrates, beginning from first principles. Now, they differ from each other in three ways, from which, blended together, all the varieties which can be imagined arise. The first of these differences is in those who appoint the magistrates, the second consists in those who are appointed, the third in the mode of appointment; and each of these three differ in three manners; for either all the citizens may appoint collectively, or some out of their whole body, or some out of a particular order in it, according to fortune, family, or virtue, or some other rule (as at Megara, where the right of election was amongst those

who had returned together to their country, and had
reinstated themselves by force of arms) and this either
by vote or lot. Again, these several modes may be
differently formed together, as some magistrates may
be chosen by part of the community, others by the whole;
some out of part, others out of the whole; some by vote,
others by lot: and each of these different modes admit
of a four-fold subdivision; for either all may elect all by
vote or by lot; and when all elect, they may either proceed
without any distinction, or they may elect by a certain
division of tribes, wards, or companies, till they have
gone through the whole community: and some magistrates may be elected one way, and others another.
Again, if some magistrates are elected either by vote or
lot of all the citizens, or by the vote of some and the lot
of some, or some one way and some another; that is to
say, some by the vote of all, others by the lot of all, there
will then be twelve different methods of electing the
magistrates, without blending the two together. Of
these there are two adapted to a democracy; namely,
to have all the magistrates chosen out of all the people,
either by vote or lot, or both; that is to say, some of
them by lot, some by vote. In a free state the whole
community should not elect at the same time, but some
out of the whole, or out of some particular rank; and
this either by lot, or vote, or both: and they should elect
either out of the whole community, or out of some particular persons in it, and this both by lot and vote. In
an oligarchy it is proper to choose some magistrates out
of the whole body of the citizens, some by vote, some by
lot, others by both: by lot is most correspondent to that
form of government. In a free aristocracy, some magis- 1300*b*
trates should be chosen out of the community in general,
others out of a particular rank, or these by choice, those
by lot. In a pure oligarchy, the magistrates should be
chosen out of certain ranks, and by certain persons, and
some of those by lot, others by both methods; but to
choose them out of the whole community is not correspondent to the nature of this government. It is proper
in an aristocracy for the whole community to elect their

magistrates out of particular persons, and this by vote. These then are all the different ways of electing of magistrates; and they have been allotted according to the nature of the different communities; but what mode of proceeding is proper for different communities, or how the offices ought to be established, or with what powers, shall be particularly explained. I mean by the powers of a magistrate, what should be his particular province, as the management of the finances or the laws of the state; for different magistrates have different powers, as that of the general of the army differs from the clerk of the market.

CHAPTER XVI

OF the three parts of which a government is formed, we now come to consider the judicial; and this also we shall divide in the same manner as we did the magisterial, into three parts. Of whom the judges shall consist, and for what causes, and how. When I say of whom, I mean whether they shall be the whole people, or some particulars; by for what causes I mean, how many different courts shall be appointed; by how, whether they shall be elected by vote or lot. Let us first determine how many different courts there ought to be. Now these are eight. The first of these is the court of inspection over the behaviour of the magistrates when they have quitted their office; the second is to punish those who have injured the public; the third is to take cognisance of those causes in which the state is a party; the fourth is to decide between magistrates and private persons, who appeal from a fine laid upon them; the fifth is to determine disputes which may arise concerning contracts of great value; the sixth is to judge between foreigners, and of murders, of which there are different species; and these may all be tried by the same judges or by different ones; for there are murders of malice prepense and of chance-medley; there is also justifiable homicide, where the fact is admitted, and the legality of it disputed.

There is also another court called at Athens the Court of Phreattæ, which determines points relating to a murder committed by one who has run away, to decide whether he shall return; though such an affair happens but seldom, and in very large cities; the seventh, to determine causes wherein strangers are concerned, and this whether they are between stranger and stranger or between a stranger and a citizen. The eighth and last is for small actions, from one to five drachma's, or a little more; for these ought also to be legally determined, but not to be brought before the whole body of the judges. But without entering into any particulars concerning actions for murder, and those wherein strangers are the parties, let us particularly treat of those courts which have the jurisdiction of those matters which more particularly relate to the affairs of the community and which if not well conducted occasion seditions and commotions in the state. Now, of necessity, either all persons must have a right to judge of all these different causes, appointed for that purpose, either by vote or lot, or all of all, some of them by vote, and others by lot, or in some causes by vote, in others by lot. Thus there will be four sorts of judges. There 1301a will be just the same number also if they are chosen out of part of the people only; for either all the judges must be chosen out of that part either by vote or lot, or some by lot and some by vote, or the judges in particular causes must be chosen some by vote, others by lot; by which means there will be the same number of them also as was mentioned. Besides, different judges may be joined together; I mean those who are chosen out of the whole people or part of them or both; so that all three may sit together in the same court, and this either by vote, lot, or both. And thus much for the different sorts of judges. Of these appointments that which admits all the community to be judges in all causes is most suitable to a democracy; the second, which appoints that certain persons shall judge all causes, to an oligarchy; the third, which appoints the whole community to be judges in some causes, but particular persons in others, to an aristocracy or free state.

BOOK V

CHAPTER I

WE have now gone through those particulars we proposed
to speak of; it remains that we next consider from what
causes and how alterations in government arise, and of
what nature they are, and to what the destruction of each
state is owing; and also to what form any form of polity
is most likely to shift into, and what are the means to be
used for the general preservation of governments, as well
as what are applicable to any particular state; and also
of the remedies which are to be applied either to all in
general, or to any one considered separately, when they
are in a state of corruption: and here we ought first to
lay down this principle, that there are many governments,
all of which approve of what is just and what is analogi-
cally equal; and yet have failed from attaining thereunto,
as we have already mentioned; thus democracies have
arisen from supposing that those who are equal in one
thing are so in every other circumstance; as, because
they are equal in liberty, they are equal in everything
else; and oligarchies, from supposing that those who are
unequal in one thing are unequal in all; that when men
are so in point of fortune, that inequality extends to
everything else. Hence it follows, that those who in some
respects are equal with others think it right to endeavour
to partake of an equality with them in everything; and
those who are superior to others endeavour to get still
more; and it is this *more* which is the inequality: thus
most states, though they have some notion of what is
just, yet are almost totally wrong; and, upon this account,
when either party has not that share in the administration
which answers to his expectations, he becomes seditious:
1301*b* but those who of all others have the greatest right to be

142

so are the last that are; namely, those who excel in virtue; for they alone can be called generally superior. There are, too, some persons of distinguished families who, because they are so, disdain to be on an equality with others, for those esteem themselves noble who boast of their ancestors' merit and fortune: these, to speak truth, are the origin and fountain from whence seditions arise. The alterations which men may propose to make in governments are two; for either they may change the state already established into some other, as when they propose to erect an oligarchy where there is a democracy; or a democracy, or free state, where there is an oligarchy, or an aristocracy from these, or those from that; or else, when they have no objection to the established government, which they like very well, but choose to have the sole management in it themselves; either in the hands of a few or one only. They will also raise commotions concerning the degree in which they would have the established power; as if, for instance, the government is an oligarchy, to have it more purely so, and in the same manner if it is a democracy, or else to have it less so; and, in like manner, whatever may be the nature of the government, either to extend or contract its powers; or else to make some alterations in some parts of it; as to establish or abolish a particular magistracy, as some persons say Lysander endeavoured to abolish the kingly power in Sparta; and Pausanias that of the ephori. Thus in Epidamnus there was an alteration in one part of the constitution, for instead of the philarchi they established a senate. It is also necessary for all the magistrates at Athens to attend in the court of the Heliæa when any new magistrate is created: the power of the archon also in that state partakes of the nature of an oligarchy: inequality is always the occasion of sedition, but not when those who are unequal are treated in a different manner correspondent to that inequality. Thus kingly power is unequal when exercised over equals. Upon the whole, those who aim after an equality are the cause of seditions. Equality is twofold, either in number or value. Equality in number is when two things contain the same parts or

the same quantity; equality in value is by proportion, as two exceeds one, and three two by the same number; thus by proportion four exceeds two, and two one in the same degree, for two is the same part of four that one is of two; that is to say, half. Now, all agree in what is absolutely and simply just; but, as we have already said, they dispute concerning proportionate value; for some persons, if they are equal in one respect, think themselves equal in all; others, if they are superior in one thing, think they may claim the superiority in all; from whence chiefly arise two sorts of governments, a democracy and an oligarchy; for nobility and virtue are to be found only
1302a amongst a few; the contrary amongst the many; there being in no place a hundred of the first to be met with, but enough of the last everywhere. But to establish a government entirely upon either of these equalities is wrong, and this the example of those so established makes evident, for none of them have been stable; and for this reason, that it is impossible that whatever is wrong at the first and in its principles should not at last meet with a bad end: for which reason in some things an equality of numbers ought to take place, in others an equality in value. However, a democracy is safer and less liable to sedition than an oligarchy; for in this latter it may arise from two causes, for either the few in power may conspire against each other or against the people; but in a democracy only one; namely, against the few who aim at exclusive power; but there is no instance worth speaking of, of a sedition of the people against themselves. Moreover, a government composed of men of moderate fortunes comes much nearer to a democracy than an oligarchy, and is the safest of all such states.

CHAPTER II

Since we are inquiring into the causes of seditions and revolutions in governments, we must begin entirely with the first principles from whence they arise. Now these, so to speak, are nearly three in number; which we must

first distinguish in general from each other, and endeavour
to show in what situation people are who begin a sedition;
and for what causes; and thirdly, what are the beginnings
of political troubles and mutual quarrels with each other.
Now that cause which of all others most universally
inclines men to desire to bring about a change in government is that which I have already mentioned; for those
who aim at equality will be ever ready for sedition, if they
see those whom they esteem their equals possess more
than they do, as well as those also who are not content
with equality but aim at superiority, if they think that
while they deserve more than, they have only equal with,
or less than, their inferiors.　Now, what they aim at may
be either just or unjust; just, when those who are inferior
are seditious, that they may be equal; unjust, when those
who are equal are so, that they may be superior.　These,
then, are the situations in which men will be seditious:
the causes for which they will be so are profit and honour;
and their contrary: for, to avoid dishonour or loss of
fortune by mulcts, either on their own account or their
friends, they will raise a commotion in the state.　The
original causes which dispose men to the things which I
have mentioned are, taken in one manner, seven in
number, in another they are more; two of which are the
same with those that have been already mentioned: but
influencing in a different manner; for profit and honour
sharpen men against each other; not to get the possession
of them for themselves (which was what I just now
supposed), but when they see others, some justly, others 1302*b*
unjustly, engrossing them.　The other causes are haughtiness, fear, eminence, contempt, disproportionate increase
in some part of the state.　There are also other things
which in a different manner will occasion revolutions in
governments;　as election intrigues, neglect, want of
numbers, a too great dissimilarity of circumstances.

CHAPTER III

WHAT influence ill-treatment and profit have for this purpose, and how they may be the causes of sedition, is almost self-evident; for when the magistrates are haughty and endeavour to make greater profits than their office gives them, they not only occasion seditions amongst each other, but against the state also who gave them their power; and this their avarice has two objects, either private property or the property of the state. What influence honours have, and how they may occasion sedition, is evident enough; for those who are themselves unhonoured while they see others honoured, will be ready for any disturbance: and these things are done unjustly when any one is either honoured or discarded contrary to their deserts, justly when they are according to them. Excessive honours are also a cause of sedition when one person or more are greater than the state and the power of the government can permit; for then a monarchy or a dynasty is usually established: on which account the ostracism was introduced in some places, as at Argos and Athens: though it is better to guard against such excesses in the founding of a state, than when they have been permitted to take place, to correct them afterward. Those who have been guilty of crimes will be the cause of sedition, through fear of punishment; as will those also who expect an injury, that they may prevent it; as was the case at Rhodes, when the nobles conspired against the people on account of the decrees they expected would pass against them. Contempt also is a cause of sedition and conspiracies; as in oligarchies, where there are many who have no share in the administration. The rich also even in democracies, despising the disorder and anarchy which will arise, hope to better themselves by the same means which happened at Thebes after the battle of Oenophyta, where, in consequence of bad administration, the democracy was destroyed; as it was at Megara, where the power of the people was lost

through anarchy and disorder; the same thing happened
at Syracuse before the tyranny of Gelon; and at Rhodes
there was the same sedition before the popular government was overthrown. Revolutions in state will also
arise from a disproportionate increase; for as the body
consists of many parts, it ought to increase proportion-
ably to preserve its symmetry, which would otherwise
be destroyed; as if the foot was to be four cubits long,
and the rest of the body but two palms; it might other- 1303a
wise be changed into an animal of a different form, if it
increase beyond proportion not only in quantity, but
also in disposition of parts; so also a city consists of parts,
some of which may often increase without notice, as the
number of poor in democracies and free states. They
will also sometimes happen by accident, as at Tarentum,
a little after the Median war, where so many of the
nobles were killed in a battle by the Iapygi, that from
a free state the government was turned into a democracy;
and at Argos, where so many of the citizens were killed
by Cleomenes the Spartan, that they were obliged to admit
several husbandmen to the freedom of the state: and
at Athens, through the unfortunate event of the infantry
battles, the number of the nobles was reduced by the soldiers
being chosen from the list of citizens in the Lacedæmonian
wars. Revolutions also sometimes take place in a democracy, though seldomer; for where the rich grow numerous
or properties increase, they become oligarchies or dynasties. Governments also sometimes alter without seditions
by a combination of the meaner people; as at Heræa:
for which purpose they changed the mode of election
from votes to lots, and thus got themselves chosen:
and by negligence, as when the citizens admit those who
are not friends to the constitution into the chief offices
of the state, which happened at Orus, when the oligarchy
of the archons was put an end to at the election of
Heracleodorus, who changed that form of government
into a democratic free state. By little and little, I mean
by this, that very often great alterations silently take
place in the form of government from people's overlooking
small matters; as at Ambracia, where the census was

originally small, but at last became nothing at all, as if a little and nothing at all were nearly or entirely alike. That state also is liable to seditions which is composed of different nations, till their differences are blended together and undistinguishable; for as a city cannot be composed of every multitude, so neither can it in every given time; for which reason all those republics which have hitherto been originally composed of different people, or afterwards admitted their neighbours to the freedom of their city, have been most liable to revolutions; as when the Achæans joined with the Træzenians in founding Sybaris; for soon after, growing more powerful than the Træzenians, they expelled them from the city; from whence came the proverb of Sybarite wickedness: and again, disputes from a like cause happened at Thurium between the Sybarites and those who had joined with them in building the city; for they assuming upon these, on account of the country being their own, were driven out. And at Byzantium the new citizens, being detected in plots against the state, were driven out of the city by force of arms. The Antisseans also, having taken in those who were banished from Chios, afterwards did the same thing; and also the Zancleans, after having taken in the people of Samos. The Appolloniats, in the Euxine Sea, having admitted their sojourners to the freedom of their city, were troubled with seditions: and the Syracusians, after the expulsion of their tyrants, having enrolled 1303b strangers and mercenaries amongst their citizens, quarrelled with each other and came to an open rupture: and the people of Amphipolis, having taken in a colony of Chalcidians, were the greater part of them driven out of the city by them. Many persons occasion seditions in oligarchies because they think themselves ill-used in not sharing the honours of the state with their equals, as I have already mentioned; but in democracies the principal people do the same because they have not more than an equal share with others who are not equal to them. The situation of the place will also sometimes occasion disturbances in the state when the ground is not well adapted for one city; as at Clazomene, where the people who lived in that part of the town called Chytrum quarrelled with them who lived in the island, and the Colophonians with the Notians. At Athens too the disposition of the citizens is not the same, for those who live in the Piræus are more attached to a popular government than those who live in the city properly so called; for as the interposition of a rivulet, however small, will occasion the line of the phalanx to fluctuate, so any trifling disagreement will be the cause of seditions; but they will not so soon flow from anything else as from the disagreement between virtue and vice, and next to that between poverty and riches, and so on in order, one cause having more influence than another; one of which that I last mentioned.

CHAPTER IV

But seditions in government do not arise for little things, but from them; for their immediate cause is something of moment. Now, trifling quarrels are attended with the greatest consequences when they arise between persons of the first distinction in the state, as was the case with the Syracusians in a remote period; for a revolution in the government was brought about by a quarrel between two young men who were in office, upon a love affair; for one of them being absent, the other seduced his mistress; he in his turn, offended with this, persuaded his friend's wife to come and live with him; and upon this the whole city took part either with the one or the other, and the government was overturned: therefore every one at the beginning of such disputes ought to take care to avoid the consequences; and to smother up all quarrels which may happen to arise amongst those in power, for the mischief lies in the beginning; for the beginning is said to be half of the business, so that what was then but a little fault will be found afterwards to bear its full proportion to what follows. Moreover, disputes between men of note involve the whole city in their consequences; as in Hestiæa, after the Median war: two brothers having a dispute about their paternal estate; he who was the poorer, from the other's having concealed part of the effects, and some money which his father had found, engaged the popular party on his side, while the other, who was rich, the men of fashion. And at Delphos, 1304a a quarrel about a wedding was the beginning of all the seditions that afterwards arose amongst them; for the bridegroom, being terrified by some unlucky omen upon waiting upon the bride, went away without marrying her; which her relations resenting, contrived secretly to convey some sacred money into his pocket while he was sacrificing, and then killed him as an impious person. At Mitylenè also, a dispute, which arose concerning a right of heritage, was the beginning of great evils, and a war with the Athenians, in which Paches took their city, for Timophanes, a man of fortune, leaving two daughters, Doxander, who was circumvented in procuring them in marriage for his two sons, began a sedition, and excited the Athenians to attack them, being the host of that state. There was also a dispute at Phocea, concerning a right of inheritance, between Mnasis, the father of Mnasis, and Euthucrates, the father of Onomarchus, which brought on the Phoceans the sacred war. The government too of Epidamnus was changed from a quarrel that arose from an intended marriage; for a certain man having contracted his daughter in marriage, the father of the young person to whom she was contracted, being archon, punishes him, upon which account he, resenting the affront, associated himself with those who were excluded from any share in the government, and brought about a revolution. A government may be changed either into an oligarchy, democracy, or a free state; when the magistrates, or any part of the city acquire great credit, or are increased in power, as the court of Areopagus at Athens, having procured great credit during the Median war, added firmness to their administration; and, on the other hand, the maritime force, composed of the commonalty, having gained the victory at Salamis, by their power at sea, got the lead in the state, and strengthened the popular party: and at Argos, the

nobles, having gained great credit by the battle of Man-
tinea against the Lacedæmonians, endeavoured to dissolve
the democracy.   And at Syracuse, the victory in their war
with the Athenians being owing to the common people,
they changed their free state into a democracy: and at
Chalcis, the people having taken off the tyrant Phocis,
together with the nobles, immediately seized the government: and at Ambracia also the people, having expelled
the tyrant Periander, with his party, placed the supreme
power in themselves.   And this in general ought to be
known, that whosoever has been the occasion of a state
being powerful, whether private persons, or magistrates,
a certain tribe, or any particular part of the citizens, or
the multitude, be they who they will, will be the cause
of disputes in the state.   For either some persons, who
envy them the honours they have acquired, will begin to
be seditious, or they, on account of the dignity they have
acquired, will not be content with their former equality.
A state is also liable to commotions when those parts of
it which seem to be opposite to each other approach to an 1304b
equality, as the rich and the common people; so that
the part which is between them both is either nothing
at all, or too little to be noticed; for if one party is so
much more powerful than the other, as to be evidently
stronger, that other will not be willing to hazard the
danger: for which reason those who are superior in
excellence and virtue will never be the cause of seditions;
for they will be too few for that purpose when compared
to the many.   In general, the beginning and the causes
of seditions in all states are such as I have now described,
and revolutions therein are brought about in two ways,
either by violence or fraud. if by violence, either at first
by compelling them to submit to the change when it is
made.   It may also be brought about by fraud in two
different ways, either when the people, being at first
deceived, willingly consent to an alteration in their
government, and are afterwards obliged by force to abide
by it: as, for instance, when the four hundred imposed
upon the people by telling them that the king of Persia
would supply them with money for the war against the

Lacedæmonians; and after they had been guilty of this falsity, they endeavoured to keep possession of the supreme power; or when they are at first persuaded, and afterwards consent to be governed: and by one of these methods which I have mentioned are all revolutions in governments brought about.

CHAPTER V

We ought now to inquire into those events which will arise from these causes in every species of government. Democracies will be most subject to revolutions from the dishonesty of their demagogues; for partly, by informing against men of property, they induce them to join together through self-defence, for a common fear will make the greatest enemies unite; and partly by setting the common people against them: and this is what any one may continually see practised in many states. In the island of Cos, for instance, the democracy was subverted by the wickedness of the demagogues, for the nobles entered into a combination with each other. And at Rhodes the demagogues, by distrib· ting of bribes, prevented the people from paying the trierarchs what was owing to them, who were obliged by the number of actions they were harassed with to conspire together and destroy the popular state. The same thing was brought about at Heraclea, soon after the settlement of the city, by the same persons; for the citizens of note, being ill treated by them, quitted the city, but afterwards joining together they returned and overthrew the popular state. Just in the same manner the democracy was destroyed in Megara; for there the demagogues, to procure money by confiscations, drove out the nobles, till the number of those who were banished was considerable, who, 1305a returning, got the better of the people in a battle, and established an oligarchy. The like happened at Cumè, during the time of the democracy, which Thrasymachus destroyed; and whoever considers what has happened in other states may perceive the same revolutions to have arisen from the same causes. The demagogues, to curry favour with the people, drive the nobles to conspire together, either by dividing their estates, or obliging them to spend them on public services, or by banishing them, that they may confiscate the fortunes of the wealthy. In former times, when the same person was both demagogue and general, the democracies were changed into tyrannies; and indeed most of the ancient tyrannies arose from those states: a reason for which then subsisted, but not now; for at that time the demagogues were of the soldiery; for they were not then powerful by their eloquence; but, now the art of oratory is cultivated, the able speakers are at present the demagogues; but, as they are unqualified to act in a military capacity, they cannot impose themselves on the people as tyrants, if we except in one or two trifling instances. Formerly, too, tyrannies were more common than now, on account of the very extensive powers with which some magistrates were entrusted: as the prytanes at Miletus; for they were supreme in many things of the last consequence; and also because at that time the cities were not of that very great extent, the people in general living in the country, and being employed in husbandry, which gave them, who took the lead in public affairs, an opportunity, if they had a turn for war, to make themselves tyrants; which they all did when they had gained the confidence of the people; and this confidence was their hatred to the rich. This was the case of Pisistratus at Athens, when he opposed the Pediaci: and of Theagenes in Megara, who slaughtered the cattle belonging to the rich, after he had seized those who kept them by the riverside. Dionysius also, for accusing Daphnæus and the rich, was thought worthy of being raised to a tyranny, from the confidence which the people had of his being a popular man in consequence of these enmities. A government shall also alter from its ancient and approved democratic form into one entirely new, if there is no census to regulate the election of magistrates; for, as the election is with the people, the demagogues who are desirous of being in office, to flatter them, will endeavour with all their power to make the people superior even to the laws. To prevent this entirely, or at least in a great measure, the magistrates should be elected by the tribes, and not by the people at large. These are nearly the revolutions to which democracies are liable, and also the causes from whence they arise.

CHAPTER VI

THERE are two things which of all others most evidently occasion a revolution in an oligarchy; one is, when the people are ill used, for then every individual is ripe for sedition; more particularly if one of the oligarchy should happen to be their leader; as Lygdamis, at Naxus, who was afterwards tyrant of that island. Seditions also which arise from different causes will differ from each other; for sometimes a revolution is brought about by the rich who have no share in the administration, which is in the hands of a very few indeed: and this happened at Massilia, Ister, Heraclea, and other cities; for those who had no share in the government ceased not to raise disputes till they were admitted to it: first the elder brothers, and then the younger also: for in some places the father and son are never in office at the same time; in others the elder and younger brother: and where this is observed the oligarchy partakes something of a free state. At Ister it was changed into a democracy; in Heraclea, instead of being in the hands of a few, it consisted of six hundred. At Cnidus the oligarchy was destroyed by the nobles quarrelling with each other, because the government was in the hands of so few: for there, as we have just mentioned, if the father was in office, the son could not; or, if there were many brothers, the eldest only; for the people, taking advantage of their disputes, elected one of the nobles for their general, and got the victory: for where there are seditions government is weak. And formerly at Erithria, during the oligarchy

1305b

of the Basilides, although the state flourished greatly
under their excellent management, yet because the people
were displeased that the power should be in the hands of
so few, they changed the government. Oligarchies also
are subject to revolutions, from those who are in office
therein, from the quarrels of the demagogues with each
other. The demagogues are of two sorts; one who flatter
the few when they are in power: for even these have their
demagogues; such was Charicles at Athens, who had
great influence over the thirty; and, in the same manner,
Phrynichus over the four hundred. The others are those
demagogues who have a share in the oligarchy, and flatter
the people: such were the state-guardians at Larissa,
who flattered the people because they were elected by
them. And this will always happen in every oligarchy
where the magistrates do not elect themselves, but are
chosen out of men either of great fortune or certain ranks,
by the soldiers or by the people; as was the custom at
Abydos. And when the judicial department is not in
the hands of the supreme power, the demagogues, favour-
ing the people in their causes, overturn the government;
which happened at Heraclea in Pontus: and also when
some desire to contract the power of the oligarchy into
fewer hands; for those who endeavour to support an
equality are obliged to apply to the people for assistance.
An oligarchy is also subject to revolutions when the
nobility spend their fortunes by luxury; for such persons
are desirous of innovations, and either endeavour to be
tyrants themselves or to support others in being so, as 1306a
Hypparinus supported Dionysius of Syracuse. And at
Amphipolis one Cleotimus collected a colony of Chalcidians, and when they came set them to quarrel with the
rich: and at Ægina a certain person who brought an
action against Chares attempted on that account to alter
the government. Sometimes they will try to raise commotions, sometimes they will rob the public, and then
quarrel with each other, or else fight with those who
endeavour to detect them; which was the case at
Apollonia in Pontus. But if the members of an oligarchy
agree among themselves the state is not very easily

destroyed without some external force. Pharsalus is a
proof of this, where, though the place is small, yet the
citizens have great power, from the prudent use they make
of it.   An oligarchy also will be destroyed when they
create another oligarchy under it; that is, when the
management of public affairs is in the hands of a few, and
not equally, but when all of them do not partake of the
supreme power, as happened once at Elis, where the
supreme power in general was in the hands of a very few,
out of whom a senate was chosen, consisting but of ninety,
who held their places for life; and their mode of election
was calculated to preserve the power amongst each other's
families, like the senators at Lacedæmon.   An oligarchy
is liable to a revolution both in time of war and peace; in
war, because through a distrust in the citizens the government is obliged to employ mercenary troops, and he to
whom they give the command of the army will very often
assume the tyranny, as Timophanes did at Corinth; and
if they appoint more than one general, they will very
probably establish a dynasty: and sometimes, through
fear of this, they are forced to let the people in general have
some share in the government, because they are obliged
to employ them.   In peace, from their want of confidence
in each other, they will entrust the guardianship of the
state to mercenaries and their general, who will be an
arbiter between them, and sometimes become master of
both, which happened at Larissa, when Simos and the
Aleuadæ had the chief power.   The same thing happened at
Abydos, during the time of the political clubs, of which
Iphiades' was one.   Commotions also will happen in an
oligarchy from one party's overbearing and insulting
another, or from their quarrelling about their law-suits or
marriages.   How their marriages, for instance, will have
that effect has been already shown: and in Eretria,
Diagoras destroyed the oligarchy of the knights upon the
same account.   A sedition also arose at Heraclea, from
a certain person being condemned by the court; and at
Thebes, in consequence of a man's being guilty of adultery;
1306b the punishment indeed which Eurytion suffered at
Heraclea was just, yet it was illegally executed: as was

that at Thebes upon Archias; for their enemies endeavoured to have them publicly bound in the pillory.
Many revolutions also have been brought about in
oligarchies by those who could not brook the despotism
which those persons assumed who were in power, as at
Cnidus and Chios.   Changes also may happen by accident
in what we call a free state and in an oligarchy; wheresoever the senators, judges, and magistrates are chosen
according to a certain census; for it often happens that
the highest census is fixed at first; so that a few only
could have a share in the government, in an oligarchy,
or in a free state those of moderate fortunes only;
when the city grows rich, through peace or some other
happy cause, it becomes so little that every one's fortune
is equal to the census, so that the whole community may
partake of all the honours of government; and this change
sometimes happens by little and little, and insensible
approaches, sometimes quicker.   These are the revolutions and seditions that arise in oligarchies, and the causes
to which they are owing: and indeed both democracies
and oligarchies sometimes alter, not into governments of
a contrary form, but into those of the same government;
as, for instance, from having the supreme power in the
law to vest it in the ruling party, or the contrariwise.

CHAPTER VII

Commotions also arise in aristocracies, from there being
so few persons in power (as we have already observed they
do in oligarchies, for in this particular an aristocracy is
most near an oligarchy, for in both these states the
administration of public affairs is in the hands of a few;
not that this arises from the same cause in both, though
herein they chiefly seem alike): and these will necessarily
be most likely to happen when the generality of the people
are high-spirited and think themselves equal to each other
in merit; such were those at Lacedæmon, called the
Partheniæ (for these were, as well as others, descendants

of citizens), who being detected in a conspiracy against
the state, were sent to found Tarentum. They will happen
also when some great men are disgraced by those who
have received higher honours than themselves, to whom
they are no ways inferior in abilities, as Lysander by the
kings: or when an ambitious man cannot get into power,
as Cinadon, who, in the reign of Agesilaus, was chief in a
conspiracy against the Spartans: and also when some are
too poor and others too rich, which will most frequently
happen in time of war; as at Lacedæmon during the
Messenian war, which is proved by a poem of Tyrtæus,
1307a called "Eunomia;" for some persons being reduced
thereby, desired that the lands might be divided: and also
when some person of very high rank might still be higher
if he could rule alone, which seemed to be Pausanias's intention at Lacedæmon, when he was their general in the
Median war, and Anno's at Carthage. But free states and
aristocracies are mostly destroyed from want of a fixed
administration of public affairs; the cause of which evil
arises at first from want of a due mixture of the democratic
and the oligarchic parts in a free state; and in an aristocracy from the same causes, and also from virtue not
being properly joined to power; but chiefly from the two
first, I mean the undue mixture of the democratic and
oligarchic parts; for these two are what all free states
endeavour to blend together, and many of those which
we call aristocracies, in this particular these states differ
from each other, and on this account the one of them is
less stable than the other, for that state which inclines
most to an oligarchy is called an aristocracy, and that
which inclines most to a democracy is called a free state;
on which account this latter is more secure than the
former, for the wider the foundation the securer the
building, and it is ever best to live where equality prevails.
But the rich, if the community gives them rank, very
often endeavour to insult and tyrannise over others. On
the whole, whichever way a government inclines, in that
it will settle, each party supporting their own. Thus a
free state will become a democracy; an aristocracy an
oligarchy; or the contrary, an aristocracy may change

into a democracy (for the poor, if they think themselves injured, directly take part with the contrary side) and a free state into an oligarchy. The only firm state is that where every one enjoys that equality he has a right to and fully possesses what is his own. And what I have been speaking of happened to the Thurians; for the magistrates being elected according to a very high census, it was altered to a lower, and they were subdivided into more courts, but in consequence of the nobles possessing all the land, contrary to law; the state was too much of an oligarchy, which gave them an opportunity of encroaching greatly on the rest of the people; but these, after they had been well inured to war, so far got the better of their guards as to expel every one out of the country who possessed more than he ought. Moreover, as all aristocracies are free oligarchies, the nobles therein endeavour to have rather too much power, as at Lacedæmon, where property is now in the hands of a few, and the nobles have too much liberty to do as they please and make such alliances as they please. Thus the city of the Locrians was ruined from an alliance with Dionysius; which state was neither a democracy nor well-tempered aristocracy. But an aristocracy chiefly approaches to a secret change by its being destroyed by degrees, as we **1307b** have already said of all governments in general; and this happens from the cause of the alteration being trifling; for whenever anything which in the least regards the state is treated with contempt, after that something else, and this of a little more consequence, will be more easily altered, until the whole fabric of government is entirely subverted, which happened in the government of Thurium; for the law being that they should continue soldiers for five years, some young men of a martial disposition, who were in great esteem amongst their officers, despising those who had the management of public affairs, and imagining they could easily accomplish their intention, first endeavoured to abolish this law, with a view of having it lawful to continue the same person perpetually in the military, perceiving that the people would readily appoint them. Upon this, the magistrates who are called coun-

sellors first joined together with an intention to oppose it,
but were afterwards induced to agree to it, from a belief,
that if that law was not repealed they would permit the
management of all other public affairs to remain in their
hands; but afterwards, when they endeavoured to restrain
some fresh alterations that were making, they found that
they could do nothing, for the whole form of government
was altered into a dynasty of those who first introduced
the innovations.   In short, all governments are liable to
be destroyed either from within or from without; from
without when they have for their neighbour a state whose
policy is contrary to theirs, and indeed if it has great
power the same thing will happen if it is not their neighbour; of which both the Athenians and the Lacedæmonians are a proof; for the one, when conquerors,
everywhere destroyed the oligarchies; the other the
democracies.   These are the chief causes of revolutions
and dissensions in governments.

CHAPTER VIII

WE are now to consider upon what the preservation of
governments in general and of each state in particular
depends; and, in the first place, it is evident that if we
are right in the causes we have assigned for their destruction, we know also the means of their preservation; for
things contrary produce contraries: but destruction and
preservation are contrary to each other.   In well-tempered governments it requires as much care as anything
whatsoever, that nothing be done contrary to law: and
this ought chiefly to be attended to in matters of small
consequence; for an illegality that approaches insensibly,
approaches secretly, as in a family small expenses continually repeated consume a man's income; for the
understanding is deceived thereby, as by this false
argument; if every part is little, then the whole is little:
now, this in one sense is true, in another is false, for the
whole and all the parts together are large, though made

up of small parts.   The first therefore of anything is what the state ought to guard against.   In the next place, no credit ought to be given to those who endeavour to deceive the people with false pretences; for they will be 1308a confuted by facts.   The different ways in which they will attempt to do this have been already mentioned. You may often perceive both aristocracies and oligarchies continuing firm, not from the stability of their forms of government, but from the wise conduct of the magistrates, both towards those who have a part in the management of public affairs, and those also who have not: towards those who have not, by never injuring them; and also introducing those who are of most consequence amongst them into office; nor disgracing those who are desirous of honour; or encroaching on the property of individuals; towards those who have, by behaving to each other upon an equality; for that equality which the favourers of a democracy desire to have established in the state is not only just, but convenient also, amongst those who are of the same rank: for which reason, if the administration is in the hands of many, those rules which are established in democracies will be very useful; as to let no one continue in office longer than six months: that all those who are of the same rank may have their turn; for between these there is a sort of democracy: for which reason demagogues are most likely to arise up amongst them, as we have already mentioned: besides, by this means both aristocracies and democracies will be the less liable to be corrupted into dynasties, because it will not be so easy for those who are magistrates for a little to do as much mischief as they could in a long time: for it is from hence that tyrannies arise in democracies and oligarchies; for either those who are most powerful in each state establish a tyranny, as the demagogues in the one, the dynastics in the other, or the chief magistrates who have been long in power.   Governments are sometimes preserved not only by having the means of their corruption at a great distance, but also by its being very near them; for those who are alarmed at some impending evil keep a stricter hand over the state; for which reason it is necessary for those who have the guardianship of the constitution to be able to awaken the fears of the people, that they may preserve it, and not like a night-guard to be remiss in protecting the state, but to make the distant danger appear at hand.   Great care ought also to be used to endeavour to restrain the quarrels and disputes of the nobles by laws, as well as to prevent those who are not already engaged in them from taking a part therein; for to perceive an evil at its very first approach is not the lot of every one, but of the politician.   To prevent any alteration taking place in an oligarchy or free state on account of the census, if that happens to continue the same while the quantity of money is increased, it will be useful to take a general account of the whole amount of it in former times, to compare it with the present, and to do this every year in those cities where the census is yearly, 1308b in larger communities once in three or five years; and if the whole should be found much larger or much less than it was at the time when the census was first established in the state, let there be a law either to extend or contract it, doing both these according to its increase or decrease; if it increases making the census larger, if it decreases smaller: and if this latter is not done in oligarchies and free states, you will have a dynasty arise in the one, an oligarchy in the other: if the former is not, free states will be changed into democracies, and oligarchies into free states or democracies.   It is a general maxim in democracies, oligarchies, monarchies, and indeed in all governments, not to let any one acquire a rank far superior to the rest of the community, but rather to endeavour to confer moderate honours for a continuance than great ones for a short time; for these latter spoil men, for it is not every one who can bear prosperity: but if this rule is not observed, let not those honours which were conferred all at once be all at once taken away, but rather by degrees.   But, above all things, let this regulation be made by the law, that no one shall have too much power, either by means of his fortune or friends; but if he has, for his excess therein, let it be contrived that he shall quit the country.   Now, as many persons promote innovations, that they may enjoy their own particular manner of living, there ought to be a particular officer to inspect the manners of every one, and see that these are not contrary to the genius of the state in which he lives, whether it may be an oligarchy, a democracy, or any other form of government; and, for the same reason, those should be guarded against who are most prosperous in the city: the means of doing which is by appointing those who are otherwise to the business and the offices of the state. I mean, to oppose men of account to the common people, the poor to the rich, and to blend both these into one body, and to increase the numbers of those who are in the middle rank; and this will prevent those seditions which arise from an inequality of condition. But above all, in every state it is necessary, both by the laws and every other method possible, to prevent those who are employed by the public from being venal, and this particularly in an oligarchy; for then the people will not be so much displeased from seeing themselves excluded from a share in the government (nay, they will rather be glad to have leisure to attend their private affairs) as at suspecting that the officers of the state steal the public money, then indeed they are afflicted with double concern, both because they are deprived of the honours of the state, and pillaged by those who enjoy them. There is one method of blending together a democracy and an aris- 1309a tocracy, if office brought no profit; by which means both the rich and the poor will enjoy what they desire; for to admit all to a share in the government is democratical; that the rich should be in office is aristocratical. This must be done by letting no public employment whatsoever be attended with any emolument; for the poor will not desire to be in office when they can get nothing by it, but had rather attend to their own affairs: but the rich will choose it, as they want nothing of the community. Thus the poor will increase their fortunes by being wholly employed in their own concerns; and the principal part of the people will not be governed by the lower sort. To prevent the exchequer from being defrauded, let all public money be delivered out openly in the face of the whole city, and let copies of the accounts be deposited in the different wards, tribes, and divisions. But, as the magistrates are to execute their offices without any advantages, the law ought to provide proper honours for those who execute them well. In democracies also it is necessary that the rich should be protected, by not permitting their lands to be divided, nor even the produce of them, which in some states is done unperceivably. It would be also better if the people would prevent them when they offer to exhibit a number of unnecessary and yet expensive public entertainments of plays, music, processions, and the like. In an oligarchy it is necessary to take great care of the poor, and allot them public employments which are gainful; and, if any of the rich insult them, to let their punishment be severer than if they insulted one of their own rank; and to let estates pass by affinity, and not gift: nor to permit any person to have more than one; for by this means property will be more equally divided, and the greater part of the poor get into better circumstances. It is also serviceable in a democracy and an oligarchy to allot those who take no part in public affairs an equality or a preference in other things; the rich in a democracy, to the poor in an oligarchy: but still all the principal offices in the state to be filled only by those who are best qualified to discharge them.

CHAPTER IX

THERE are three qualifications necessary for those who fill the first departments in government; first of all, an affection for the established constitution; second place, abilities every way completely equal to the business of their office; in the third, virtue and justice correspondent to the nature of that particular state they are placed in; for if justice is not the same in all states, it is evident that there must be different species thereof. There may be some doubt, when all these qualifications do not

meet in the same persons, in what manner the choice shall
be made; as for instance, suppose that one person is an
accomplished general, but a bad man and no friend to the 1309b
constitution; another is just and a friend to it, which
shall one prefer? we should then consider of two qualities,
which of them the generality possess in a greater degree,
which in a less; for which reason in the choice of a general
we should regard his courage more than his virtue as the
more uncommon quality; as there are fewer capable of
conducting an army than there are good men: but, to
protect the state or manage the finances, the contrary
rule should be followed; for these require greater virtue
than the generality are possessed of, but only that knowledge which is common to all.　It may be asked, if a man
has abilities equal to his appointment in the state, and is
affectionate to the constitution, what occasion is there
for being virtuous, since these two things alone are
sufficient to enable him to be useful to the public? it is,
because those who possess those qualities are often
deficient in prudence; for, as they often neglect their
own affairs, though they know them and love themselves,
so nothing will prevent their serving the public in the
same manner.　In short, whatsoever the laws contain
which we allow to be useful to the state contributes to
its preservation: but its first and principal support is
(as has been often insisted upon) to have the number of
those who desire to preserve it greater than those who
wish to destroy it.　Above all things that ought not to
be forgotten which many governments now corrupted
neglect; namely, to preserve a mean.　For many
things seemingly favourable to a democracy destroy a
democracy, and many things seemingly favourable to
an oligarchy destroy an oligarchy.　Those who think
this the only virtue extend it to excess, not considering
that as a nose which varies a little from perfect straight-
ness, either towards a hook nose or a flat one, may yet
be beautiful and agreeable to look at; but if this par-
ticularity is extended beyond measure, first of all the
properties of the part is lost, but at last it can hardly
be admitted to be a nose at all, on account of the excess

of the rise or sinking: thus it is with other parts of the human body; so also the same thing is true with respect to states; for both an oligarchy and a democracy may something vary from their most perfect form and yet be well constituted; but if any one endeavours to extend either of them too far, at first he will make the government the worse for it, but at last there will be no government at all remaining. The lawgiver and the politician therefore should know well what preserves and what destroys a democracy or an oligarchy, for neither the one nor the other can possibly continue without rich and poor: but that whenever an entire equality of circum-

1310a stances prevails, the state must necessarily become of another form; so that those who destroy these laws, which authorise an inequality in property, destroy the government. It is also an error in democracies for the demagogues to endeavour to make the common people superior to the laws; and thus by setting them at variance with the rich, dividing one city into two; whereas they ought rather to speak in favour of the rich. In oligarchies, on the contrary, it is wrong to support those who are in administration against the people. The oaths also which they take in an oligarchy ought to be contrary to what they now are; for, at present, in some places they swear, " I will be adverse to the common people, and contrive all I can against them; " whereas they ought rather to suppose and pretend the contrary; expressing in their oaths, that they will not injure the people. But of all things which I have mentioned, that which contributes most to preserve the state is, what is now most despised, to educate your children for the state; for the most useful laws, and most approved by every statesman, will be of no service if the citizens are not accustomed to and brought up in the principles of the constitution; of a democracy, if that is by law established; of an oligarchy, if that is; for if there are bad morals in one man, there are in the city. But to educate a child fit for the state, it must not be done in the manner which would please either those who have the power in an oligarchy or those who desire a democracy, but so as they may be able to conduct either of these forms of governments.   But now the children of the magistrates in an oligarchy are brought up too delicately, and the children of the poor hardy with exercise and labour; so that they are both desirous of and able to promote innovations.   In democracies of the purest form they pursue a method which is contrary to their welfare; the reason of which is, that they define liberty wrong: now, there are two things which seem to be the objects of a democracy, that the people in general should possess the supreme power, and all enjoy freedom; for that which is just seems to be equal, and what the people think equal, that is a law: now, their freedom and equality consists in every one's doing what they please: that is in such a democracy every one may live as he likes; " as his inclination guides," in the words of Euripides: but this is wrong, for no one ought to think it slavery to live in subjection to government, but protection.   Thus I have mentioned the causes of corruption in different states, and the means of their preservation.

CHAPTER X

It now remains that we speak of monarchies, their causes of corruption, and means of preservation; and indeed almost the same things which have been said of other governments happen to kingdoms and tyrannies; for 1310b a kingdom partakes of an aristocracy, a tyranny of the worst species of an oligarchy and democracy; for which reason it is the worst that man can submit to, as being composed of two, both of which are bad, and collectively retains all the corruptions and all the defects of both these states.   These two species of monarchies arise from principles contrary to each other: a kingdom is formed to protect the better sort of people against the multitude, and kings are appointed out of those, who are chosen either for their superior virtue and actions flowing from virtuous principles, or else from their noble descent; but a tyrant is chosen out of the meanest populace; an

enemy to the better sort, that the common people may
not be oppressed by them. That this is true experience
convinces us; for the generality of tyrants were indeed
mere demagogues, who gained credit with the people by
oppressing the nobles. Some tyrannies were established
in this manner after the cities were considerably enlarged;
others before that time, by kings who exceeded the power
which their country allowed them, from a desire of
governing despotically: others were founded by those
who were elected to the superior offices in the state; for
formerly the people appointed officers for life, who came
to be at the head of civil and religious affairs, and these
chose one out of their body in whom the supreme power
over all the magistrates was placed. By all these means
it was easy to establish a tyranny, if they chose it; for
their power was ready at hand, either by their being
kings, or else by enjoying the honours of the state; thus
Phidon at Argos and other tyrants enjoyed originally the
kingly power; Phalaris and others in Ionia, the honours
of the state. Panætius at Leontium, Cypselus at Corinth,
Pisistratus at Athens, Dionysius at Syracuse, and others,
acquired theirs by having been demagogues. A kingdom,
as we have said, partakes much of the nature of an
aristocracy, and is bestowed according to worth, as either
virtue, family, beneficent actions, or these joined with
power; for those who have been benefactors to cities
and states, or have it in their powers to be so, have
acquired this honour, and those who have prevented
a people from falling into slavery by war, as Codrus, or
those who have freed them from it, as Cyrus, or the
founders of cities, or settlers of colonies, as the kings of
Sparta, Macedon, and Molossus. A king desires to be the
1311a guardian of his people, that those who have property
may be secure in the possession of it, and that the people
in general meet with no injury; but a tyrant, as has been
often said, has no regard to the common good, except
for his own advantage; his only object is pleasure, but
a king's is virtue: what a tyrant therefore is ambitious
of engrossing is wealth, but a king rather honour. The
guards too of a king are citizens, a tyrant's foreigners.

That a tyranny contains all that is bad both in a democracy and an oligarchy is evident; with an oligarchy it has for its end gain, as the only means of providing the tyrant with guards and the luxuries of life; like that it places no confidence in the people; and therefore deprives them of the use of arms: it is also common to them both to persecute the populace, to drive them out of the city and their own habitations.   With a democracy it quarrels with the nobles, and destroys them both publicly and privately, or drives them into banishment, as rivals and an impediment to the government; hence naturally arise conspiracies both amongst those who desire to govern and those who desire not to be slaves; hence arose Periander's advice to Thrasybulus to take off the tallest stalks, hinting thereby, that it was necessary to make away with the eminent citizens.   We ought then in reason, as has been already said, to account for the changes which arise in a monarchy from the same causes which produce them in other states: for, through injustice received, fear, and contempt, many of those who are under a monarchical government conspire against it; but of all species of injustice, injurious contempt has most influence on them for that purpose: sometimes it is owing to their being deprived of their private fortunes.   The dissolution too of a kingdom and a tyranny are generally the same; for monarchs abound in wealth and honour, which all are desirous to obtain.   Of plots: some aim at the life of those who govern, others at their government; the first arises from hatred to their persons; which hatred may be owing to many causes, either of which will be sufficient to excite their anger, and the generality of those who are under the influence of that passion will join in a conspiracy, not for the sake of their own advancement, but for revenge.   Thus the plot against the children of Pisistratus arose from their injurious treatment of Harmodius's sister, and insulting him also; for Harmodius resenting the injury done to his sister, and Aristogiton the injury done to Harmodius.   Periander the tyrant of Ambracia also lost his life by a conspiracy, for some improper liberties he took with a boy in his cups: and 1311b

Philip was slain by Pausanias for neglecting to revenge
him of the affront he had received from Attalus; as was
Amintas the Little by Darda, for insulting him on account
of his age; and the eunuch by Evagoras the Cyprian,
in revenge for having taken his son's wife away from
him. . . .

Many also who have had their bodies scourged with
stripes have, through resentment, either killed those who
caused them to be inflicted or conspired against them,
even when they had kingly power, as at Mitylene,
Megacles, joining with his friends, killed the Penthelidæ,
who used to go about striking those they met with
clubs. Thus, in later times, Smendes killed Penthilus for
whipping him and dragging him away from his wife.
Decamnichus also was the chief cause of the conspiracy
against Archelaus, for he urged others on: the occasion of his resentment was his having delivered him to
Euripides the poet to be scourged; for Euripides was
greatly offended with him for having said something of
the foulness of his breath. And many others have been
killed or conspired against on the same account. Fear
too is a cause which produces the same effects, as well
in monarchies as in other states: thus Artabanes conspired against Xerxes through fear of punishment for
having hanged Darius according to his orders, whom
he supposed he intended to pardon, as the order was
given at supper-time. Some kings also have been
1312a dethroned and killed in consequence of the contempt
they were held in by the people; as some one conspired
against Sardanapalus, having seen him spinning with
his wife, if what is related of him is true, or if not of
him, it may very probably be true of some one else.
Dion also conspired against Dionysius the Younger,
seeing his subjects desirous of a conspiracy, and that
he himself was always drunk: and even a man's friends
will do this if they despise him; for from the confidence
he places in them, they think that they shall not be found
out. Those also who think they shall gain his throne
will conspire against a king through contempt; for as
they are powerful themselves, and despise the danger,

on account of their own strength, they will readily attempt it.   Thus a general at the head of his army will endeavour to dethrone the monarch, as Cyrus did Astyages, despising both his manner of life and his forces; his forces for want of action, his life for its effeminacy: thus Suthes, the Thracian, who was general to Amadocus, conspired against him.   Sometimes more than one of these causes will excite men to enter into conspiracies, as contempt and desire of gain; as in the instance of Mithridates against Ariobarzanes.   Those also who are of a bold disposition, and have gained military honours amongst kings, will of all others be most like to engage in sedition; for strength and courage united inspire great bravery: whenever, therefore, these join in one person, he will be very ready for conspiracies, as he will easily conquer. Those who conspire against a tyrant through love of glory and honour have a different motive in view from what I have already mentioned; for, like all others who embrace danger, they have only glory and honour in view, and think, not as some do, of the wealth and pomp they may acquire, but engage in this as they would in any other noble action, that they may be illustrious and distinguished, and destroy a tyrant, not to succeed in his tyranny, but to acquire renown.   No doubt but the number of those who act upon this principle is small, for we must suppose they regard their own safety as nothing in case they should not succeed, and must embrace the opinion of Dion (which few can do) when he made war upon Dionysius with a very few troops; for he said, that let the advantage he made be ever so little it would satisfy him to have gained it; and that, should it be his lot to die the moment he had gained footing in his country, he should think his death sufficiently glorious.   A tyranny also is exposed to the same destruction as all other states 1312b are, from too powerful neighbours: for it is evident, that an opposition of principles will make them desirous of subverting it; and what they desire, all who can, do: and there is a principle of opposition in one state to another, as a democracy against a tyranny, as says Hesiod, "a potter against a potter;" for the extreme of a democracy is a tyranny; a kingly power against an aristocracy, from their different forms of government: for which reason the Lacedæmonians destroyed many tyrannies; as did the Syracusians during the prosperity of their state. Nor are they only destroyed from without, but also from within, when those who have no share in the power bring about a revolution, as happened to Gelon, and lately to Dionysius; to the first, by means of Thrasybulus, the brother of Hiero, who flattered Gelon's son, and induced him to lead a life of pleasure, that he himself might govern; but the family joined together and endeavoured to support the tyranny and expel Thrasybulus; but those whom they made of their party seized the opportunity and expelled the whole family. Dion made war against his relation Dionysius, and being assisted by the people, first expelled and then killed him. As there are two causes which chiefly induce men to conspire against tyrants, hatred and contempt, one of these, namely hatred, seems inseparable from them. Contempt also is often the cause of their destruction: for though, for instance, those who raised themselves to the supreme power generally preserved it; but those who received it from them have, to speak truth, almost immediately all of them lost it; for, falling into an effeminate way of life, they soon grew despicable, and generally fell victims to conspiracies. Part of their hatred may be very fitly ascribed to anger; for in some cases this is their motive to action: for it is often a cause which impels them to act more powerfully than hatred, and they proceed with greater obstinacy against those whom they attack, as this passion is not under the direction of reason. Many persons also indulge this passion through contempt; which occasioned the fall of the Pisistratidæ and many others. But hatred is more powerful than anger; for anger is accompanied with grief, which prevents the entrance of reason; but hatred is free from it. In short, whatever causes may be assigned as the destruction of a pure oligarchy unmixed with any other government and an extreme democracy, the same may be applied to a tyranny; for these are divided tyrannies.

Kingdoms are seldom destroyed by any outward attack; for which reason they are generally very stable; but they have many causes of subversion within; of which two are the principal; one is when those who are in power 1313*a* excite a sedition, the other when they endeavour to establish a tyranny by assuming greater power than the law gives them. A kingdom, indeed, is not what we ever see erected in our times, but rather monarchies and tyrannies; for a kingly government is one that is voluntarily submitted to, and its supreme power admitted upon great occasions: but where many are equal, and there are none in any respect so much better than another as to be qualified for the greatness and dignity of government over them, then these equals will not willingly submit to be commanded; but if any one assumes the government, either by force or fraud, this is a tyranny. To what we have already said we shall add, the causes of revolutions in an hereditary kingdom. One of these is, that many of those who enjoy it are naturally proper objects of contempt only: another is, that they are insolent while their power is not despotic; but they possess kingly honours only. Such a state is soon destroyed; for a king exists but while the people are willing to obey, as their submission to him is voluntary, but to a tyrant involuntary. These and such-like are the causes of the destruction of monarchies.

CHAPTER XI

Monarchies, in a word, are preserved by means contrary to what I have already mentioned as the cause of their destruction; but to speak to each separately: the stability of a kingdom will depend upon the power of the king's being kept within moderate bounds; for by how much the less extensive his power is, by so much the longer will his government continue; for he will be less despotic and more upon an equality of condition with those he governs; who, on that account, will envy him the less.

It was on this account that the kingdom of the Molossi continued so long; and the Lacedæmonians from their government's being from the beginning divided into two parts, and also by the moderation introduced into the other parts of it by Theopompus, and his establishment of the ephori; for by taking something from the power he increased the duration of the kingdom, so that in some measure he made it not less, but bigger; as they say he replied to his wife, who asked him if he was not ashamed to deliver down his kingdom to his children reduced from what he received it from his ancestors? No, says he, I give it him more lasting. Tyrannies are preserved two ways most opposite to each other, one of which is when the power is delegated from one to the other, and in this manner many tyrants govern in their states. Report says that Periander founded many of these. There are also many of them to be met with amongst the Persians. What has been already mentioned is as conducive as anything can be to preserve a tyranny; namely, to keep down those who are of an aspiring disposition, to take off those who will not submit, to allow no public meals, no clubs, no education, nothing at all, but to guard against everything that gives rise to high spirits or mutual confidence; nor to suffer the learned meetings of those who are at leisure to hold conversation with each other; and to endeavour by every means possible to keep all the people strangers to each other; for knowledge increases mutual confidence; and to oblige all strangers to appear in public, and to live near the city-gate, that all their actions may be sufficiently seen; for those who are kept like slaves seldom entertain any noble thoughts: in short, to imitate everything which the Persians and barbarians do, for they all contribute to support slavery; and to endeavour to know what every one who is under their power does and says; and for this purpose to employ spies: such were those women whom the Syracusians called ποταγωγίδες. Hiero also used to send out listeners wherever there was any meeting or conversation; for the people dare not speak with freedom for fear of such persons; and if any

1313ᵇ

one does, there is the less chance of its being concealed; and to endeavour that the whole community should mutually accuse and come to blows with each other, friend with friend, the commons with the nobles, and the rich with each other. It is also advantageous for a tyranny that all those who are under it should be oppressed with poverty, that they may not be able to compose a guard; and that, being employed in procuring their daily bread, they may have no leisure to conspire against their tyrants. The Pyramids of Egypt are a proof of this, and the votive edifices of the Cyposelidæ, and the temple of Jupiter Olympus, built by the Pisistratidæ, and the works of Polycrates at Samos; for all these produced one end, the keeping the people poor. It is necessary also to multiply taxes, as at Syracuse; where Dionysius in the space of five years collected all the private property of his subjects into his own coffers. A tyrant also should endeavour to engage his subjects in a war, that they may have employment and continually depend upon their general. A king is preserved by his friends, but a tyrant is of all persons the man who can place no confidence in friends, as every one has it in his desire and these chiefly in their power to destroy him. All these things also which are done in an extreme democracy should be done in a tyranny, as permitting great licentiousness to the women in the house, that they may reveal their husbands' secrets; and showing great indulgence to slaves also for the same reason; for slaves and women conspire not against tyrants: but when they are treated with kindness, both of them are abettors of tyrants, and extreme democracies also; and the people too in such a state desire to be despotic. For which reason flatterers are in repute in both these: the demagogue in the democracy, for he is the proper flatterer of the people; among tyrants, he who will servilely adapt himself to their humours; for this is the business of 1314a flatterers. And for this reason tyrants always love the worst of wretches, for they rejoice in being flattered, which no man of a liberal spirit will submit to; for they love the virtuous, but flatter none. Bad men too are fit

for bad purposes; "like to like," as the proverb says.
A tyrant also should show no favour to a man of worth
or a freeman; for he should think, that no one deserved
to be thought these but himself; for he who supports his
dignity, and is a friend to freedom, encroaches upon the
superiority and the despotism of the tyrant: such men,
therefore, they naturally hate, as destructive to their
government. A tyrant also should rather admit strangers
to his table and familiarity than citizens, as these are his
enemies, but the others have no design against him.
These and such-like are the supports of a tyranny, for
it comprehends whatsoever is wicked. But all these
things may be comprehended in three divisions, for there
are three objects which a tyranny has in view; one of
which is, that the citizens should be of poor abject dispositions; for such men never propose to conspire against
any one. The second is, that they should have no confidence in each other; for while they have not this, the
tyrant is safe enough from destruction. For which
reason they are always at enmity with those of merit, as
hurtful to their government; not only as they scorn to be
governed despotically, but also because they can rely
upon each other's fidelity, and others can rely upon theirs,
and because they will not inform against their associates,
nor any one else. The third is, that they shall be totally
without the means of doing anything; for no one under-
takes what is impossible for him to perform: so that
without power a tyranny can never be destroyed. These,
then, are the three objects which the inclinations of
tyrants desire to see accomplished; for all their tyrannical
plans tend to promote one of these three ends, that their
people may neither have mutual confidence, power, nor
spirit. This, then, is one of the two methods of preserving
tyrannies: the other proceeds in a way quite contrary
to what has been already described, and which may be
discerned from considering to what the destruction of
a kingdom is owing; for as one cause of that is, making
the government approach near to a tyranny, so the safety
of a tyranny consists in making the government nearly
kingly; preserving only one thing, namely power, that

not only the willing, but the unwilling also, must be obliged to submit; for if this is once lost, the tyranny is at an end. This, then, as the foundation, must be preserved: in other particulars carefully do and affect to seem like a king; first, appear to pay a great attention 1314b to what belongs to the public; nor make such profuse presents as will offend the people; while they are to supply the money out of the hard labour of their own hands, and see it given in profusion to mistresses, foreigners, and fiddlers; keeping an exact account both of what you receive and pay; which is a practice some tyrants do actually follow, by which means they seem rather fathers of families than tyrants: nor need you ever fear the want of money while you have the supreme power of the state in your own hands. It is also much better for those tyrants who quit their kingdom to do this than to leave behind them money they have hoarded up; for their regents will be much less desirous of making innovations, and they are more to be dreaded by absent tyrants than the citizens; for such of them as he suspects he takes with him, but these regents must be left behind. He should also endeavour to appear to collect such taxes and require such services as the exigencies of the state demand, that whenever they are wanted they may be ready in time of war; and particularly to take care that he appear to collect and keep them not as his own property, but the public's. His appearance also should not be severe, but respectable, so that he should inspire those who approach him with veneration and not fear; but this will not be easily accomplished if he is despised. If, therefore, he will not take the pains to acquire any other, he ought to endeavour to be a man of political abilities, and to fix that opinion of himself in the judgment of his subjects. He should also take care not to appear to be guilty of the least offence against modesty, nor to suffer it in those under him: nor to permit the women of his family to treat others haughtily; for the haughtiness of women has been the ruin of many tyrants. With respect to the pleasures of sense, he ought to do directly contrary to the practice of some tyrants at present; for they

do not only continually indulge themselves in them for
many days together, but they seem also to desire to have
other witnesses of it, that they may wonder at their
happiness; whereas he ought really to be moderate in
these, and, if not, to appear to others to avoid them;
for it is not the sober man who is exposed either to plots
or contempt, but the drunkard; not the early riser, but
the sluggard. His conduct in general should also be
contrary to what is reported of former tyrants; for he
ought to improve and adorn his city, so as to seem a
guardian and not a tyrant; and, moreover, always to
1315a seem particularly attentive to the worship of the gods;
for from persons of such a character men entertain less
fears of suffering anything illegal while they suppose
that he who governs them is religious and reverences the
gods; and they will be less inclined to raise insinuations
against such a one, as being peculiarly under their protection: but this must be so done as to give no occasion
for any suspicion of hypocrisy. He should also take
care to show such respect to men of merit in every particular, that they should not think they could be treated
with greater distinction by their fellow-citizens in a free
state. He should also let all honours flow immediately
from himself, but every censure from his subordinate
officers and judges. It is also a common protection of
all monarchies not to make one person too great, or,
certainly, not many; for they will support each other:
but, if it is necessary to entrust any large powers to one
person, to take care that it is not one of an ardent spirit;
for this disposition is upon every opportunity most ready
for a revolution: and, if it should seem necessary to deprive any one of his power, to do it by degrees, and not
reduce him all at once. It is also necessary to abstain
from all kinds of insolence; more particularly from
corporal punishment; which you must be most cautious
never to exercise over those who have a delicate sense
of honour; for, as those who love money are touched to
the quick when anything affects their property, so are
men of honour and principle when they receive any
disgrace: therefore, either never employ personal punish-

ment, or, if you do, let it be only in the manner in which
a father would correct his son, and not with contempt;
and, upon the whole, make amends for any seeming
disgrace by bestowing greater honours. But of all
persons who are most likely to entertain designs against
the person of a tyrant, those are chiefly to be feared and
guarded against who regard as nothing the loss of their
own lives, so that they can but accomplish their purpose:
be very careful therefore of those who either think themselves affronted, or those who are dear to them; for
those who are excited by anger to revenge regard as
nothing their own persons: for, as Heraclitus says, it is
dangerous to fight with an angry man who will purchase
with his life the thing he aims at. As all cities are composed of two sorts of persons, the rich and the poor, it is
necessary that both these should find equal protection
from him who governs them, and that the one party
should not have it in their power to injure the other;
but that the tyrant should attach to himself that party
which is the most powerful; which, if he does, he will
have no occasion either to make his slaves free, or to
deprive citizens of their arms; for the strength of either
of the parties added to his own forces will render him
superior to any conspiracy.—It would be superfluous
to go through all particulars; for the rule of conduct
which the tyrant ought to pursue is evident enough, and
that is, to affect to appear not the tyrant, but the king;
the guardian of those he governs, not their plunderer, 1315*b*
but their protector, and to affect the middle rank in life,
not one superior to all others: he should, therefore,
associate his nobles with him and soothe his people; for
his government will not only be necessarily more honourable and worthy of imitation, as it will be over men of
worth, and not abject wretches who perpetually both
hate and fear him; but it will be also more durable.
Let him also frame his life so that his manners may be
consentaneous to virtue, or at least let half of them be
so, that he may not be altogether wicked, but only so
in part.

CHAPTER XII

INDEED an oligarchy and a tyranny are of all governments of the shortest duration. The tyranny of Orthagoras and his family at Sicyon, it is true, continued longer than any other: the reason for which was, that they used their power with moderation, and were in many particulars obedient to the laws; and, as Clisthenes was an able general, he never fell into contempt, and by the care he took that in many particulars his government should be popular. He is reported also to have presented a person with a crown who adjudged the victory to another; and some say that it is the statue of that judge which is placed in the forum.

They say also, that Pisistratus submitted to be summoned into the court of the Areopagites. The second that we shall mention is the tyranny of the Cypselidæ, at Corinth, which continued seventy-seven years and six months; for Cypselus was tyrant there thirty years, Periander forty-four, and Psammetichus, the son of Georgias, three years; the reason for which was, that Cypselus was a popular man, and governed without guards. Periander indeed ruled like a tyrant, but then he was an able general. The third was that of the Pisistradidæ at Athens; but it was not continual: for Pisistratus himself was twice expelled; so that out of thirty-three years he was only fifteen in power, and his son eighteen; so that the whole time was thirty-three years. Of the rest we shall mention that of Hiero, and Gelo at Syracuse; and this did not continue long, for both their reigns were only eighteen years; for Gelo died in the eighth year of his tyranny, and Hiero in his tenth. Thrasybulus fell in his eleventh month, and many other tyrannies have continued a very short time. We have now gone through the general cases of corruption and 1316a means of preservation both in free states and monarchies. In Plato's *Republic*, Socrates is introduced treating upon the changes which different governments are liable to: but his discourse is faulty; for he does not particularly

mention what changes the best and first governments are
liable to; for he only assigns the general cause, of nothing
being immutable, but that in time everything will alter

.   .   .   .
.   .   .   .   .¹   he conceives that
nature will then produce bad men, who will not submit to
education, and in this, probably, he is not wrong; for
it is certain that there are some persons whom it is
impossible by any education to make good men; but why
should this change be more peculiar to what he calls the
best-formed government, than to all other forms, and
indeed to all other things that exist? and in respect to
his assigned time, as the cause of the alteration of all
things, we find that those which did not begin to exist
at the same time cease to be at the same time; so that,
if anything came into beginning the day before the
solstice, it must alter at the same time. Besides, why
should such a form of government be changed into the
Lacedæmonian? for, in general, when governments alter,
they alter into the contrary species to what they before
were, and not into one like their former. And this
reasoning holds true of other changes; for he says, that
from the Lacedæmonian form it changes into an oligarchy,
and from thence into a democracy, and from a democracy
into a tyranny: and sometimes a contrary change takes
place, as from a democracy into an oligarchy, rather than
into a monarchy. With respect to a tyranny he neither
says whether there will be any change in it; or if not, to
what cause it will be owing; or if there is, into what other
state it will alter: but the reason of this is, that a tyranny
is an indeterminate government; and, according to him,
every state ought to alter into the first, and most perfect,
thus the continuity and circle would be preserved. But
one tyranny often changed into another; as at Syria,
from Myron's to Clisthenes'; or into an oligarchy, as was
Antileo's at Chalcas; or into a democracy, as was Gelo's
at Syracuse; or into an aristocracy, as was Charilaus's at
Lacedæmon, and at Carthage. An oligarchy is also
changed into a tyranny; such was the rise of most of the
ancient tyrannies in Sicily; at Leontini, into the tyranny

¹ A few lines are omitted, as the text is unintelligible.

of Panætius; at Gela, into that of Cleander; at Rhegium,
into that of Anaxilaus; and the like in many other cities.
It is absurd also to suppose, that a state is changed into
an oligarchy because those who are in power are avaricious
and greedy of money, and not because those who are by
1316b far richer than their fellow citizens think it unfair that
those who have nothing should have an equal share in the
rule of the state with themselves, who possess so much;
for in many oligarchies it is not allowable to be employed
in money-getting, and there are many laws to prevent it.
But in Carthage, which is a democracy, money-getting is
creditable, and yet their form of government remains
unaltered. It is also absurd to say, that in an oligarchy
there are two cities, one of the poor and another of the
rich; for why should this happen to them more than to
the Lacedæmonians, or any other state where all possess
not equal property, or where all are not equally good?
for though no one member of the community should be
poorer than he was before, yet a democracy might nevertheless change into an oligarchy; if the rich should be more
powerful than the poor, and the one too negligent, and
the other attentive: and though these changes are owing
to many causes, yet he mentions but one only, that the
citizens become poor by luxury, and paying interest-
money; as if at first they were all rich, or the greater part
of them: but this is not so, but when some of those who
have the principal management of public affairs lose their
fortunes, they will endeavour to bring about a revolution;
but when others do, nothing of consequence will follow,
nor when such states do alter is there any more reason
for their altering into a democracy than any other.
Besides, though some of the members of the community
may not have spent their fortunes, yet if they share not
in the honours of the state, or if they are ill-used and
insulted, they will endeavour to raise seditions, and bring
about a revolution, that they may be allowed to do as
they like; which, Plato says, arises from too much
liberty. Although there are many oligarchies and democracies, yet Socrates, when he is treating of the changes
they may undergo, speaks of them as if there was but
one of each sort.

BOOK VI

CHAPTER I

We have already shown what is the nature of the supreme
council in the state, and wherein one may differ from
another, and how the different magistrates should be
regulated; and also the judicial department, and what is
best suited to what state; and also to what causes both
the destruction and preservation of governments are
owing.

As there are very many species of democracies, as well
as of other states, it will not be amiss to consider at the
same time anything which we may have omitted to
mention concerning either of them, and to allot to each
that mode of conduct which is peculiar to and advantageous for them; and also to inquire into the combinations of all these different modes of government which we 1317a
have mentioned; for as these are blended together the
government is altered, as from an aristocracy to be an
oligarchy, and from a free state to be a democracy.   Now,
I mean by those combinations of government (which I
ought to examine into, but have not yet done), namely,
whether the deliberative department and the election of
magistrates is regulated in a manner correspondent to an
oligarchy, or the judicial to an aristocracy, or the deliberative part only to an oligarchy, and the election of magistrates to an aristocracy, or whether, in any other manner,
everything is not regulated according to the nature of the
government.   But we will first consider what particular
sort of democracy is fitted to a particular city, and also
what particular oligarchy to a particular people; and of
other states, what is advantageous to what.   It is also
necessary to show clearly, not only which of these governments is best for a state, but also how it ought to be
established there, and other things we will treat of briefly.

And first, we will speak of a democracy; and this will at the same time show clearly the nature of its opposite, which some persons call an oligarchy; and in doing this we must examine into all the parts of a democracy, and everything that is connected therewith; for from the manner in which these are compounded together different species of democracies arise: and hence it is that they are more than one, and of various natures. Now, there are two causes which occasion there being so many democracies; one of which is that which we have already mentioned; namely, there being different sorts of people; for in one country the majority are husbandmen, in another mechanics, and hired servants; if the first of these is added to the second, and the third to both of them, the democracy will not only differ in the particular of better or worse, but in this, that it will be no longer the same government; the other is that which we will now speak of. The different things which are connected with democracies and seem to make part of these states, do, from their being joined to them, render them different from others: this attending a few, that more, and another all. It is necessary that he who would found any state which he may happen to approve of, or correct one, should be acquainted with all these particulars. All founders of states endeavour to comprehend within their own plan everything of nearly the same kind with it; but in doing this they err, in the manner I have already described in treating of the preservation and destruction of governments. I will now speak of these first principles and manners, and whatever else a democratical state requires.

CHAPTER II

Now the foundation of a democratical state is liberty, and 1317b people have been accustomed to say this as if here only liberty was to be found; for they affirm that this is the end proposed by every democracy. But one part of liberty is to govern and be governed alternately; for, according to democratical justice, equality is measured by numbers, and not by worth: and this being just, it is necessary that the supreme power should be vested in the people at large; and that what the majority determine should be final: so that in a democracy the poor ought to have more power than the rich, as being the greater number; for this is one mark of liberty which all framers of a democracy lay down as a criterion of that state; another is, to live as every one likes; for this, they say, is a right which liberty gives, since he is a slave who must live as he likes not. This, then, is another criterion of a democracy. Hence arises the claim to be under no command whatsoever to any one, upon any account, any otherwise than by rotation, and that just as far only as that person is, in his turn, under his also. This also is conducive to that equality which liberty demands. These things being premised, and such being the government, it follows that such rules as the following should be observed in it, that all the magistrates should be chosen out of all the people, and all to command each, and each in his turn all: that all the magistrates should be chosen by lot, except to those offices only which required some particular knowledge and skill: that no census, or a very small one, should be required to qualify a man for any office: that none should be in the same employment twice, or very few, and very seldom, except in the army: that all their appointments should be limited to a very short time, or at least as many as possible: that the whole community should be qualified to judge in all causes whatsoever, let the object be ever so extensive, ever so interesting, or of ever so high a nature; as at Athens, where the people at large judge the magistrates when they come out of office, and decide concerning public affairs as well as private contracts: that the supreme power should be in the public assembly; and that no magistrate should be allowed any discretionary power but in a few instances, and of no consequence to public business. Of all magistrates a senate is best suited to a democracy, where the whole community is not paid for giving their attendance; for in that case it loses its power; for then the people will

bring all causes before them, by appeal, as we have already
mentioned in a former book. In the next place, there
should, if possible, be a fund to pay all the citizens who
have any share in the management of public affairs, either
as members of the assembly, judges, and magistrates; but
if this cannot be done, at least the magistrates, the judges,
the senators, and members of the supreme assembly, and
also those officers who are obliged to eat at a common
table ought to be paid. Moreover, as an oligarchy is said
to be a government of men of family, fortune, and education; so, on the contrary, a democracy is a government
in the hands of men of no birth, indigent circumstances,
and mechanical employments. In this state also no office
1318a should be for life; and, if any such should remain after
the government has been long changed into a democracy,
they should endeavour by degrees to diminish the power;
and also elect by lot instead of vote. These things, then,
appertain to all democracies; namely, to be established
on that principle of justice which is homogeneous to those
governments; that is, that all the members of the state,
by number, should enjoy an equality, which seems chiefly
to constitute a democracy, or government of the people:
for it seems perfectly equal that the rich should have no
more share in the government than the poor, nor be alone
in power; but that all should be equal, according to
number; for thus, they think, the equality and liberty
of the state best preserved.

CHAPTER III

In the next place we must inquire how this equality
is to be procured. Shall the qualifications be divided
so that five hundred rich should be equal to a thousand
poor, or shall the thousand have equal power with
the five hundred? or shall we not establish our equality
in this manner? but divide indeed thus, and afterwards taking an equal number both out of the five
hundred and the thousand, invest them with the power of
creating the magistrates and judges. Is this state then

established according to perfect democratical justice, or rather that which is guided by numbers only? For the defenders of a democracy say, that that is just which the majority approve of: but the favourers of an oligarchy say, that that is just which those who have most approve of; and that we ought to be directed by the value of property. Both the propositions are unjust; for if we agree with what the few propose we erect a tyranny: for if it should happen that an individual should have more than the rest who are rich, according to oligarchical justice, this man alone has a right to the supreme power; but if superiority of numbers is to prevail, injustice will then be done by confiscating the property of the rich, who are few, as we have already said. What then that equality is, which both parties will admit, must be collected from the definition of right which is common to them both; for they both say that what the majority of the state approves of ought to be established. Be it so; but not entirely: but since a city happens to be made up of two different ranks of people, the rich and the poor, let that be established which is approved of by both these, or the greater part: but should there be opposite sentiments, let that be established which shall be approved of by the greater part: but let this be according to the census; for instance, if there should be ten of the rich and twenty of the poor, and six of the first and fifteen of the last should agree upon any measure, and the remaining four of the rich should join with the remaining five of the poor in opposing it, that party whose census when added together should determine which opinion should be law, and should these happen to be equal, it should be regarded as a case similar to an assembly or court of justice dividing equally upon any question that comes before them, who either determine it by lot or some such method. But although, with 1318*b* respect to what is equal and just, it may be very difficult to establish the truth, yet it is much easier to do than to persuade those who have it in their power to encroach upon others to be guided thereby; for the weak always desire what is equal and just, but the powerful pay no regard thereunto.

CHAPTER IV

THERE are four kinds of democracies. The best is that
which is composed of those first in order, as we have
already said, and this also is the most ancient of any.   I
call that the first which every one would place so, was he
to divide the people; for the best part of these are the
husbandmen.   We see, then, that a democracy may be
framed where the majority live by tillage or pasturage:
for, as their property is but small, they will not be at
leisure perpetually to hold public assemblies, but will be
continually employed in following their own business, not
having otherwise the means of living; nor will they be
desirous of what another enjoys, but will rather like to
follow their own business than meddle with state affairs
and accept the offices of government, which will be
attended with no great profit; for the major part of mankind are rather desirous of riches than honour (a proof of
this is, that they submitted to the tyrannies in ancient
times, and do now submit to the oligarchies, if no one
hinders them in their usual occupations, or deprives them
of their property; for some of them soon get rich, others
are removed from poverty); besides, their having the
right of election and calling their magistrates to account
for their conduct when they come out of office, will satisfy
their desire of honours, if any of them entertain that
passion: for in some states, though the commonalty have
not the right of electing the magistrates, yet it is vested
in part of that body chosen to represent them: and it is
sufficient for the people at large to possess the deliberative
power: and this ought to be considered as a species of
democracy; such was that formerly at Mantinæa: for
which reason it is proper for the democracy we have been
now treating of to have a power (and it has been usual for
them to have it) of censuring their magistrates when out
of office, and sitting in judgment upon all causes: but
that the chief magistrates should be elected, and according
to a certain census, which should vary with the rank of

their office, or else not by a census, but according to their abilities for their respective appointments. A state thus constituted must be well constituted; for the magistracies will be always filled with the best men with the approbation of the people; who will not envy their superiors: and these and the nobles should be content with this part in the administration; for they will not be governed by their inferiors. They will be also careful to use their power with moderation, as there are others to whom full power is delegated to censure their conduct; for it is very serviceable to the state to have them dependent upon others, and not to be permitted to do whatsoever they choose; for with such a liberty there would be no check to that evil particle there is in every one: therefore it is 1319a necessary and most for the benefit of the state that the offices thereof should be filled by the principal persons in it, whose characters are unblemished, and that the people are not oppressed. It is now evident that this is the best species of democracy, and on what account; because the people are such and have such powers as they ought to have. To establish a democracy of husbandmen some of those laws which were observed in many ancient states are universally useful; as, for instance, on no account to permit any one to possess more than a certain quantity of land, or within a certain distance from the city. Formerly also, in some states, no one was allowed to sell their original lot of land. They also mention a law of one Oxylus, which forbade any one to add to their patrimony by usury. We ought also to follow the law of the Aphutæans, as useful to direct us in this particular we are now speaking of; for they having but very little ground, while they were a numerous people, and at the same time were all husbandmen, did not include all their lands within the census, but divided them in such a manner that, according to the census, the poor had more power than the rich. Next to the commonalty of husbandmen is one of shepherds and herdsmen; for they have many things in common with them, and, by their way of life, are excellently qualified to make good soldiers, stout in body, and able to continue in the open air all night. The generality

of the people of whom other democracies are composed
are much worse than these; for their lives are wretched,
nor have they any business with virtue in anything they
do; these are your mechanics, your exchange-men, and
hired servants; as all these sorts of men frequent the
exchange and the citadel, they can readily attend the
public assembly; whereas the husbandmen, being more
dispersed in the country, cannot so easily meet together;
nor are they equally desirous of doing it with these others.
When a country happens to be so situated that a great
part of the land lies at a distance from the city, there
it is easy to establish a good democracy or a free state,
for the people in general will be obliged to live in the
country; so that it will be necessary in such a democracy,
though there may be an exchange-mob at hand, never to
allow a legal assembly without the inhabitants of the
country attend.   We have shown in what manner the
first and best democracy ought to be established, and it
will be equally evident as to the rest, for from these we
1319*b* should proceed as a guide, and always separate the
meanest of the people from the rest.   But the last and
worst, which gives to every citizen without distinction a
share in every part of the administration, is what few
citizens can bear, nor is it easy to preserve for any long
time, unless well supported by laws and manners.   We
have already noticed almost every cause that can destroy
either this or any other state.   Those who have taken the
lead in such a democracy have endeavoured to support
it, and make the people powerful by collecting together
as many persons as they could and giving them their
freedom, not only legitimately but naturally born, and also
if either of their parents were citizens, that is to say, if
either their father or mother; and this method is better
suited to this state than any other: and thus the demagogues have usually managed.   They ought, however, to
take care, and do this no longer than the common people
are superior to the nobles and those of the middle rank,
and then stop; for, if they proceed still further, they will
make the state disorderly, and the nobles will ill brook
the power of the common people, and be full of resentment

against it; which was the cause of an insurrection at Cyrene: for a little evil is overlooked, but when it becomes a great one it strikes the eye. It is, moreover, very useful in such a state to do as Clisthenes did at Athens, when he was desirous of increasing the power of the people, and as those did who established the democracy in Cyrene; that is, to institute many tribes and fraternities, and to make the religious rites of private persons few, and those common; and every means is to be contrived to associate and blend the people together as much as possible; and that all former customs be broken through. Moreover, whatsoever is practised in a tyranny seems adapted to a democracy of this species; as, for instance, the licentiousness of the slaves, the women, and the children; for this to a certain degree is useful in such a state; and also to overlook every one's living as they choose; for many will support such a government: for it is more agreeable to many to live without any control than as prudence would direct.

CHAPTER V

It is also the business of the legislator and all those who would support a government of this sort not to make it too great a work, or too perfect; but to aim only to render it stable: for, let a state be constituted ever so badly, there is no difficulty in its continuing a few days: they should therefore endeavour to procure its safety by all those ways which we have described in assigning the causes of the preservation and destruction of governments; avoiding what is hurtful, and by framing such laws, written and unwritten, as contain those things which chiefly tend to the preservation of the state; nor to suppose that that is useful either for a democratic or 1320a an oligarchic form of government which contributes to make them more purely so, but what will contribute to their duration: but our demagogues at present, to flatter the people, occasion frequent confiscations in the courts;

for which reason those who have the welfare of the state
really at heart should act directly opposite to what they
do, and enact a law to prevent forfeitures from being
divided amongst the people or paid into the treasury,
but to have them set apart for sacred uses: for those
who are of a bad disposition would not then be the less
cautious, as their punishment would be the same; and
the community would not be so ready to condemn those
whom they sat in judgment on when they were to get
nothing by it: they should also take care that the causes
which are brought before the public should be as few as
possible, and punish with the utmost severity those who
rashly brought an action against any one; for it is not
the commons but the nobles who are generally prosecuted:
for in all things the citizens of the same state ought to be
affectionate to each other, at least not to treat those
who have the chief power in it as their enemies. Now,
as the democracies which have been lately established
are very numerous, and it is difficult to get the common
people to attend the public assemblies without they are
paid for it, this, when there is not a sufficient public
revenue, is fatal to the nobles; for the deficiencies therein
must be necessarily made up by taxes, confiscations,
and fines imposed by corrupt courts of justice: which
things have already destroyed many democracies. Whenever, then, the revenues of the state are small, there
should be but few public assemblies and but few courts
of justice: these, however, should have very extensive
jurisdictions, but should continue sitting a few days only,
for by this means the rich would not fear the expense,
although they should receive nothing for their attendance,
though the poor did; and judgment also would be given
much better; for the rich will not choose to be long
absent from their own affairs, but will willingly be so
for a short time: and, when there are sufficient revenues,
a different conduct ought to be pursued from what the
demagogues at present follow; for now they divide the
surplus of the public money amongst the poor; these
receive it and again want the same supply, while the
giving it is like pouring water into a sieve: but the true

patriot in a democracy ought to take care that the majority of the community are not too poor, for this is the cause of rapacity in that government; he therefore should endeavour that they may enjoy perpetual plenty; and as this also is advantageous to the rich, what can be saved out of the public money should be put by, and then divided at once amongst the poor, if possible, in such a quantity as may enable every one of them to purchase a little field, and, if that cannot be done, at least to give each of them enough to procure the imple- 1320*b* ments of trade and husbandry; and if there is not enough for all to receive so much at once, then to divide it according to tribes or any other allotment. In the meantime let the rich pay them for necessary services, but not be obliged to find them in useless amusements. And something like this was the manner in which they managed at Carthage, and preserved the affections of the people; for by continually sending some of their community into colonies they procured plenty. It is also worthy of a sensible and generous nobility to divide the poor amongst them, and supplying them with what is necessary, induce them to work; or to imitate the conduct of the people at Tarentum: for they, permitting the poor to partake in common of everything which is needful for them, gain the affections of the commonalty. They have also two different ways of electing their magistrates; for some are chosen by vote, others by lot; by the last, that the people at large may have some share in the administration; by the former, that the state may be well governed: the same may be accomplished if of the same magistrates you choose some by vote, others by lot. And thus much for the manner in which democracies ought to be established.

CHAPTER VI

WHAT has been already said will almost of itself sufficiently show how an oligarchy ought to be founded; for he who would frame such a state should have in his view a democracy to oppose it; for every species of oligarchy should be founded on principles diametrically opposite to some species of democracy.

The first and best-framed oligarchy is that which approaches near to what we call a free state; in which there ought to be two different census, the one high, the other low: from those who are within the latter the ordinary officers of the state ought to be chosen; from the former the supreme magistrates: nor should any one be excluded from a part of the administration who was within the census; which should be so regulated that the commonalty who are included in it should by means thereof be superior to those who have no share in the government; for those who are to have the management of public affairs ought always to be chosen out of the better sort of the people. Much in the same manner ought that oligarchy to be established which is next in order: but as to that which is most opposite to a pure democracy, and approaches nearest to a dynasty and a tyranny, as it is of all others the worst, so it requires the greatest care and caution to preserve it: for as bodies of sound and healthy constitutions and ships which are well manned and well found for sailing can bear many injuries without perishing, while a diseased body or a leaky ship with an indifferent crew cannot support the 1321a least shock; so the worst-established governments want most looking after. A number of citizens is the preservation of a democracy; for these are opposed to those rights which are founded in rank: on the contrary, the preservation of an oligarchy depends upon the due regulation of the different orders in the society.

CHAPTER VII

As the greater part of the community are divided into four sorts of people; husbandmen, mechanics, traders, and hired servants; and as those who are employed in war may likewise be divided into four; the horsemen, the heavy-armed soldier, the light-armed, and the sailor,

where the nature of the country can admit a great number
of horse; there a powerful oligarchy may be easily established: for the safety of the inhabitants depends upon
a force of that sort; but those who can support the
expense of horsemen must be persons of some considerable
fortune. Where the troops are chiefly heavy-armed,
there an oligarchy, inferior in power to the other, may
be established; for the heavy-armed are rather made up
of men of substance than the poor: but the light-armed
and the sailors always contribute to support a democracy:
but where the number of these is very great and a sedition
arises, the other parts of the community fight at a dis-
advantage; but a remedy for this evil is to be learned
from skilful generals, who always mix a proper number
of light-armed soldiers with their horse and heavy-armed:
for it is with those that the populace get the better of the
men of fortune in an insurrection; for these being lighter
are easily a match for the horse and the heavy-armed:
so that for an oligarchy to form a body of troops from
these is to form it against itself: but as a city is composed
of persons of different ages, some young and some old,
the fathers should teach their sons, while they were very
young, a light and easy exercise; but, when they are
grown up, they should be perfect in every warlike exercise.
Now, the admission of the people to any share in the
government should either be (as I said before) regulated
by a census, or else, as at Thebes, allowed to those who
for a certain time have ceased from any mechanic employment, or as at Massalia, where they are chosen according
to their worth, whether citizens or foreigners. With
respect to the magistrates of the highest rank which it
may be necessary to have in a state, the services they
are bound to do the public should be expressly laid down,
to prevent the common people from being desirous of
accepting their employments, and also to induce them to
regard their magistrates with favour when they know
what a price they pay for their honours. It is also
necessary that the magistrates, upon entering into their
offices, should make magnificent sacrifices and erect
some public structure, that the people partaking of the

entertainment, and seeing the city ornamented with votive gifts in their temples and public structures, may see with pleasure the stability of the government: add to this also, that the nobles will have their generosity recorded: but now this is not the conduct which those who are at present at the head of an oligarchy pursue, but the contrary; for they are not more desirous of honour than of gain; for which reason such oligarchies may more properly be called little democracies. Thus 1321b we have explained on what principles a democracy and an oligarchy ought to be established.

CHAPTER VIII

AFTER what has been said I proceed next to treat particularly of the magistrates; of what nature they should be, how many, and for what purpose, as I have already mentioned: for without necessary magistrates no state can exist, nor without those which contribute to its dignity and good order can exist happily: now it is necessary that in small states the magistrates should be few; in a large one, many: also to know well what offices may be joined together, and what ought to be separated.

The first thing necessary is to establish proper regulators in the markets; for which purpose a certain magistrate should be appointed to inspect their contracts and preserve good order; for of necessity, in almost every city there must be both buyers and sellers to supply each other's mutual wants: and this is what is most productive of the comforts of life; for the sake of which men seem to have joined together in one community. A second care, and nearly related to the first, is to have an eye both to the public and private edifices in the city, that they may be an ornament; and also to take care of all buildings which are likely to fall: and to see that the highways are kept in proper repair; and also that the landmarks between different estates are preserved, that there may be no disputes on that account; and all other business of the same nature. Now, this business may be divided into several branches, over each of which in populous cities they appoint a separate person; one to inspect the buildings, another the fountains, another the harbours; and they are called the inspectors of the city. A third, which is very like the last, and conversant nearly about the same objects, only in the country, is to take care of what is done out of the city. The officers who have this employment we call inspectors of the lands, or inspectors of the woods; but the business of all three of them is the same. There must also be other officers appointed to receive the public revenue and to deliver it out to those who are in the different departments of the state: these are called receivers or quæstors. There must also be another, before whom all private contracts and sentences of courts should be enrolled, as well as proceedings and declarations. Sometimes this employment is divided amongst many, but there is one supreme over the rest; these are called proctors, notaries, and the like. Next to these is an officer whose business is of all others the most necessary, and yet most difficult; namely, to take care that sentence is executed upon those who are condemned; and that every one pays the fines laid on him; and also to have the charge of those who are in prison. 1322a This office is very disagreeable on account of the odium attending it, so that no one will engage therein without it is made very profitable, or, if they do, will they be willing to execute it according to law; but it is most necessary, as it is of no service to pass judgment in any cause without that judgment is carried into execution: for without this human society could not subsist: for which reason it is best that this office should not be executed by one person, but by some of the magistrates of the other courts. In like manner, the taking care that those fines which are ordered by the judges are levied should be divided amongst different persons. And as different magistrates judge different causes, let the causes of the young be heard by the young: and as to those which are already brought to a hearing, let one person pass sentence, and another see it executed:

as, for instance, let the magistrates who have the care of the public buildings execute the sentence which the inspectors of the markets have passed, and the like in other cases: for by so much the less odium attends those who carry the laws into execution, by so much the easier will they be properly put in force: therefore for the same persons to pass the sentence and to execute it will subject them to general hatred; and if they pass it upon all, they will be considered as the enemies of all. Thus one person has often the custody of the prisoner's body, while another sees the sentence against him executed, as the eleven did at Athens: for which reason it is prudent to separate these offices, and to give great attention thereunto as equally necessary with anything we have already mentioned; for it will certainly happen that men of character will decline accepting this office, and worthless persons cannot properly be entrusted with it, as having themselves rather an occasion for a guard than being qualified to guard others. This, therefore, ought by no means to be a separate office from others; nor should it be continually allotted to any individuals, but the young men; where there is a city-guard, the youths ought in turns to take these offices upon them. These, then, as the most necessary magistrates, ought to be first mentioned: next to these are others no less necessary, but of much higher rank, for they ought to be men of great skill and fidelity. These are they who have the guard of the city, and provide everything that is necessary for war; whose business it is, both in war and peace, to defend the walls and the gates, and to take care to muster and marshal the citizens. Over all these there are sometimes more officers, sometimes fewer: thus in little cities there is only one whom they call either general or 1322b polemarch; but where there are horse and light-armed troops, and bowmen, and sailors, they sometimes put distinct commanders over each of these; who again have others under them, according to their different divisions; all of which join together to make one military body: and thus much for this department. Since some of the magistrates, if not all, have business with the public money, it is necessary that there should be other officers, whose employment should be nothing else than to take an account of what they have, and correct any mismanagement therein. But besides all these magistrates there is one who is supreme over them all, who very often has in his own power the disposal of the public revenue and taxes; who presides over the people when the supreme power is in them; for there must be some magistrate who has a power to summon them together, and to preside as head of the state. These are sometimes called preadvisers; but where there are many, more properly a council. These are nearly the civil magistrates which are requisite to a government: but there are other persons whose business is confined to religion; as the priests, and those who are to take care of the temples, that they are kept in proper repair, or, if they fall down, that they may be rebuilt; and whatever else belongs to public worship. This charge is sometimes entrusted to one person, as in very small cities: in others it is delegated to many, and these distinct from the priesthood, as the builders or keepers of holy places, and officers of the sacred revenue. Next to these are those who are appointed to have the general care of all those public sacrifices to the tutelar god of the state, which the laws do not entrust to the priests: and these in different states have different appellations. To enumerate in few words the different departments of all those magistrates who are necessary: these are either religion, war, taxes, expenditures, markets, public buildings, harbours, highways. Belonging to the courts of justice there are scribes to enroll private contracts; and there must also be guards set over the prisoners, others to see the law is executed, council on either side, and also others to watch over the conduct of those who are to decide the causes. Amongst the magistrates also may finally be reckoned those who are to give their advice in public affairs. But separate states, who are peculiarly happy and have leisure to attend to more minute particulars, and are very attentive to good order, require particular magistrates for themselves; such as those who have the government of the women; who are to see the laws are executed; who take care of the boys and preside over their education. To these may be added those who have the care of their gymnastic exercises, their theatres, and every other public spectacle which there may happen to be. Some of these, however, are not of general use; as the governors of the women: for the poor are obliged to employ their wives and children in servile offices for want of slaves. As there are three magistrates to whom some states entrust the supreme power; namely, guardians of the laws, preadvisers, and senators; guardians of the laws suit best to an aristocracy, preadvisers to an oligarchy, and a senate to a democracy. And thus much briefly concerning all magistrates.

BOOK VII

CHAPTER I

HE who proposes to make that inquiry which is necessary concerning what government is best, ought first to determine what manner of living is most eligible; for while this remains uncertain it will also be equally uncertain what government is best: for, provided no unexpected accidents interfere, it is highly probable, that those who enjoy the best government will live the most happily according to their circumstances; he ought, therefore, first to know what manner of life is most desirable for all; and afterwards whether this life is the same to the man and the citizen, or different. As I imagine that I have already sufficiently shown what sort of life is best in my popular discourses on that subject, I think I may very properly repeat the same here; as most certainly no one ever called in question the propriety of one of the divisions; namely, that as what is good, relative to man, may be divided into three sorts, what is external, what appertains to the body, and what to the soul, it is evident that all these must conspire to make a man happy: for no one would say that a man was happy who had no fortitude, no temperance, no justice, no prudence; but was afraid of the flies that flew round him: nor would abstain from the meanest theft if he was either hungry or dry, or would murder his dearest friend for a farthing; and also was in every particular as wanting in his understanding as an infant or an idiot. These truths are so evident that all must agree to them; though some may dispute about the quantity and the degree: for they may think, that a very little virtue is sufficient for happiness; but for riches, property, power, honour, and all such things, they endeavour to increase them without bounds: but to such we reply, that it is easy to prove from what experience teaches us in these cases, that these external goods produce not virtue, but virtue them. As to a happy life, whether it is to be found in pleasure or virtue, or both, certain it is, that those whose morals are most pure, and whose understandings are best cultivated, will enjoy more of it, although their fortune is but moderate, than those do who own an exuberance of wealth, are deficient in those; and this utility any one who reflects may easily convince himself of; for whatsoever is external has its boundary, as a machine, and whatsoever is useful, in its excess is either necessarily hurtful, or at best useless to the possessor; but every good quality of the soul, the higher it is in degree, so much the more useful it is, if it is permitted on this subject to use the word useful, as well as noble. It is also very evident, that the accidents of each subject take place of each other, as the subjects themselves, of which we allow they are accidents, differ from each other in value; so that if the soul is more noble than any outward possession, as the body, both in itself and with respect to us, it must be admitted of course that the best accidents of each must follow the same analogy. Besides, it is for the sake of the soul that these things are desirable; and it is on this account that wise men should desire them, not the soul for them. Let us therefore be well assured, that every one enjoys as much happiness as he possesses virtue and wisdom, and acts according to their dictates; since for this we have the example of GOD Himself, WHO IS COMPLETELY HAPPY, NOT FROM ANY EXTERNAL GOOD; BUT IN HIMSELF, AND BECAUSE SUCH IS HIS NATURE. For good fortune is something different from happiness, as every good which depends not on the mind is owing to chance or fortune; but it is not from fortune that any one is wise and just: hence it follows, that that city is happiest which is the best and acts best: for no one can do well who acts not well; nor can the deeds either of man or city be praiseworthy without virtue and wisdom; for whatsoever is just, or wise, or prudent in a man, the same things are just, wise, and prudent in a city.

1323*b*

Thus much by way of introduction; for I could not but just touch upon this subject, though I could not go through a complete investigation of it, as it properly belongs to another question: let us at present suppose so much, that a man's happiest life, both as an individual and as a citizen, is a life of virtue, accompanied with those enjoyments which virtue usually procures. If 1324*a* there are any who are not convinced by what I have said, their doubts shall be answered hereafter, at present we shall proceed according to our intended method.

CHAPTER II

It now remains for us to say whether the happiness of any individual man and the city is the same or different: but this also is evident; for whosoever supposes that riches will make a person happy, must place the happiness of the city in riches if it possesses them; those who prefer a life which enjoys a tyrannic power over others will also think, that the city which has many others under its command is most happy: thus also if any one approves a man for his virtue, he will think the most worthy city the happiest: but here there are two particulars which require consideration, one of which is, whether it is the most eligible life to be a member of the community and enjoy the rights of a citizen, or whether to live as a stranger, without interfering in public affairs; and also what form of government is to be preferred, and what disposition of the state is best; whether the whole community should be eligible to a share in the administration, or only the greater part, and some only: as this, therefore, is a subject of political examination and speculation, and not what concerns the individual, and the first of these is what we are at present engaged in, the one of these I am not obliged to speak to, the other is the proper business of my present design. It is evident that government must be the best which is so established, that every one therein may have it in his power to act virtuously and live happily: but some, who admit that a life of virtue is most eligible, still doubt which is preferable, a public life of active virtue, or one entirely disengaged from what is without and spent in contemplation; which some say is the only one worthy of a philosopher; and one of these two different modes of life both now and formerly seem to have been chosen by all those who were the most virtuous men; I mean the public or philosophic. And yet it is of no little consequence on which side the truth lies; for a man of sense must naturally incline to the better choice; both as an individual and a citizen. Some think that a tyrannic government over those near us is the greatest injustice; but that a political one is not unjust: but that still is a restraint on the pleasures and tranquillity of life. Others hold the quite contrary opinion, and think that a public and active life is the only life for man: for that private persons have no opportunity of practising any one virtue, more than they have who are engaged in public life the management of the state. These are their sentiments; others say, that a tyrannical and despotical mode of government is the only happy one; for even amongst some free states the object of their laws seems to be to tyrannise over their neighbours: so that the generality of political institutions, wheresoever dispersed, if they have any one common object in view, have all of them this, to conquer and govern. It is evident, both from the laws of the Lacedæmonians and Cretans, as well as by the manner in which they educated their children, that all which they had in view was to make them soldiers: besides, among all nations, those who have power enough and reduce others to servitude are honoured on that account; as were the Scythians, Persians, Thracians, and Gauls: with some there are laws to heighten the virtue of courage; thus they tell us that at Carthage they allowed every person to wear as many rings for distinction as he had served campaigns. There was also a law in Macedonia, that a man who had not himself killed an enemy should be obliged to wear a halter; among the Scythians, at a festival, none were permitted to drink out of the cup which was carried about who had not done the same thing. Among the Iberians, a warlike nation, they fixed as many columns upon a man's tomb as he had slain enemies: and among different nations different things of this sort prevail, some of them established by law, others by custom. Probably it may seem too absurd to those who are willing to take this subject into their consideration to inquire whether it is the business of a legislator to be able to point out by what means a state may govern and tyrannise over its neighbours, whether they will, or will not: for how can that belong either to the politician or legislator which is unlawful? for that cannot be lawful which is done not only justly, but unjustly also: for a conquest may be unjustly made. But we see nothing of this in the arts: for it is the business neither of the physician nor the pilot to use either persuasion or force, the one to his patients, the other to his passengers: and yet many seem to think a despotic government is a political one, and what they would not allow to be just or proper, if exercised over themselves, they will not blush to exercise over others; for they endeavour to be wisely governed themselves, but think it of no consequence whether others are so or not: but a despotic power is absurd, except only where nature has framed the one party for dominion, the other for subordination; and therefore no one ought to assume it over all in general, but those only which are the proper objects thereof: thus no one should hunt men either for food or sacrifice, but what is fit for those purposes, and these are wild animals which are eatable.

Now a city which is well governed might be very 1325a happy in itself while it enjoyed a good system of laws, although it should happen to be so situated as to have no connection with any other state, though its constitution should not be framed for war or conquest; for it would then have no occasion for these. It is evident therefore that the business of war is to be considered as commendable, not as a final end, but as the means of procuring it. It is the duty of a good legislator to examine carefully into his state; and the nature of the people, and how they may partake of every intercourse, of a good life, and of the happiness which results from it: and in this respect some laws and customs differ from others. It is also the duty of a legislator, if he has any neighbouring states, to consider in what manner he shall oppose each of them, or what good offices he shall show them. But what should be the final end of the best governments will be considered hereafter.

CHAPTER III

WE will now speak to those who, while they agree that a life of virtue is most eligible, yet differ in the use of it, addressing ourselves to both these parties; for there are some who disapprove of all political governments, and think that the life of one who is really free is different from the life of a citizen, and of all others most eligible: others again think that the citizen is the best; and that it is impossible for him who does nothing to be well employed; but that virtuous activity and happiness are the same thing. Now both parties in some particulars say what is right, in others what is wrong, thus, that the life of a freeman is better than the life of a slave is true, for a slave, as a slave, is employed in nothing honourable; for the common servile employments which he is commanded to perform have nothing virtuous in them; but, on the other hand, it is not true that a submission to all sorts of governments is slavery; for the government of freemen differs not more from the government of slaves than slavery and freedom differ from each other in their nature; and how they do has been already mentioned. To prefer doing of nothing to virtuous activity is also wrong, for happiness consists in action, and many noble ends are produced by the actions of the just and wise. From what we have already determined on this subject, some one probably may think, that supreme power is of all things best, as that will enable a man to command very many useful services from others; so that he who

can obtain this ought not to give it up to another, but
rather to seize it: and, for this purpose, the father should
have no attention or regard for the son, or the son for
the father, or friend for friend; for what is best is most
eligible: but to be a member of the community and be
in felicity is best. What these persons advance might
probably be true, if the supreme good was certainly
theirs who plunder and use violence to others: but it is 1325b
most unlikely that it should be so; for it is a mere sup-
position: for it does not follow that their actions are
honourable who thus assume the supreme power over
others, without they were by nature as superior to them
as a man to a woman, a father to a child, a master to a
slave: so that he who so far forsakes the paths of virtue
can never return back from whence he departed from
them: for amongst equals whatever is fair and just ought
to be reciprocal; for this is equal and right; but that
equals should not partake of what is equal, or like to like,
is contrary to nature: but whatever is contrary to nature
is not right; therefore, if there is any one superior to the
rest of the community in virtue and abilities for active
life, him it is proper to follow, him it is right to obey,
but the one alone will not do, but must be joined to the
other also: and, if we are right in what we have now
said, it follows that happiness consists in virtuous activity,
and that both with respect to the community as well as
the individual an active life is the happiest: not that an
active life must necessarily refer to other persons, as some
think, or that those studies alone are practical which are
pursued to teach others what to do; for those are much
more so whose final object is in themselves, and to improve
the judgment and understanding of the man; for virtuous
activity has an end, therefore is something practical;
nay, those who contrive the plan which others follow are
more particularly said to act, and are superior to the
workmen who execute their designs. But it is not necessary that states which choose to have no intercourse with
others should remain inactive; for the several members
thereof may have mutual intercourse with each other;
for there are many opportunities for this among the

different citizens; the same thing is true of every individual: for, was it otherwise, neither could the Deity
nor the universe be perfect; to neither of whom can
anything external separately exist. Hence it is evident,
that that very same life which is happy for each individual
is happy also for the state and every member of it.

CHAPTER IV

As I have now finished what was introductory to this
subject, and considered at large the nature of other states,
it now remains that I should first say what ought to be
the establishment of a city which one should form according to one's wish; for no good state can exist without
a moderate proportion of what is necessary. Many
things therefore ought to be forethought of as desirable,
but none of them such as are impossible: I mean relative
to the number of citizens and the extent of the territory:
for as other artificers, such as the weaver and the shipwright, ought to have such materials as are fit for their
work, since so much the better they are, by so much
1326a superior will the work itself necessarily be; so also ought
the legislator and politician endeavour to procure proper
materials for the business they have in hand. Now the
first and principal instrument of the politician is the
number of the people; he should therefore know how
many, and what they naturally ought to be: in like
manner the country, how large, and what it is. Most
persons think that it is necessary for a city to be large
to be happy: but, should this be true, they cannot tell
what is a large one and what a small one; for according
to the multitude of the inhabitants they estimate the
greatness of it; but they ought rather to consider its
strength than its numbers; for a state has a certain
object in view, and from the power which it has in itself
of accomplishing it, its greatness ought to be estimated;
as a person might say, that Hippocrates was a greater
physician, though not a greater man, than one that

exceeded him in the size of his body: but if it was proper
to determine the strength of the city from the number
of the inhabitants, it should never be collected from the
multitude in general who may happen to be in it; for
in a city there must necessarily be many slaves, sojourners,
and foreigners; but from those who are really part of the
city and properly constitute its members; a multitude
of these is indeed a proof of a large city, but in a state
where a large number of mechanics inhabit, and but few
soldiers, such a state cannot be great; for the greatness
of the city, and the number of men in it, are not the same
thing. This too is evident from fact, that it is very difficult, if not impossible, to govern properly a very numerous
body of men; for of all the states which appear well
governed we find not one where the rights of a citizen
are open to an indiscriminate multitude. And this is
also evident from the nature of the thing; for as law is
a certain order, so good law is of course a certain good
order: but too large a multitude are incapable of this,
unless under the government of that DIVINE POWER
which comprehends the universe. Not but that, as
quantity and variety are usually essential to beauty, the
perfection of a city consists in the largeness of it as far
as that largeness is consistent with that order already
mentioned: but still there is a determinate size to all
cities, as well as everything else, whether animals, plants,
or machines, for each of these, if they are neither too little
nor too big, have their proper powers; but when they
have not their due growth, or are badly constructed, as
a ship a span long is not properly a ship, nor one of two
furlongs length, but when it is of a fit size; for either
from its smallness or from its largeness it may be quite
useless: so is it with a city; one that is too small has not 1326b
in itself the power of self-defence, but this is essential
to a city: one that is too large is capable of self-defence
in what is necessary; but then it is a nation and not a
city: for it will be very difficult to accommodate a form
of government to it: for who would choose to be the
general of such an unwieldy multitude, or who could be
their herald but a stentor? The first thing therefore

necessary is, that a city should consist of such numbers as will be sufficient to enable the inhabitants to live happily in their political community: and it follows, that the more the inhabitants exceed that necessary number, the greater will the city be: but this must not be, as we have already said, without bounds; but what is its proper limit experience will easily show, and this experience is to be collected from the actions both of the governors and the governed. Now, as it belongs to the first to direct the inferior magistrates and to act as judges, it follows that they can neither determine causes with justice nor issue their orders with propriety without they know the characters of their fellow-citizens: so that whenever this happens not to be done in these two particulars, the state must of necessity be badly managed; for in both of them it is not right to determine too hastily and without proper knowledge, which must evidently be the case where the number of the citizens is too many: besides, it is more easy for strangers and sojourners to assume the rights of citizens, as they will easily escape detection in so great a multitude. It is evident, then, that the best boundary for a city is that wherein the numbers are the greatest possible, that they may be the better able to be sufficient in themselves, while at the same time they are not too large to be under the eye and government of the magistrates. And thus let us determine the extent of a city.

CHAPTER V

What we have said concerning a city may nearly be applied to a country; for as to what soil it should be, every one evidently will commend it if it is such as is sufficient in itself to furnish what will make the inhabitants happy; for which purpose it must be able to supply them with all the necessaries of life; for it is the having these in plenty, without any want, which makes them content. As to its extent, it should be such as may enable the inhabitants to live at their ease with freedom and temperance. Whether we have done right or wrong in fixing this limit to the territory shall be considered more minutely hereafter, when we come particularly to inquire into property, and what fortune is requisite for a man to live on, and how and in what manner they ought to employ it; for there are many doubts upon this question, while each party insists upon their own plan of life being carried to an excess, the one of severity, the other of indulgence. What the situation of the country should be it is not difficult to determine, in some particulars respecting that we ought to be advised by those who are skilful in military affairs. It should be difficult of access to an enemy, but easy to the inhabitants: and as we said, that the number of 1327a inhabitants ought to be such as can come under the eye of the magistrate, so should it be with the country; for then it is easily defended. As to the position of the city, if one could place it to one's wish, it is convenient to fix it on the seaside: with respect to the country, one situation which it ought to have has been already mentioned, namely, that it should be so placed as easily to give assistance to all places, and also to receive the necessaries of life from all parts, and also wood, or any other materials which may happen to be in the country.

CHAPTER VI

But with respect to placing a city in the neighbourhood of the sea, there are some who have many doubts whether it is serviceable or hurtful to a well-regulated state; for they say, that the resort of persons brought up under a different system of government is disserviceable to the state, as well by impeding the laws as by their numbers; for a multitude of merchants must necessarily arise from their trafficking backward and forward upon the seas, which will hinder the well-governing of the city: but if this inconvenience should not arise, it is evident that it

is better, both on account of safety and also for the easier
acquisition of the necessaries of life, that both the city
and the country should be near the sea; for it is necessary
that those who are to sustain the attack of the enemy
should be ready with their assistance both by land and
by sea, and to oppose any inroad, both ways if possible,
but if not, at least where they are most powerful, which
they may do while they possess both. A maritime
situation is also useful for receiving from others what
your own country will not produce, and exporting those
necessaries of your own growth which are more than you
have occasion for; but a city ought to traffic to supply
its own wants, and not the wants of others; for those who
themselves furnish an open market for every one, do it
for the sake of gain; which it is not proper for a well-
established state to do, neither should they encourage
such a commerce. Now, as we see that many places and
cities have docks and harbours lying very convenient for
the city, while those who frequent them have no com-
munication with the citadel, and yet they are not too far
off, but are surrounded by walls and such-like fortifica-
tions, it is evident, that if any good arises from such an
intercourse the city will receive it, but if anything hurtful,
it will be easy to restrain it by a law declaring and
deputing whom the state will allow to have an intercourse
with each other, and whom not. As to a naval power, it
is by no means doubtful that it is necessary to have one
to a certain degree; and this not only for the sake of the
1327b city itself, but also because it may be necessary to appear
formidable to some of the neighbouring states, or to be
able to assist them as well by sea as by land; but to
know how great that force should be, the health of the
state should be inquired into, and if that appears vigorous
and enables her to take the lead of other communities, it
is necessary that her force should correspond with her
actions. As for that multitude of people which a maritime
power creates, they are by no means necessary to a state,
nor ought they to make a part of the citizens; for the
mariners and infantry, who have the command, are freemen, and upon these depends a naval engagement: but

when there are many servants and husbandmen, there they will always have a number of sailors, as we now see happens to some states, as in Heraclea, where they man many triremes, though the extent of their city is much inferior to some others. And thus we determine concerning the country, the port, the city, the sea, and a maritime power: as to the number of the citizens, what that ought to be we have already said.

CHAPTER VII

WE now proceed to point out what natural disposition the members of the community ought to be of: but this any one will easily perceive who will cast his eye over the states of Greece, of all others the most celebrated, and also the other different nations of this habitable world. Those who live in cold countries, as the north of Europe, are full of courage, but wanting in understanding and the arts: therefore they are very tenacious of their liberty; but, not being politicians, they cannot reduce their neighbours under their power: but the Asiatics, whose understandings are quick, and who are conversant in the arts, are deficient in courage; and therefore are always conquered and the slaves of others: but the Grecians, placed as it were between these two boundaries, so partake of them both as to be at the same time both courageous and sensible; for which reason Greece continues free, and governed in the best manner possible, and capable of commanding the whole world, could they agree upon one system of policy. Now this is the difference between the Grecians and other nations, that the latter have but one of these qualities, whereas in the former they are both happily blended together. Hence it is evident, that those persons ought to be both sensible and courageous who will readily obey a legislator, the object of whose laws is virtue.—As to what some persons say, that the military must be mild and tender to those they know, but severe and cruel to those they know not, it is courage which 1328a makes any one lovely; for that is the faculty of the soul which we most admire: as a proof of this, our resentment rises higher against our friends and acquaintance than against those we know not: for which reason Archilaus accusing his friends says very properly to himself, Shall my friends insult me? The spirit of freedom and command also is what all inherit who are of this disposition; for courage is commanding and invincible. It also is not right for any one to say, that you should be severe to those you know not; for this behaviour is proper for no one: nor are those who are of a noble disposition harsh in their manners, excepting only to the wicked; and when they are particularly so, it is, as has been already said, against their friends, when they think they have injured them; which is agreeable to reason: for when those who think they ought to receive a favour from any one do not receive it, beside the injury done them, they consider what they are deprived of: hence the saying, " Cruel are the wars of brothers; " and this, " Those who have greatly loved do greatly hate." And thus we have nearly determined how many the inhabitants of a city ought to be, and what their natural disposition, and also the country how large, and of what sort is necessary; I say nearly, because it is needless to endeavour at as great accuracy in those things which are the objects of the senses as in those which are inquired into by the understanding only.

CHAPTER VIII

As in natural bodies those things are not admitted to be parts of them without which the whole would not exist, so also it is evident that in a political state everything that is necessary thereunto is not to be considered as a part of it, nor any other community from whence one whole is made; for one thing ought to be common and the same to the community, whether they partake of it equally or unequally, as, for instance, food, land, or the like; but when one thing is for the benefit of one person, and another for the benefit of another, in this there is nothing like a community, excepting that one makes it and the other uses it; as, for instance, between any instrument employed in making any work, and the workmen, as there is nothing common between the house and the builder, but the art of the builder is employed on the house. Thus property is necessary for states, but property is no part of the state, though many species of it have life; but a city is a community of equals, for the purpose of enjoying the best life possible: but the happiest life is the best which consists in the perfect practice of virtuous energies: as therefore some persons have great, others little or no opportunity of being employed in these, it is evident that this is the cause of the difference there is between the different cities and communities there are to be found; for while each of these endeavour to acquire what is best by various and different means, they give 1328*b* rise to different modes of living and different forms of government. We are now to consider what those things are without which a city cannot possibly exist; for what we call parts of the city must of necessity inhere in it: and this we shall plainly understand, if we know the number of things necessary to a city: first, the inhabitants must have food: secondly, arts, for many instruments are necessary in life: thirdly, arms, for it is necessary that the community should have an armed force within themselves, both to support their government against those of their own body who might refuse obedience to it, and also to defend it from those who might attempt to attack it from without: fourthly, a certain revenue, as well for the internal necessities of the state as for the business of war: fifthly, which is indeed the chief concern, a religious establishment: sixthly in order, but first of all in necessity, a court to determine both criminal and civil causes. These things are absolutely necessary, so to speak, in every state; for a city is a number of people not accidentally met together, but with a purpose of ensuring to themselves sufficient independency and self-protection; and if anything necessary for these purposes is wanting, it is impossible that in such a situation these ends can be obtained. It is necessary therefore that a city should be capable of acquiring all these things: for this purpose a proper number of husbandmen are necessary to procure food, also artificers and soldiers, and rich men, and priests, and judges, to determine what is right and proper.

CHAPTER IX

HAVING determined thus far, it remains that we consider whether all these different employments shall be open to all; for it is possible to continue the same persons always husbandmen, artificers, judges, or counsellors; or shall we appoint different persons to each of those employments which we have already mentioned; or shall some of them be appropriated to particulars, and others of course common to all? but this does not take place in every state, for, as we have already said, it is possible that all may be common to all, or not, but only common to some: and this is the difference between one government and another: for in democracies the whole community partakes of everything, but in oligarchies it is different.

Since we are inquiring what is the best government possible, and it is admitted to be that in which the citizens are happy; and that, as we have already said, it is impossible to obtain happiness without virtue; it follows, that in the best-governed states, where the citizens are really men of intrinsic and not relative goodness, none of them should be permitted to exercise any mechanic employment or follow merchandise, as being ignoble and destructive to virtue; neither should they be husband-

1329a men, that they may be at leisure to improve in virtue and perform the duty they owe to the state. With respect to the employments of a soldier, a senator, and a judge, which are evidently necessary to the community, shall they be allotted to different persons, or shall the same person execute both? This question, too, is easily answered: for in some cases the same persons may execute them, in others they should be different, where the different employments require different abilities, as when courage is wanting for one, judgment for the other, there they should be allotted to different persons; but when it is evident, that it is impossible to oblige those who have arms in their hands, and can insist on their own terms, to be always under command; there these different employments should be trusted to one person; for those who have arms in their hands have it in their option whether they will or will not assume the supreme power: to these two (namely, those who have courage and judgment) the government must be entrusted; but not in the same manner, but as nature directs; what requires courage to the young, what requires judgment to the old; for with the young is courage, with the old is wisdom: thus each will be allotted the part they are fit for according to their different merits. It is also necessary that the landed property should belong to these men; for it is necessary that the citizens should be rich, and these are the men proper for citizens; for no mechanic ought to be admitted to the rights of a citizen, nor any other sort of people whose employment is not entirely noble, honourable, and virtuous; this is evident from the principle we at first set out with; for to be happy it is necessary to be virtuous; and no one should say that a city is happy while he considers only one part of its citizens, but for that purpose he ought to examine into all of them. It is evident, therefore, that the landed property should belong to these, though it may be necessary for them to have husbandmen, either slaves, barbarians, or servants. There remains of the different classes of the people whom we have enumerated, the priests, for these evidently compose a rank by themselves; for neither are they to be reckoned amongst the husbandmen nor the mechanics; for reverence to the gods is highly becoming every state: and since the citizens have been divided into orders, the military and the council, and it is proper to offer due worship to the gods, and since it is necessary that those who are employed in their service should have nothing else to do, let the business of the priesthood be allotted to those who are in years. We have now shown what is necessary to the existence of a city, and of what parts it consists, and that husbandmen, mechanic, and mercenary servants are necessary to a city; but that the parts of it are soldiers and sailors, and that these are always different from those, but from each other only occasionally.

CHAPTER X

IT seems neither now nor very lately to have been known **1329b** to those philosophers who have made politics their study, that a city ought to be divided by families into different orders of men; and that the husbandmen and soldiers should be kept separate from each other; which custom is even to this day preserved in Egypt and in Crete; also Sesostris having founded it in Egypt, Minos in Crete. Common meals seem also to have been an ancient regulation, and to have been established in Crete during the reign of Minos, and in a still more remote period in Italy; for those who are the best judges in that country say that one Italus being king of Ænotria, from whom the people, changing their names, were called Italians instead of Ænotrians, and that part of Europe was called Italy which is bounded by the Scylletic Gulf on the one side and the Lametic on the other, the distance between which is about half a day's journey. This Italus, they relate, made the Ænotrians, who were formerly shepherds, husbandmen, and gave them different laws from what they had before, and to have been the first who established common meals, for which reason some of his descendants still use them, and observe some of his laws. The Opici inhabit that part which lies towards the Tyrrhenian Sea, who both now are and formerly were called Ausonians. The Chones inhabited the part toward Iapigia and the Ionian Sea which is called Syrtis. These Chones were descended from the Ænotrians. Hence arose the custom of common meals, but the separation of the citizens into different families from Egypt: for the reign of Sesostris is of much higher antiquity than that of Minos. As we ought to think that most other things were found out in a long, nay, even in a boundless time (reason teaching us that want would make us first invent that which was necessary, and, when that was obtained, then those things which were requisite for the conveniences and ornament of life), so should we conclude the same with respect to a political state; now everything in Egypt bears the marks of the most remote antiquity, for these people seem to be the most ancient of all others, and to have acquired laws and political order; we should therefore make a proper use of what is told us of them, and endeavour to find out what they have omitted. We have already said, that the landed property ought to belong to the military and those who partake of the government of the state; and that therefore the husbandmen should be a separate order of people; and how large and of what nature the country ought to be: we will first treat of the division of the land, and of the husbandmen, how many and of what sort they ought to be; since we by no means hold that property ought to be common, as some persons have said, only thus far, in friendship, it 1330a should be their custom to let no citizen want subsistence. As to common meals, it is in general agreed that they are proper in well-regulated cities; my reasons for approving of them shall be mentioned hereafter: they are what all the citizens ought to partake of; but it will not be easy for the poor, out of what is their own, to furnish as much as they are ordered to do, and supply their own house besides. The expense also of religious worship should be defrayed by the whole state. Of necessity therefore the land ought to be divided into two parts, one of which should belong to the community in general, the other to the individuals separately; and each of these parts should again be subdivided into two: half of that which belongs to the public should be appropriated to maintain the worship of the gods, the other half to support the common meals. Half of that which belongs to the individuals should be at the extremity of the country, the other half near the city, so that these two portions being allotted to each person, all would partake of land in both places, which would be both equal and right; and induce them

to act in concert with greater harmony in any war with
their neighbours: for when the land is not divided in this
manner, one party neglects the inroads of the enemy on
the borders, the other makes it a matter of too much
consequence and more than is necessary; for which reason,
in some places there is a law which forbids the inhabitants
of the borders to have any vote in the council when they
are debating upon a war which is made against them,
as their private interest might prevent their voting im-
partially.   Thus therefore the country ought to be divided,
and for the reasons before mentioned.   Could one have
one's choice, the husbandmen should by all means be
slaves, not of the same nation, or men of any spirit; for
thus they would be laborious in their business, and safe
from attempting any novelties: next to these barbarian
servants are to be preferred, similar in natural disposition
to these we have already mentioned.   Of these, let those
who are to cultivate the private property of the individual
belong to that individual, and those who are to cultivate the public territory belong to the public.   In what
manner these slaves ought to be used, and for what reason
it is very proper that they should have the promise of
their liberty made them, as a reward for their services,
shall be mentioned hereafter.

CHAPTER XI

We have already mentioned, that both the city and all
the country should communicate both with the sea and
the continent as much as possible.   There are these four
things which we should be particularly desirous of in the
position of the city with respect to itself: in the first place,
health is to be consulted as the first thing necessary: now
a city which fronts the east and receives the winds which
blow from thence is esteemed most healthful; next to
this that which has a northern position is to be preferred,
as best in winter.   It should next be contrived that it
may have a proper situation for the business of govern-

ment and for defence in war: that in war the citizens may 1330b
have easy access to it; but that it may be difficult of
access to, and hardly to be taken by, the enemy. In the
next place particularly, that there may be plenty of water,
and rivers near at hand: but if those cannot be found,
very large cisterns must be prepared to save rain-water,
so that there may be no want of it in case they should be
driven into the town in time of war. And as great care
should be taken of the health of the inhabitants, the first
thing to be attended to is, that the city should have a
good situation and a good position; the second is, that
they may have good water to drink; and this not be
negligently taken care of; for what we chiefly and most
frequently use for the support of the body must principally
influence the health of it; and this influence is what the
air and water naturally have: for which reason in all wise
governments the waters ought to be appropriated to
different purposes, and if they are not equally good, and
if there is not a plenty of necessary water, that which
is to drink should be separated from that which is
for other uses. As to fortified places, what is proper for
some governments is not proper for all; as, for instance, a
lofty citadel is proper for a monarchy and an oligarchy;
a city built upon a plain suits a democracy; neither of
these for an aristocracy, but rather many strong places.
As to the form of private houses, those are thought to be
best and most useful for their different purposes which
are distinct and separate from each other, and built in
the modern manner, after the plan of Hippodamus: but
for safety in time of war, on the contrary, they should be
built as they formerly were; for they were such that
strangers could not easily find their way out of them, and
the method of access to them such as an enemy could
with difficulty find out if he proposed to besiege them.
A city therefore should have both these sorts of buildings,
which may easily be contrived if any one will so regulate
them as the planters do their rows of vines; not that the
buildings throughout the city should be detached from
each other, only in some parts of it; thus elegance and
safety will be equally consulted. With respect to walls,

those who say that a courageous people ought not to have any, pay too much respect to obsolete notions; particularly as we may see those who pride themselves therein continually confuted by facts. It is indeed disreputable for those who are equal, or nearly so, to the enemy, to endeavour to take refuge within their walls; but since it very often happens, that those who make the attack are too powerful for the bravery and courage of those few who oppose them to resist, if you would not suffer the calamities of war and the insolence of the 1331a enemy, it must be thought the part of a good soldier to seek for safety under the shelter and protection of walls, more especially since so many missile weapons and machines have been most ingeniously invented to besiege cities with. Indeed to neglect surrounding a city with a wall would be similar to choosing a country which is easy of access to an enemy, or levelling the eminences of it; or as if an individual should not have a wall to his house, lest it should be thought that the owner of it was a coward: nor should this be left unconsidered, that those who have a city surrounded with walls may act both ways, either as if it had or as if it had not; but where it has not they cannot do this. If this is true, it is not only necessary to have walls, but care must be taken that they may be a proper ornament to the city, as well as a defence in time of war; not only according to the old methods, but the modern improvements also: for as those who make offensive war endeavour by every way possible to gain advantages over their adversaries, so should those who are upon the defensive employ all the means already known, and such new ones as philosophy can invent, to defend themselves: for those who are well prepared are seldom first attacked.

CHAPTER XII

As the citizens in general are to eat at public tables in
certain companies, and it is necessary that the walls
should have bulwarks and towers in proper places and
at proper distances, it is evident that it will be very
necessary to have some of these in the towers; let the
buildings for this purpose be made the ornaments of the
walls. As to temples for public worship, and the hall
for the public tables of the chief magistrates, they ought
to be built in proper places, and contiguous to each
other, except those temples which the law or the oracle
orders to be separate from all other buildings; and let
these be in such a conspicuous eminence, that they may
have every advantage of situation, and in the neighbourhood of that part of the city which is best fortified. Ad-
joining to this place there ought to be a large square, like
that which they call in Thessaly The Square of Freedom,
in which nothing is permitted to be bought or sold; into
which no mechanic nor husbandman, nor any such person,
should be permitted to enter, unless commanded by the
magistrates. It will also be an ornament to this place
if the gymnastic exercises of the elders are performed
in it. It is also proper, that for performing these exercises the citizens should be divided into distinct classes,
according to their ages, and that the young persons should
have proper officers to be with them, and that the seniors
should be with the magistrates; for having them before
their eyes would greatly inspire true modesty and
ingenuous fear. There ought to be another square 1331*b*
separate from this for buying and selling, which should
be so situated as to be commodious for the reception of
goods both by sea and land. As the citizens may be
divided into magistrates and priests, it is proper that
the public tables of the priests should be in buildings
near the temples. Those of the magistrates who preside
over contracts, indictments, and such-like, and also over
the markets, and the public streets near the square, or

some public way, I mean the square where things are bought and sold; for I intended the other for those who are at leisure, and this for necessary business. The same order which I have directed here should be observed also in the country; for there also their magistrates, such as the surveyors of the woods and overseers of the grounds, must necessarily have their common tables and their towers, for the purpose of protection against an enemy. There ought also to be temples erected at proper places, both to the gods and the heroes; but it is unnecessary to dwell longer and most minutely on these particulars; for it is by no means difficult to plan these things, it is rather so to carry them into execution; for the theory is the child of our wishes, but the practical part must depend upon fortune; for which reason we shall decline saying anything farther upon these subjects.

CHAPTER XIII

WE will now show of what numbers and of what sort of people a government ought to consist, that the state may be happy and well administered. As there are two particulars on which the excellence and perfection of everything depend, one of these is, that the object and end proposed should be proper; the other, that the means to accomplish it should be adapted to that purpose; for it may happen that these may either agree or disagree with each other; for the end we propose may be good, but in taking the means to obtain it we may err; at other times we may have the right and proper means in our power, but the end may be bad, and sometimes we may mistake in both; as in the art of medicine the physician does not sometimes know in what situation the body ought to be, to be healthy; nor what to do to procure the end he aims at. In every art and science, therefore, we should be master of this knowledge, namely, the proper end, and the means to obtain it. Now it is evident that all persons are desirous to live well and be happy; but that some have the means thereof in their own power, others not; and this either through nature 1332a or fortune; for many ingredients are necessary to a happy life; but fewer to those who are of a good than to those who are of a bad disposition. There are others who continually have the means of happiness in their own power, but do not rightly apply them. Since we propose to inquire what government is best, namely, that by which a state may be best administered, and that state is best administered where the people are the happiest, it is evident that happiness is a thing we should not be unacquainted with. Now, I have already said in my treatise on Morals (if I may here make any use of what I have there shown), that happiness consists in the energy and perfect practice of virtue; and this not relatively, but simply; I mean by relatively, what is necessary in some certain circumstances; by simply, what is good and fair in itself: of the first sort are just punishments, and restraints in a just cause; for they arise from virtue and are necessary, and on that account are virtuous; though it is more desirable that neither any state nor any individual should stand in need of them; but those actions which are intended either to procure honour or wealth are simply good; the others eligible only to remove an evil; these, on the contrary, are the foundation and means of relative good. A worthy man indeed will bear poverty, disease, and other unfortunate accidents with a noble mind; but happiness consists in the contrary to these (now we have already determined in our treatise on Morals, that he is a man of worth who considers what is good because it is virtuous as what is simply good; it is evident, therefore, that all the actions of such a one must be worthy and simply good): this has led some persons to conclude, that the cause of happiness was external goods; which would be as if any one should suppose that the playing well upon the lyre was owing to the instrument, and not to the art. It necessarily follows from what has been said, that some things should be ready at hand and others procured by the legislator; for which reason in founding a city we earnestly wish

that there may be plenty of those things which are supposed to be under the dominion of fortune (for some things we admit her to be mistress over); but for a state to be worthy and great is not only the work of fortune, but of knowledge and judgment also. But for a state to be worthy it is necessary that those citizens which are in the administration should be worthy also; but as in our city every citizen is to be so, we must consider how this may be accomplished; for if this is what every one could be, and not some individuals only, it would be more desirable; for then it would follow, that what might be done by one might be done by all. Men are worthy and good three ways; by nature, by custom, by reason. In the first place, a man ought to be born a man, and not any other animal; that is to say, he ought to have both a body and soul; but it avails not to be only born
1332*b* with some things, for custom makes great alterations; for there are some things in nature capable of alteration either way which are fixed by custom, either for the better or the worse. Now, other animals live chiefly a life of nature; and in very few things according to custom; but man lives according to reason also, which he alone is endowed with; wherefore he ought to make all these accord with each other; for if men followed reason, and were persuaded that it was best to obey her, they would act in many respects contrary to nature and custom. What men ought naturally to be, to make good members of a community, I have already determined; the rest of this discourse therefore shall be upon education; for some things are acquired by habit, others by hearing them.

CHAPTER XIV

As every political community consists of those who govern and of those who are governed, let us consider whether during the continuance of their lives they ought to be the same persons or different; for it is evident that the mode of education should be adapted to this dis-

tinction.   Now, if one man differed from another as much,
as we believe, the gods and heroes differ from men: in
the first place, being far their superiors in body; and,
secondly, in the soul: so that the superiority of the
governors over the governed might be evident beyond a
doubt, it is certain that it would be better for the one
always to govern, the other always to be governed: but,
as this is not easy to obtain, and kings are not so superior
to those they govern as Scylax informs us they are in
India, it is evident that for many reasons it is necessary
that all in their turns should both govern and be governed:
for it is just that those who are equal should have everything alike; and it is difficult for a state to continue which
is founded in injustice; for all those in the country who
are desirous of innovation will apply themselves to those
who are under the government of the rest, and such will
be their numbers in the state, that it will be impossible for
the magistrates to get the better of them.   But that the
governors ought to excel the governed is beyond a doubt;
the legislator therefore ought to consider how this shall
be, and how it may be contrived that all shall have their
equal share in the administration.   Now, with respect to
this it will be first said, that nature herself has directed us
in our choice, laying down the selfsame thing when she
has made some young, others old: the first of whom it
becomes to obey, the latter to command; for no one when
he is young is offended at his being under government, or
thinks himself too good for it; more especially when he
considers that he himself shall receive the same honours
which he pays when he shall arrive at a proper age.   In
some respects it must be acknowledged that the governors
and the governed are the same, in others they are different;
it is therefore necessary that their education should be in 1333a
some respect the same, in others different: as they say,
that he will be a good governor who has first learnt to
obey.   Now of governments, as we have already said,
some are instituted for the sake of him who commands;
others for him who obeys: of the first sort is that of the
master over the servant; of the latter, that of freemen
over each other.   Now some things which are commanded

differ from others; not in the business, but in the end
proposed thereby: for which reason many works, even of
a servile nature, are not disgraceful for young freemen to
perform; for many things which are ordered to be done
are not honourable or dishonourable so much in their own
nature as in the end which is proposed, and the reason for
which they are undertaken. Since then we have determined, that the virtue of a good citizen and good governor
is the same as of a good man; and that every one before
he commands should have first obeyed, it is the business
of the legislator to consider how his citizens may be good
men, what education is necessary to that purpose, and
what is the final object of a good life. The soul of man
may be divided into two parts; that which has reason in
itself, and that which hath not, but is capable of obeying
its dictates: and according to the virtues of these two
parts a man is said to be good: but of those virtues which
are the ends, it will not be difficult for those to determine
who adopt the division I have already given; for the
inferior is always for the sake of the superior; and this
is equally evident both in the works of art as well as in
those of nature; but that is superior which has reason.
Reason itself also is divided into two parts, in the manner
we usually divide it; the theoretic and the practical;
which division therefore seems necessary for this part also:
the same analogy holds good with respect to actions; of
which those which are of a superior nature ought always
to be chosen by those who have it in their power; for that
is always most eligible to every one which will procure the
best ends. Now life is divided into labour and rest, war
and peace; and of what we do the objects are partly
necessary and useful, partly noble: and we should give
the same preference to these that we do to the different
parts of the soul and its actions, as war to procure peace;
labour, rest; and the useful, the noble. The politician,
therefore, who composes a body of laws ought to extend
his views to everything; the different parts of the soul
and their actions; more particularly to those things which
are of a superior nature and ends; and, in the same
manner, to the lives of men and their different actions.

They ought to be fitted both for labour and war, but rather 1333*b*
for rest and peace; and also to do what is necessary and
useful, but rather what is fair and noble. It is to those
objects that the education of the children ought to tend,
and of all the youths who want instruction. All the
Grecian states which now seem best governed, and the
legislators who founded those states, appear not to have
framed their polity with a view to the best end, or to
every virtue, in their laws and education; but eagerly to
have attended to what is useful and productive of gain:
and nearly of the same opinion with these are some
persons who have written lately, who, by praising the
Lacedæmonian state, show they approve of the intention
of the legislator in making war and victory the end of his
government. But how contrary to reason this is, is easily
proved by argument, and has already been proved by
facts (but as the generality of men desire to have an
extensive command, that they may have everything
desirable in the greater abundance; so Thibron and
others who have written on that state seem to approve of
their legislator for having procured them an extensive
command by continually enuring them to all sorts of
dangers and hardships): for it is evident, since the
Lacedæmonians have now no hope that the supreme
power will be in their own hand, that neither are they
happy nor was their legislator wise. This also is ridiculous,
that while they preserved an obedience to their laws, and
no one opposed their being governed by them, they lost
the means of being honourable: but these people understand not rightly what sort of government it is which
ought to reflect honour on the legislator; for a government of freemen is nobler than despotic power, and more
consonant to virtue. Moreover, neither should a city be
thought happy, nor should a legislator be commended,
because he has so trained the people as to conquer their
neighbours; for in this there is a great inconvenience:
since it is evident that upon this principle every citizen
who can will endeavour to procure the supreme power in
his own city; which crime the Lacedæmonians accuse
Pausanias of, though he enjoyed such great honours.

Such reasoning and such laws are neither political, useful, nor true: but a legislator ought to instil those laws on the minds of men which are most useful for them, both in their public and private capacities. The rendering a people fit for war, that they may enslave their inferiors, ought not to be the care of the legislator; but that they may not themselves be reduced to slavery by others. In 1334a the next place, he should take care that the object of his government is the safety of those who are under it, and not a despotism over all: in the third place, that those only are slaves who are fit to be only so. Reason indeed concurs with experience in showing that all the attention which the legislator pays to the business of war, and all other rules which he lays down, should have for their object rest and peace; since most of those states (which we usually see) are preserved by war; but, after they have acquired a supreme power over those around them, are ruined; for during peace, like a sword, they lose their brightness: the fault of which lies in the legislator, who never taught them how to be at rest.

CHAPTER XV

As there is one end common to a man both as an individual and a citizen, it is evident that a good man and a good citizen must have the same object in view; it is evident that all the virtues which lead to rest are necessary; for, as we have often said, the end of war is peace, of labour, rest; but those virtues whose object is rest, and those also whose object is labour, are necessary for a liberal life and rest; for we want a supply of many necessary things that we may be at rest. A city therefore ought to be temperate, brave, and patient; for, according to the proverb, "Rest is not for slaves;" but those who cannot bravely face danger are the slaves of those who attack them. Bravery, therefore, and patience are necessary for labour, philosophy for rest, and temperance and justice in both; but these chiefly in time of peace and rest; for war obliges men to be just and temperate; but the enjoyment of pleasure, with the rest of peace, is more apt to produce insolence; those indeed who are easy in their circumstances, and enjoy everything that can make them happy, have great occasion for the virtues of temperance and justice.   Thus if there are, as the poets tell us, any inhabitants in the happy isles, to these a higher degree of philosophy, temperance, and justice will be necessary, as they live at their ease in the full plenty of every sensual pleasure.   It is evident, therefore, that these virtues are necessary in every state that would be happy or worthy; for he who is worthless can never enjoy real good, much less is he qualified to be at rest; but can appear good only by labour and being at war, but in peace and at rest the meanest of creatures.   For which reason virtue should not be cultivated as the Lacedæmonians did; for they did not differ from others in their opinion concerning the supreme good, but in **1334b** imagining this good was to be procured by a particular virtue; but since there are greater goods than those of war, it is evident that the enjoyment of those which are valuable in themselves should be desired, rather than those virtues which are useful in war; but how and by what means this is to be acquired is now to be considered. We have already assigned three causes on which it will depend; nature, custom, and reason, and shown what sort of men nature must produce for this purpose; it remains then that we determine which we shall first begin by in education, reason or custom, for these ought always to preserve the most entire harmony with each other; for it may happen that reason may err from the end proposed, and be corrected by custom.   In the first place, it is evident that in this as in other things, its beginning or production arises from some principle, and its end also arises from another principle, which is itself an end.   Now, with us, reason and intelligence are the end of nature; our production, therefore, and our manners ought to be accommodated to both these.   In the next place, as the soul and the body are two distinct things, so also we see that the soul is divided into two parts, the reasoning and not-reasoning, with their habits, which are two in number, one belonging to each, namely, appetite and intelligence; and as the body is in production before the soul, so is the not-reasoning part of the soul before the reasoning; and this is evident; for anger, will, and desire are to be seen in children nearly as soon as they are born; but reason and intelligence spring up as they grow to maturity. The body, therefore, necessarily demands our care before the soul; next the appetites, for the sake of the mind; the body for the sake of the soul.

CHAPTER XVI

IF then tne legislator ought to take care that the bodies of the children are as perfect as possible, his first attention ought to be given to matrimony; at what time and in what situation it is proper that the citizens should engage in the nuptial contract. Now, with respect to this alliance, the legislator ought both to consider the parties and their time of life, that they may grow old at the same part of time, and that their bodily powers may not be different; that is to say, the man being able to have children, but the woman too old to bear them; or, on the contrary, the woman be young enough to produce children, but the man too old to be a father; for from such a situation discords and disputes continually arise. In the next place, with respect to the succession of children, there ought not to be too great an interval of time between them and their parents; for when there is, the parent can receive no benefit from his child's affection, or the child any advantage from his father's protection; 1335*a* neither should the difference in years be too little, as great inconveniences may arise from it; as it prevents that proper reverence being shown to a father by a boy who considers him as nearly his equal in age, and also from the disputes it occasions in the economy of the family. But, to return from this digression, care ought to be taken that the bodies of the children may be such as will answer the expectations of the legislator; and this also will be affected by the same means. Since the season for the production of children is determined (not exactly, but to speak in general), namely, for the man till seventy years, and the woman till fifty, the entering into the marriage state, as far as time is concerned, should be regulated by these periods. It is extremely bad for the children when the father is too young; for in all animals whatsoever the parts of the young are imperfect, and are more likely to be productive of females than males, and diminutive also in size; the same thing of course necessarily holds true in men; as a proof of this you may see in those cities where the men and women usually marry very young, the people in general are very small and ill framed; in child-birth also the women suffer more, and many of them die. And thus some persons tell us the oracle of Træzenium should be explained, as if it referred to the many women who were destroyed by too early marriages, and not their gathering their fruits too soon. It is also conducive to temperance not to marry too soon; for women who do so are apt to be intemperate. It also prevents the bodies of men from acquiring their full size if they marry before their growth is completed; for this is the determinate period, which prevents any further increase; for which reason the proper time for a woman to marry is eighteen, for a man thirty-seven, a little more or less; for when they marry at that time their bodies are in perfection, and they will also cease to have children at a proper time; and moreover with respect to the succession of the children, if they have them at the time which may reasonably be expected, they will be just arriving into perfection when their parents are sinking down under the load of seventy years. And thus much for the time which is proper for marriage; but moreover a proper season of the year should be observed, as many persons do now, and appropriate the winter for this business. The married couple ought also to regard the precepts of physicians and naturalists, each of whom have treated on these 1335b subjects. What is the fit disposition of the body will be

better mentioned when we come to speak of the education of the child;. we will just slightly mention a few particulars. Now, there is no occasion that any one should have the habit of body of a wrestler to be either a good citizen, or to enjoy a good constitution, or to be the father of healthy children; neither should he be infirm or too much dispirited by misfortunes, but between both these. He ought to have a habit of labour, but not of too violent labour; nor should that be confined to one object only, as the wrestler's is; but to such things as are proper for freemen. These things are equally necessary both for men and women. Women with child should also take care that their diet is not too sparing, and that they use sufficient exercise; which it will be easy for the legislator to effect if he commands them once every day to repair to the worship of the gods who are supposed to preside over matrimony. But, contrary to what is proper for the body, the mind ought to be kept as tranquil as possible; for as plants partake of the nature of the soil, so does the child receive much of the disposition of the mother. With respect to the exposing or bringing up of children, let it be a law, that nothing imperfect or maimed shall be brought up, ... As the proper time has been pointed out for a man and a woman to enter into the marriage state, so also let us determine how long it is advantageous for the community that they should have children; for as the children of those who are too young are imperfect both in body and mind, so also those whose parents are too old are weak in both: while therefore the body continues in perfection, which (as some poets say, who reckon the different periods of life by sevens) is till fifty years, or four or five more, the children may be equally perfect; but when the parents are past that age it is better they should have no more. With respect to any connection between a man and a woman, or a woman and a man, when either of the parties are betrothed, let it be held in utter detesta-
1336a tion on any pretext whatsoever; but should any one be guilty of such a thing after the marriage is consummated, let his infamy be as great as his guilt deserves.

CHAPTER XVII

WHEN a child is born it must be supposed that the
strength of its body will depend greatly upon the quality
of its food. Now whoever will examine into the nature
of animals, and also observe those people who are very
desirous their children should acquire a warlike habit,
will find that they feed them chiefly with milk, as being
best accommodated to their bodies, but without wine,
to prevent any distempers: those motions also which
are natural to their age are very serviceable; and to
prevent any of their limbs from being crooked, on account
of their extreme ductility, some people even now use
particular machines that their bodies may not be dis-
torted. It is also useful to enure them to the cold when
they are very little; for this is very serviceable for their
health; and also to enure them to the business of war;
for which reason it is customary with many of the barbarians to dip their children in rivers when the water is
cold; with others to clothe them very slightly, as among
the Celts; for whatever it is possible to accustom children
to, it is best to accustom them to it at first, but to do
it by degrees: besides, boys have naturally a habit of
loving the cold, on account of the heat. These, then,
and such-like things ought to be the first object of our
attention: the next age to this continues till the child
is five years old; during which time it is best to teach
him nothing at all, not even necessary labour, lest it
should hinder his growth; but he should be accustomed
to use so much motion as not to acquire a lazy habit of
body; which he will get by various means and by play
also: his play also ought to be neither illiberal nor too
laborious nor lazy. Their governors and preceptors also
should take care what sort of tales and stories it may be
proper for them to hear; for all these ought to pave the
way for their future instruction: for which reason the
generality of their play should be imitations of what they
are afterwards to do seriously. They too do wrong who

forbid by laws the disputes between boys and their quarrels, for they contribute to increase their growth; as they are a sort of exercise to the body: for the struggles of the heart and the compression of the spirits give strength to those who labour, which happens to boys in their disputes. The preceptors also ought to have an eye upon their manner of life, and those with whom they converse; and to take care that they are never in the company of slaves. At this time and till they are seven **1336b** years old it is necessary that they should be educated at home. It is also very proper to banish, both from their hearing and sight, everything which is illiberal and the like. Indeed it is as much the business of the legislator as anything else, to banish every indecent expression out of the state: for from a permission to speak whatever is shameful, very quickly arises the doing it, and this particularly with young people: for which reason let them never speak nor hear any such thing: but if it appears that any freeman has done or said anything that is forbidden before he is of age to be thought fit to partake of the common meals, let him be punished by disgrace and stripes; but if a person above that age does so, let him be treated as you would a slave, on account of his being infamous. Since we forbid his speaking everything which is forbidden, it is necessary that he neither sees obscene stories nor pictures; the magistrates therefore are to take care that there are no statues or pictures of anything of this nature, except only to those gods to whom the law permits them, and to which the law allows persons of a certain age to pay their devotions, for themselves, their wives, and children. It should also be illegal for young persons to be present either at iambics or comedies before they are arrived at that age when they are allowed to partake of the pleasures of the table: indeed a good education will preserve them from all the evils which attend on these things. We have at present just touched upon this subject; it will be our business hereafter, when we properly come to it, to determine whether this care of children is unnecessary, or, if necessary, in what manner it must be done; at present we have only mentioned it as necessary. Probably the saying of Theodorus, the tragic actor, was not a bad one —That he would permit no one, not even the meanest actor, to go upon the stage before him, that he might first engage the ear of the audience.   The same thing happens both in our connections with men and things: what we meet with first pleases best; for which reason children should be kept strangers to everything which is bad, more particularly whatsoever is loose and offensive to good manners.   When five years are accomplished, the two next may be very properly employed in being spectators of those exercises they will afterwards have to learn.   There are two periods into which education ought to be divided, according to the age of the child; the one is from his being seven years of age to the time of puberty; the other from thence till he is one-and-twenty: for those who divide ages by the number seven 1337a are in general wrong: it is much better to follow the division of nature; for every art and every instruction is intended to complete what nature has left defective: we must first consider if any regulation whatsoever is requisite for children; in the next place, if it is advantageous to make it a common care, or that every one should act therein as he pleases, which is the general practice in most cities; in the third place, what it ought to be.

BOOK VIII

CHAPTER I

No one can doubt that the maigstrate ought greatly to interest himself in the care of youth; for where it is neglected it is hurtful to the city, for every state ought to be governed according to its particular nature; for the form and manners of each government are peculiar to itself; and these, as they originally established it, so they usually still preserve it. For instance, democratic forms and manners a democracy; oligarchic, an oligarchy: but, universally, the best manners produce the best government. Besides, as in every business and art there are some things which men are to learn first and be made accustomed to, which are necessary to perform their several works; so it is evident that the same thing is necessary in the practice of virtue. As there is one end in view in every city, it is evident that education ought to be one and the same in each; and that this should be a common care, and not the individual's, as it now is, when every one takes care of his own children separately; and their instructions are particular also, each person teaching them as they please; but what ought to be engaged in ought to be common to all. Besides, no one ought to think that any citizen belongs to him in particular, but to the state in general; for each one is a part of the state, and it is the natural duty of each part to regard the good of the whole: and for this the Lacedæmonians may be praised; for they give the greatest attention to education, and make it public. It is evident, then, that there should be laws concerning education, and that it should be public.

CHAPTER II

WHAT education is, and how children ought to be instructed, is what should be well known; for there are doubts concerning the business of it, as all people do not agree in those things they would have a child taught, both with respect to their improvement in virtue and a happy life: nor is it clear whether the object of it should be to improve the reason or rectify the morals. From the present mode of education we cannot determine with certainty to which men incline, whether to instruct a child in what will be useful to him in life; or what tends to virtue, and what is excellent: for all these things have their separate defenders. As to virtue, there is no par- 1337*b* ticular in which they all agree: for as all do not equally esteem all virtues, it reasonably follows that they will not cultivate the same. It is evident that what is necessary ought to be taught to all: but that which is necessary for one is not necessary for all; for there ought to be a distinction between the employment of a freeman and a slave. The first of these should be taught everything useful which will not make those who know it mean. Every work is to be esteemed mean, and every art and every discipline which renders the body, the mind, or the understanding of freemen unfit for the habit and practice of virtue: for which reason all those arts which tend to deform the body are called mean, and all those employments which are exercised for gain; for they take off from the freedom of the mind and render it sordid. There are also some liberal arts which are not improper for freemen to apply to in a certain degree; but to endeavour to acquire a perfect skill in them is exposed to the faults I have just mentioned; for there is a great deal of difference in the reason for which any one does or learns anything: for it is not illiberal to engage in it for one's self, one's friend, or in the cause of virtue; while, at the same time, to do it for the sake of another may seem to be acting the part of a servant and a slave. The mode of instruction which now prevails seems to partake of both parts.

CHAPTER III

THERE are four things which it is usual to teach children; reading, gymnastic exercises, and music, to which (in the fourth place) some add painting. Reading and painting are both of them of singular use in life, and gymnastic exercises, as productive of courage. As to music, some persons may doubt, as most persons now use it for the sake of pleasure: but those who originally made it part of education did it because, as has been already said, nature requires that we should not only be properly employed, but to be able to enjoy leisure honourably: for this (to repeat what I have already said) is of all things the principal. But, though both labour and rest are necessary, yet the latter is preferable to the first; and by all means we ought to learn what we should do when at rest: for we ought not to employ that time at play; for then play would be the necessary business of our lives. But if this cannot be, play is more necessary for those who labour than those who are at rest: for he who labours requires relaxation; which play will supply: for as labour is attended with pain and continued exertion, it is necessary that play should be introduced, under proper regulations, as a medicine: for such an employment of the mind is a relaxation to it, and eases with pleasure.
1338a Now rest itself seems to partake of pleasure, of happiness, and an agreeable life: but this cannot be theirs who labour, but theirs who are at rest; for he who labours, labours for the sake of some end which he has not: but happiness is an end which all persons think is attended with pleasure and not with pain: but all persons do not agree in making this pleasure consist in the same thing; for each one has his particular standard, correspondent to his own habits; but the best man proposes the best pleasure, and that which arises from the noblest actions. But it is evident, that to live a life of rest there are some things which a man must learn and be instructed in; and that the object of this learning and this instruction centres in their acquisition: but the learning and instruction

which is given for labour has for its object other things; for which reason the ancients made music a part of education; not as a thing necessary, for it is not of that nature, nor as a thing useful, as reading, in the common course of life, or for managing of a family, or for learning anything as useful in public life. Painting also seems useful to enable a man to judge more accurately of the productions of the finer arts: nor is it like the gymnastic exercises, which contribute to health and strength; for neither of these things do we see produced by music; there remains for it then to be the employment of our rest, which they had in view who introduced it; and, thinking it a proper employment for freemen, to them they allotted it; as Homer sings:

> " How right to call Thalia to the feast: "

and of some others he says:

> " The bard was call'd, to ravish every ear: "

and, in another place, he makes Ulysses say the happiest part of man's life is

> " When at the festal board, in order plac'd,
> They hear the song."

It is evident, then, that there is a certain education in which a child may be instructed, not as useful nor as necessary, but as noble and liberal: but whether this is one or more than one, and of what sort they are, and how to be taught, shall be considered hereafter: we are now got so far on our way as to show that we have the testimony of the ancients in our favour, by what they have delivered down upon education—for music makes this plain. Moreover, it is necessary to instruct children in what is useful, not only on account of its being useful in itself, as, for instance, to learn to read, but also as the means of acquiring other different sorts of instruction: thus they should be instructed in painting, not only to prevent their being mistaken in purchasing pictures, or in buying or selling of vases, but rather as it makes 1338*b* them judges of the beauties of the human form; for to be always hunting after the profitable ill agrees with great

and freeborn souls.   As it is evident whether a boy should
be first taught morals or reasoning, and whether his body
or his understanding should be first cultivated, it is plain
that boys should be first put under the care of the different
masters of the gymnastic arts, both to form their bodies
and teach them their exercises.

CHAPTER IV

Now those states which seem to take the greatest care of
their children's education, bestow their chief attention on
wrestling, though it both prevents the increase of the
body and hurts the form of it.   This fault the Lacedæmonians did not fall into, for they made their children
fierce by painful labour, as chiefly useful to inspire them
with courage: though, as we have already often said, this
is neither the only thing nor the principal thing necessary
to attend to; and even with respect to this they may not
thus attain their end; for we do not find either in other
animals, or other nations, that courage necessarily attends
the most cruel, but rather the milder, and those who have
the dispositions of lions: for there are many people who
are eager both to kill men and to devour human flesh, as
the Achæans and Heniochi in Pontus, and many others in
Asia, some of whom are as bad, others worse than these,
who indeed live by tyranny, but are men of no courage.
Nay, we know that the Lacedæmonians themselves, while
they continued those painful labours, and were superior
to all others (though now they are inferior to many, both
in war and gymnastic exercises), did not acquire their
superiority by training their youth to these exercises, but
because those who were disciplined opposed those who
were not disciplined at all.   What is fair and honourable
ought then to take place in education of what is fierce
and cruel: for it is not a wolf, nor any other wild beast,
which will brave any noble danger, but rather a good
man.   So that those who permit boys to engage too
earnestly in these exercises, while they do not take care

to instruct them in what is necessary to do, to speak the
real truth, render them mean and vile, accomplished only
in one duty of a citizen, and in every other respect, as
reason evinces, good for nothing.   Nor should we form
our judgments from past events, but from what we see at
present: for now they have rivals in their mode of education, whereas formerly they had not.   That gymnastic
exercises are useful, and in what manner, is admitted;
for during youth it is very proper to go through a course
of those which are most gentle, omitting that violent diet
and those painful exercises which are prescribed as necessary; that they may not prevent the growth of the body:
and it is no small proof that they have this effect, that
amongst the Olympic candidates we can scarce find two 1339a
or three who have gained a victory both when boys and
men: because the necessary exercises they went through
when young deprived them of their strength.   When they
have allotted three years from the time of puberty to
other parts of education, they are then of a proper age to
submit to labour and a regulated diet; for it is impossible
for the mind and body both to labour at the same time,
as they are productive of contrary evils to each other;
the labour of the body preventing the progress of the
mind, and the mind of the body.

CHAPTER V

WITH respect to music we have already spoken a little in
a doubtful manner upon this subject.   It will be proper
to go over again more particularly what we then said,
which may serve as an introduction to what any other
person may choose to offer thereon; for it is no easy
matter to distinctly point out what power it has, nor on
what accounts one should apply it, whether as an amusement and refreshment, as sleep or wine; as these are
nothing serious, but pleasing, and the killers of care, as
Euripides says; for which reason they class in the same
order and use for the same purpose all these, namely,

sleep, wine, and music, to which some add dancing; or
shall we rather suppose that music tends to be productive
of virtue, having a power, as the gymnastic exercises have,
to form the body in a certain way, to influence the manners
so as to accustom its professors to rejoice rightly? or shall
we say, that it is of any service in the conduct of life, and
an assistant to prudence? for this also is a third property
which has been attributed to it. Now that boys are not
to be instructed in it as play is evident; for those who
learn don't play, for to learn is rather troublesome; neither
is it proper to permit boys at their age to enjoy perfect
leisure; for to cease to improve is by no means fit for
what is as yet imperfect; but it may be thought that the
earnest attention of boys in this art is for the sake of that
amusement they will enjoy when they come to be men
and completely formed; but, if this is the case, why are
they themselves to learn it, and not follow the practice
of the kings of the Medes and Persians, who enjoy the
pleasure of music by hearing others play, and being shown
its beauties by them; for of necessity those must be better
skilled therein who make this science their particular
study and business, than those who have only spent so
much time at it as was sufficient just to learn the principles
of it. But if this is a reason for a child's being taught
anything, they ought also to learn the art of cookery, but
this is absurd. The same doubt occurs if music has a
power of improving the manners; for why should they
on this account themselves learn it, and not reap every
advantage of regulating the passions or forming a judg-
1339*b* ment on the merits of the performance by hearing others,
as the Lacedæmonians; for they, without having ever
learnt music, are yet able to judge accurately what is good
and what is bad; the same reasoning may be applied if
music is supposed to be the amusement of those who live
an elegant and easy life, why should they learn themselves,
and not rather enjoy the benefit of others' skill. Let us
here consider what is our belief of the immortal gods in
this particular. Now we find the poets never represent
Jupiter himself as singing and playing; nay, we ourselves
treat the professors of these arts as mean people, and say

that no one would practise them but a drunkard or a
buffoon. But probably we may consider this subject
more at large hereafter. The first question is, whether
music is or is not to make a part of education? and of
those three things which have been assigned as its proper
employment, which is the right? Is it to instruct, to
amuse, or to employ the vacant hours of those who live
at rest? or may not all three be properly allotted to it?
for it appears to partake of them all; for play is necessary
for relaxation, and relaxation pleasant, as it is a medicine
for that uneasiness which arises from labour. It is
admitted also that a happy life must be an honourable
one, and a pleasant one too, since happiness consists in
both these; and we all agree that music is one of the most
pleasing things, whether alone or accompanied with a
voice; as Musæus says, " Music's the sweetest joy of
man; " for which reason it is justly admitted into every
company and every happy life, as having the power of
inspiring joy. So that from this any one may suppose
that it is necessary to instruct young persons in it; for all
those pleasures which are harmless are not only conducive
to the final end of life, but serve also as relaxations; and,
as men are but rarely in the attainment of that final end,
they often cease from their labour and apply to amusement, with no further view than to acquire the pleasure
attending it. It is therefore useful to enjoy such
pleasures as these. There are some persons who make
play and amusement their end, and probably that end
has some pleasure annexed to it, but not what should be;
but while men seek the one they accept the other for it;
because there is some likeness in human actions to the
end; for the end is pursued for the sake of nothing else
that attends it; but for itself only; and pleasures like
these are sought for, not on account of what follows them,
but on account of what has gone before them, as labour
and grief; for which reason they seek for happiness in
these sort of pleasures; and that this is the reason any one
may easily perceive. That music should be pursued, not
on this account only, but also as it is very serviceable
during the hours of relaxation from labour, probably no

1340a one doubts; we should also inquire whether besides this use it may not also have another of nobler nature; and we ought not only to partake of the common pleasure arising from it (which all have the sensation of, for music naturally gives pleasure, therefore the use of it is agreeable to all ages and all dispositions); but also to examine if it tends anything to improve our manners and our souls. And this will be easily known, if we feel our dispositions any way influenced thereby; and that they are so is evident from many other instances, as well as the music at the Olympic games; and this confessedly fills the soul with enthusiasm; but enthusiasm is an affection of the soul which strongly agitates the disposition. Besides, all those who hear any imitations sympathise therewith; and this when they are conveyed even without rhythm or verse. Moreover, as music is one of those things which are pleasant, and as virtue itself consists in rightly enjoying, loving, and hating, it is evident that we ought not to learn or accustom ourselves to anything so much as to judge right and rejoice in honourable manners and noble actions. But anger and mildness, courage and modesty, and their contraries, as well as all other dispositions of the mind, are most naturally imitated by music and poetry; which is plain by experience, for when we hear these our very soul is altered; and he who is affected either with joy or grief by the imitation of any objects, is in very nearly the same situation as if he was affected by the objects themselves; thus, if any person is pleased with seeing a statue of any one on no other account but its beauty, it is evident that the sight of the original from whence it was taken would also be pleasing; now it happens in the other senses there is no imitation of manners; that is to say, in the touch and the taste; in the objects of sight, a very little; for these are merely representations of things, and the perceptions which they excite are in a manner common to all. Besides, statues and paintings are not properly imitations of manners, but rather signs and marks which show the body is affected by some passion. However, the difference is not great, yet young men ought not to view the paintings of

Pauso, but of Polygnotus, or any other painter or statuary
who expresses manners.   But in poetry and music there
are imitations of manners; and this is evident, for different
harmonies differ from each other so much by nature, that
those who hear them are differently affected, and are not
in the same disposition of mind when one is performed as
when another is;   the one, for instance, occasions grief **1340b**
and contracts the soul, as the mixed Lydian: others soften
the mind, and as it were dissolve the heart: others fix
it in a firm and settled state, such is the power of the
Doric music only; while the Phrygian fills the soul with
enthusiasm, as has been well described by those who have
written philosophically upon this part of education; for
they bring examples of what they advance from the things
themselves.   The same holds true with respect to rhythm;
some fix the disposition, others occasion a change in it;
some act more violently, others more liberally.   From
what has been said it is evident what an influence music
has over the disposition of the mind, and how variously
it can fascinate it: and if it can do this, most certainly it
is what youth ought to be instructed in.   And indeed the
learning of music is particularly adapted to their disposition; for at their time of life they do not willingly attend
to anything which is not agreeable; but music is naturally
one of the most agreeable things; and there seems to be
a certain connection between harmony and rhythm; for
which reason some wise men held the soul itself to be
harmony; others, that it contains it.

CHAPTER VI

WE will now determine whether it is proper that children
should be taught to sing, and play upon any instrument,
which we have before made a matter of doubt. Now, it
is well known that it makes a great deal of difference when
you would qualify any one in any art, for the person himself
to learn the practical part of it; for it is a thing very
difficult, if not impossible, for a man to be a good judge of
what he himself cannot do. It is also very necessary that
children should have some employment which will amuse
them; for which reason the rattle of Archytas seems well
contrived, which they give children to play with, to
prevent their breaking those things which are about the
house; for at their age they cannot sit still: this therefore
is well adapted to infants, as instruction ought to be their
rattle as they grow up; hence it is evident that they
should be so taught music as to be able to practise it.
Nor is it difficult to say what is becoming or unbecoming
of their age, or to answer the objections which some make
to this employment as mean and low. In the first place,
it is necessary for them to practise, that they may be
judges of the art: for which reason this should be done
when they are young; but when they are grown older the
practical part may be dropped; while they will still
continue judges of what is excellent in the art, and take
a proper pleasure therein, from the knowledge they
acquired of it in their youth. As to the censure which
some persons throw upon music, as something mean and
low, it is not difficult to answer that, if we will but consider
how far we propose those who are to be educated so as
to become good citizens should be instructed in this art,
1341a and what music and what rhythms they should be
acquainted with; and also what instruments they should
play upon; for in these there is probably a difference.
Such then is the proper answer to that censure: for it
must be admitted, that in some cases nothing can prevent
music being attended, to a certain degree, with the bad

effects which are ascribed to it; it is therefore clear that
the learning of it should never prevent the business of
riper years; nor render the body effeminate, and unfit
for the business of war or the state; but it should be
practised by the young, judged of by the old. That
children may learn music properly, it is necessary that
they should not be employed in those parts of it which
are the objects of dispute between the masters in that
science; nor should they perform such pieces as are
wondered at from the difficulty of their execution; and
which, from being first exhibited in the public games, are
now become a part of education; but let them learn so
much of it as to be able to receive proper pleasure from
excellent music and rhythms; and not that only which
music must make all animals feel, and also slaves and
boys, but more. It is therefore plain what instruments
they should use; thus, they should never be taught to
play upon the flute, or any other instrument which
requires great skill, as the harp or the like, but on such
as will make them good judges of music, or any other
instruction: besides, the flute is not a moral instrument,
but rather one that will inflame the passions, and is therefore
rather to be used when the soul is to be animated than
when instruction is intended. Let me add also, that
there is something therein which is quite contrary to what
education requires; as the player on the flute is prevented
from speaking: for which reason our forefathers very
properly forbade the use of it to youth and freemen, though
they themselves at first used it; for when their riches
procured them greater leisure, they grew more animated
in the cause of virtue; and both before and after the
Median war their noble actions so exalted their minds
that they attended to every part of education; selecting
no one in particular, but endeavouring to collect the
whole: for which reason they introduced the flute also,
as one of the instruments they were to learn to play on.
At Lacedæmon the choregus himself played on the flute;
and it was so common at Athens that almost every freeman understood it, as is evident from the tablet which
Thrasippus dedicated when he was choregus; but after-

wards they rejected it as dangerous; having become better
judges of what tended to promote virtue and what did
not. For the same reason many of the ancient instru-
1341*b* ments were thrown aside, as the dulcimer and the lyre; as
also those which were to inspire those who played on them
with pleasure, and which required a nice finger and great
skill to play well on. What the ancients tell us, by way
of fable, of the flute is indeed very rational; namely, that
after Minerva had found it, she threw it away: nor are
they wrong who say that the goddess disliked it for
deforming the face of him who played thereon: not but
that it is more probable that she rejected it as the knowledge thereof contributed nothing to the improvement of
the mind. Now, we regard Minerva as the inventress of
arts and sciences. As we disapprove of a child's being
taught to understand instruments, and to play like a
master (which we would have confined to those who are
candidates for the prize in that science; for they play not
to improve themselves in virtue, but to please those who
hear them, and gratify their importunity); therefore we
think the practice of it unfit for freemen; but then it
should be confined to those who are paid for doing it; for
it usually gives people sordid notions, for the end they
have in view is bad: for the impertinent spectator is
accustomed to make them change their music; so that
the artists who attend to him regulate their bodies
according to his motions.

CHAPTER VII

WE are now to enter into an inquiry concerning harmony
and rhythm; whether all sorts of these are to be employed
in education, or whether some peculiar ones are to be
selected; and also whether we should give the same
directions to those who are engaged in music as part
of education, or whether there is something different
from these two. Now, as all music consists in melody
and rhythm, we ought not to be unacquainted with the

power which each of these has in education; and whether
we should rather choose music in which melody prevails,
or rhythm: but when I consider how many things have
been well written upon these subjects, not only by some
musicians of the present age, but also by some philosophers who are perfectly skilled in that part of music
which belongs to education; we will refer those who desire
a very particular knowledge therein to those writers, and
shall only treat of it in general terms, without descending
to particulars. Melody is divided by some philosophers,
whose notions we approve of, into moral, practical, and
that which fills the mind with enthusiasm: they also
allot to each of these a particular kind of harmony which
naturally corresponds therewith: and we say that music
should not be applied to one purpose only, but many;
both for instruction and purifying the soul (now I use
the word purifying at present without any explanation,
but shall speak more at large of it in my *Poetics*); and,
in the third place, as an agreeable manner of spending the
time and a relaxation from the uneasiness of the mind. **1342***a*
It is evident that all harmonies are to be used; but not
for all purposes; but the most moral in education: but
to please the ear, when others play, the most active and
enthusiastic; for that passion which is to be found very
strong in some souls is to be met with also in all; but
the difference in different persons consists in its being
in a less or greater degree, as pity, fear, and enthusiasm
also; which latter is so powerful in some as to overpower
the soul: and yet we see those persons, by the application
of sacred music to soothe their mind, rendered as sedate
and composed as if they had employed the art of the
physician: and this must necessarily happen to the com-
passionate, the fearful, and all those who are subdued
by their passions: nay, all persons, as far as they are
affected with those passions, admit of the same cure,
and are restored to tranquillity with pleasure. In the
same manner, all music which has the power of purifying
the soul affords a harmless pleasure to man. Such,
therefore, should be the harmony and such the music
which those who contend with each other in the theatre

should exhibit: but as the audience is composed of two
sorts of people, the free and the well-instructed, the rude,
the mean mechanics, and hired servants, and a long
collection of the like, there must be some music and some
spectacles to please and soothe them; for as their minds
are as it were perverted from their natural habits, so also
is there an unnatural harmony, and overcharged music,
which is accommodated to their taste: but what is
according to nature gives pleasure to every one, therefore
those who are to contend upon the theatre should be
allowed to use this species of music. But in education
ethic melody and ethic harmony should be used, which
is the Doric, as we have already said, or any other which
those philosophers who are skilful in that music which
is to be employed in education shall approve of. But
Socrates, in Plato's *Republic,* is very wrong when he
1342*b* permits only the Phrygian music to be used as well as
the Doric, particularly as amongst other instruments he
banishes the flute; for the Phrygian music has the same
power in harmony as the flute has amongst the instruments; for they are both pathetic and raise the mind:
and this the practice of the poets proves; for in their
bacchanal songs, or whenever they describe any violent
emotions of the mind, the flute is the instrument they
chiefly use: and the Phrygian harmony is most suitable
to these subjects. Now, that the dithyrambic measure
is Phrygian is allowed by general consent; and those who
are conversant in studies of this sort bring many proofs
of it; as, for instance, when Philoxenus endeavoured
to compose dithyrambic music for Doric harmony, he
naturally fell back again into Phrygian, as being fittest
for that purpose; as every one indeed agrees, that the
Doric music is most serious, and fittest to inspire courage:
and, as we always commend the middle as being between
the two extremes, and the Doric has this relation with
respect to other harmonies, it is evident that is what
the youth ought to be instructed in. There are two
things to be taken into consideration, both what is possible
and what is proper; every one then should chiefly
endeavour to attain those things which contain both

these qualities: but this is to be regulated by different times of life; for instance, it is not easy for those who are advanced in years to sing such pieces of music as require very high notes, for nature points out to them those which are gentle and require little strength of voice (for which reason some who are skilful in music justly find fault with Socrates for forbidding the youth to be instructed in gentle harmony; as if, like wine, it would make them drunk, whereas the effect of that is to render men bacchanals, and not make them languid): these therefore are what should employ those who are grown old. Moreover, if there is any harmony which is proper for a child's age, as being at the same time elegant and instructive, as the Lydian of all others seems chiefly to be—These then are as it were the three boundaries of education, moderation, possibility, and decorum.

GREAT BOOKS IN PHILOSOPHY

PAPERBACK SERIES

001 — John Stuart Mill — *On Liberty*		$ 3.95
002 — John Stuart Mill — *The Subjection*		
	of Women	3.95
003 — John Locke — *Second Treatise on*		
	Civil Government	3.95
004 — Niccolo Machiavelli — *The Prince*		3.95
005 — Plato — *Republic*		5.95
006 — Aristotle — *Politics*		4.95

ORDER FORM

The books listed above can be obtained from your book dealer or directly from Prometheus Books. Please check off the appropriate books. Remittance must accompany all orders from individuals. Please include $2.00 postage and handling for the first book and .50 for each additional title. (NYS residents please add applicable sales tax.)

Send to _____
(Please type or print clearly)

Address _____

City _____ State _____ Zip _____

Amount enclosed _____

Prometheus Books
700 E. Amherst St., Buffalo, New York 14215